GIVING CREDIT WHERE DUE

A Path to Global Poverty Reduction

I0130653

Robert F. Clark

University Press of America,® Inc.
Lanham · Boulder · New York · Toronto · Oxford

Copyright © 2006 by
University Press of America,® Inc.
4501 Forbes Boulevard
Suite 200
Lanham, Maryland 20706
UPA Acquisitions Department (301) 459-3366

PO Box 317
Oxford
OX2 9RU, UK

All rights reserved
Printed in the United States of America
British Library Cataloging in Publication Information Available

Library of Congress Control Number: 2006926774
ISBN-13: 978-0-7618-3534-9 (paperback : alk. paper)
ISBN-10: 0-7618-3534-2 (paperback : alk. paper)

The paper used in this publication meets the minimum
requirements of American National Standard for Information
Sciences—Permanence of Paper for Printed Library Materials,
ANSI Z39.48—1984

For the Marzzaccos, in-laws *par excellence*

CONTENTS

Preface

A world in which an estimated one of every six human beings lives in extreme poverty is morally unacceptable. The actual figure may be less. Some researchers put it more in the range of one in twelve or even one in thirty. No matter. The contrast between the concentration of extreme wealth in the hands of a few and the precarious daily existence of hundreds of millions of our fellow human beings is too stark to ignore.

A globalizing economy has yet to operate as a positive force for all the world's people—or prove that it can and will. Economic dislocations abound in the wake of globalization. The growth of the world's wealth highlights appalling income inequalities. Hence, "market economies, particularly those undergoing processes of radical reform, need some sort of system for the protection of the poor during the adjustment process."[1]

Existing antipoverty strategies, ranging from reliance on growth alone to a laser-like focus on deserving "target groups", fall short of fundamentally altering the scale of extreme poverty. On the world's present course, that will not change. Targeted poverty alleviation programs in the aggregate continue to be but "a thin veneer" on top of conventional development strategies.[2]

A new global poverty reduction paradigm is required. In my view, it would give priority to the provision of a guaranteed minimum income that would lift the world's neediest people above the line of extreme poverty. In this book, I advocate a particular scheme to accomplish that objective.

The scheme is a global refundable tax credit that would put a floor under the income of every qualifying poor person who files a tax return. In a refundable tax credit scheme, positive tax rates are applied to income but taxpayers are allowed to deduct a credit from the taxes for which they are liable. If the tax credit exceeds the amount of the tax owed, the government makes a transfer payment to the taxpayer.

A global tax credit will not eliminate extreme poverty but it will significantly and measurably erode it. Since extreme poverty is found in financially strapped developing countries, the scheme I outline will require outside financial and technical support from the world community for those countries that adopt it.

My previous studies of antipoverty efforts, both U.S. and global, led me to wonder what could be done to alter the fate of the world's poorest people. In investigating the notion of a global refundable tax credit, I found much that aided my thinking but nothing that spoke directly to the concept itself.

Hence, as an alternative (or an addition) to existing antipoverty strategies, the concept may merit attention from social welfare policy analysts, development economists, political leaders, journalists, advocacy groups and concerned citizens who are offended by the worldwide persistence of extreme poverty, deepseated inequality and inequitable development.

Acknowledgments

Through the interlibrary loan program, staff at the Martha Washington Branch of the Fairfax County Public Library in Virginia obtained key materials I used for research. The search engine Google proved indispensable. Without the Internet, the book you have in hand would not have been possible.

The websites of the U.S. Basic Income Guarantee (USBIG) Network and the Basic Income Earth Network (BIEN) contained treasure troves of relevant resources. Thanks to Karl Widerquist, USBIG Coordinator, earlier versions of chapters 3 and 7 first appeared as discussion papers on the USBIG website.

As with my previous books, my wife Marie provided helpful comments and loving support. I am grateful to friends Jacqueline Lemire, Walter O'Brien and Thomas Sheehan, who provided very detailed and very valuable feedback on the manuscript. An early draft of the manuscript posted at my website garnered some helpful comments.

None of those acknowledged necessarily agrees in whole or in part with what is proposed here. You, dear reader, may not agree either, but if that stimulates you to come up with a better solution to extreme global poverty, the book will have served a purpose. The book remains my sole responsibility, including its errors of fact, omission or interpretation.

Robert F. Clark
Alexandria, Virginia
January 1, 2006

END NOTES

1. U.S. Agency for International Development (2004) 53. The statement is found in Chapter Five, "Targeted Programs and Social Safety Nets" whose authors are Samuel A. Morley and Gustav F. Papanek. The overall document is intended as a guide for AID officials.

2. Ul Haq, Mahbub (1976) 65. This indictment, written over twenty years ago, was directed at the situation in India and Pakistan to dramatize the failure of those two countries to attack poverty directly. It seems applicable to current conditions in the world as a whole.

Introduction

Extreme poverty in the world persists in part because of the obstacles to upward mobility, which are embedded in social and economic environments. It also persists in part due to the failure of poor individuals to seize the limited opportunities available to them. The proportion contributed by each factor varies from one person and one society to another and can change over time. No "one size fits all" approach to extreme poverty reduction is likely to succeed.

Conservatives emphasize the individual's responsibility to improve his/her lot while liberals emphasize individual rights to at least a minimally acceptable standard of living. The former, ignoring society's culpability, encourage individuals to rely on their own unaided (and hence often futile) efforts to escape poverty. The latter, downplaying the role of individual initiative, advocate forms of welfare and social services to the poor that can foster dependency.

The tax systems of developing countries provide a way to bridge the ideological divide. A global refundable tax credit would enable participating countries to offset the adverse social conditions that contribute to extreme poverty. By providing a survival-based floor under income, it would open up horizons of individual opportunity.

Thus, both liberal and conservative agendas can be, if not completely satisfied, at least satisficed.[1] The involvement of the international community would signal its complicity in current conditions and a resolve to change them for the better.

The notion of putting a publicly financed floor under the income of the poor can provoke outrage. The so-called "free rider" problem, captured in the famous image of an able-bodied Malibu surfer sponging off the rest of us, jumps to the front and center of political discourse.[2] Income redistribution under any guise is derided as diverting resources from capital investment, stunting economic growth, expropriating individual wealth unethically, rewarding laziness, and fostering social engineering at the expense of human freedom.

Even if one negotiates these hurdles, debate surfaces over the type of scheme best suited to the objective. The type of refundable tax credit described herein faces significant obstacles, most notably corruption and lack of administrative capacity in the tax systems of many developing countries.

Such obstacles coupled with resistance to income distribution broadly mean that the tax credit approach will lack political traction for some time.

But not indefinitely.

Realistically, a global tax credit will not emerge as a near-term (five to fifteen year) response to extreme poverty. Think of it as a mid-term (sixteen to twenty-five year) response. Over this period, the world will continue on the path of economic integration and the tax systems of developing countries will be under pressure to reform. Refundable tax credits for the world's poorest will become more viable. They will be seen as preferable to other universal basic income schemes that are asymptotically long-term, never quite touching the axis of political feasibility.

Like democracy as a form of government, a global refundable tax credit scheme can be criticized as an undesirable approach to global poverty reduction—until one examines the alternatives. A global tax credit approach to poverty reduction will not fit into the world as we know it. It will however fit into the world we will soon come to know.

Extreme Poverty — A Global Disgrace

According to the Universal Declaration of Human Rights, "Everyone has the right to a standard of living adequate for . . . health and well-being . . . and the right to security in the event of . . . lack of livelihood in circumstances beyond his control."[3]

We are embarrassingly far from achieving that standard for every human being. While offering undreamed-of opportunities to many people and countries, globalization has marginalized others. Perhaps as many as a billion people (one of every six on the planet) survive on less than a dollar a day. Extreme poverty affronts a world that is integrating economically and socially at a dizzying pace.

On the plus side, the processes of globalization have fostered a freer exchange of goods and ideas. They have helped promote more open economies, more open societies and a trend toward democratic accountability. They have thrown the spotlight on evils like gender inequity, social exclusion, child labor exploitation and environmental degradation.

Global competition has improved industrial productivity (that is, higher ratios of output to input), bringing down prices and making more goods and services available to more people. Advanced information and communications technologies have empowered public opinion.

At the same time, the persistence of extreme poverty and severe income inequality in a prospering world has triggered a backlash against the harsher consequences of globalization. Left unchecked, the all-out quest for economic growth and private profit overwhelms a more rounded approach that embodies sustainable development and respect for human rights.

Protesters direct their ire toward rich, mainly Western, countries and the international organizations perceived as operating under their thumb, such as the

World Bank, International Monetary Fund (IMF) and World Trade Organization (WTO). Collectively, despite their pious pronouncements and even the best of intentions, these entities are charged with exacerbating poverty on the ground.

They abet the multinational corporations that are faulted for obliterating small enterprises in developing countries and stifling small business opportunities for the poor. Economic development through massive capital investment depletes natural resources and inflicts lasting damage on fragile ecostructures. Global competition induces firms to cut costs through greater reliance on technology and the elimination of less skilled jobs.

Despite these adverse effects, few people advocate retreating into closed economies (like those of Burma and North Korea), which would only worsen the prospects of the poor.[4] Future antipoverty initiatives will therefore take place in the context of an expanding, not a contracting, global economy.

Trade—Freer But Not Always Fairer[5]

Although precise cause and effect mechanisms are elusive, trade and economic growth are closely correlated. Both are bound up with factors like prices, exchange rates and inflation. The composition and volume of its trade affects a nation's economic stability and growth prospects.

Both domestic and international trade policies can have a major impact, positive or negative, on a country's Gross Domestic Product, income distribution and poverty rates. In large part this is due to the expansion of world trade in the past half century. In 1953, the value of world merchandise trade was $58.0 billion for exports and $66.0 billion for imports; in 2003, the respective figures were $7.3 and $7.6 *trillion*.[6]

The World Trade Organization has fostered economic openness and trade liberalization. A multilateral system is preferable to a series of bilateral accords. For many countries, increased trade openness generates growth that in turn can help reduce poverty.[7] The problem lies with poor countries that function outside the global trade regimen or, although within it, are disadvantaged by its rules.

Clearly, a global rules-based trading system is more predictable and stable than one dictated by the whims of powerful interests. However, under a global system, those interests are hardly muted. They are disproportionately influential in the rules-writing and enforcement process. Thus, advanced industrialized countries "have pushed poor countries to eliminate trade barriers, while keeping up their own barriers. . . ."[8]

International trade rules disadvantage poor countries in several ways. First, with subsidies beyond $300 billion a year, rich countries promote their agricultural products in external markets, thereby undercutting imports from developing countries. Consequently, poor countries lose export income from the sale of those basic commodities on which their economies depend. In other cases, developing countries simply cannot cope with collapsed markets.[9]

Second, in the area of industrial policy, developing countries are constrained from providing subsidies or imposing local content requirements on foreign investors. They are less able to support the entry and/or expansion of domestic industries.

Third, there is increasing private sector involvement in the delivery of public and social services (such as water, energy, education and training); once a foreign service provider is established in a developing country, the General Agreement on Trade in Services mandates that it be treated the same as domestic firms. As in industry, this can work to the disadvantage of small domestic service providers.

Fourth, the WTO's Trade-Related Aspects of Intellectual Property Rights (TRIPS) agreement, designed (reasonably enough) to protect their creators' investment in new ideas, inventions, technologies, and literary and artistic productions, entails huge increases in the licensing fees paid from developing nations to suppliers of such "properties."[10]

Global trade agreements are influenced by major traders like the United States, Canada, the European Union, Japan and China. Developing countries are encouraged to make their markets more competitive by countenancing declines in real wages and wage growth rates. Collective bargaining rights have been eroded.

China, a rapidly developing nation and a huge global trading partner, entered the World Trade Organization on December 11, 2001. Its role in the organization will affect the dynamics of trade negotiations henceforth. Its impact on world trading relationships and domestic economies will be profound. Whether that impact will redound to the benefit of smaller developing nations and their poorest people remains uncertain.

Developing Nations as Prisoners of Events

At present developing countries are whipsawed by large but volatile capital flows that are geared to global economic cycles. Developing country governments are finding it harder to impose controls and restrictions on capital.[11] National policymaking capacity is further constrained by the global integration of financial markets. Following a kind of herd instinct, these markets tend to move in tandem into or out of a country or region in response to overall economic trends and unexpected shocks (e.g. sudden rapid depreciation of a country's currency).[12]

Developing countries are limited in their ability to affect global capital flows. Unregulated speculative flows of capital into and out of poor countries have "left behind collapsed currencies and weakened banking systems."[13]

All too often, World Bank and IMF loan conditionalities, laudably intended to foster stable governments and sustainable economic growth, have become self-defeating bureaucratic burdens and provoked resentment in recipient countries. Forced cuts in public expenditures have affected the poor adversely.

Few developing countries have adapted to onrushing technologies in computers, robotics, telecommunications and medicine. In exacerbation of the problem, they are encouraged by international advisers to pursue labor-intensive "pro-poor" growth strategies that are anything but.

Unquestionably poverty reduction is associated with growth in the Gross Domestic Product (GDP).[14] Some developing countries continue to "shoot themselves in the foot" by maintaining policies and practices that discourage investment and entrepreneurial opportunities. "Onerous hiring and firing regulations . . . are associated with lower Research and Development (R&D) expenditure" and retard productivity gains.[15]

The World Bank cites four key factors that chill the investment climate in developing countries: policy uncertainty, insecure property rights, macroeconomic instability, and arbitrary regulation.[16] Rent-seeking by special interests in the form of tariffs, regulatory preference, subsidies, and, for that matter, corruption (e.g. bribery) undermine government credibility and public trust.

Growth with equity in developing countries depends on open markets, increased capital investment and a strong technological orientation, with an adequate social protection scheme for each country's poorest people.

Job creation, small and medium enterprise development, microfinance schemes, and community-based health and social services can benefit any society but by themselves are insufficient for robust economic growth and the elimination of extreme poverty.[17] For business startups, "delays are greater and costs higher in low-income countries."[18]

A Shared Responsibility

The growth course developing country governments prefer may in fact prove academic. Their influence over the pace and direction of change is waning. Worldwide, in the wake of globalization, "the nation-state, as a bedrock economic political institution, is steadily losing control over international flows of people, goods, funds and technology."[19] Coping alone with extreme poverty may lie outside the capabilities of developing country governments. .

While the global poverty *rate* has fallen, the absolute number of extremely poor people remains unacceptably high. This is because of large increases in global population, the rate's denominator. The addition of 75 million people each year to the world's population exacerbates the problems of famine, unemployment and poverty. Absent concerted international action, the world's poor will continue to be whipsawed by forces outside the control not only of themselves, but their own governments.

The national security interests of rich and poor countries alike are tied to the eradication of extreme global poverty.[20] Terrorist groups find it safer to operate from poor countries. The failure of global economic growth to benefit hundreds of millions of the world's poorest people fuels social and political unrest. Economically, poor countries are becoming more marginalized as rich countries mount anti-terrorist programs but "devote insufficient resources to deal effectively with the poorer areas of the world."[21]

Poor countries make weak trading partners and offer limited opportunities for investment. "Problems such as drugs, disease, criminal trafficking, environmental degradation, and global climate change rarely stay within national borders."[22] The economic problems of developing countries often spark regional conflicts that have wider repercussions for the international community.

If the world community recognizes the right of all people to a minimally adequate standard of living, it assumes an obligation to eliminate abuses of that right. "Fighting poverty is both a moral imperative and a necessity for a stable world."[23] Because of its role in the world, the United States has a special responsibility to "spread [globalization's] benefits to all, including the poorest, while addressing its negative consequences."[24] But not alone.

The forces of globalization that exacerbate the plight of the world's poorest people transcend national borders. Hence, responsibility for alleviating their plight lies not only with the poor themselves or with their governments or, for that matter, with the governments of developed countries. It lies with the entire world community acting in concert through international organizations.

Antipoverty Initiatives — Too Small, Too Brief

The benefits of economic growth are spread unevenly throughout society. They accrue disproportionately to upper income centiles. Certain types of communities like urban areas or favorable geographic locations, such as ports, tend to prosper while others, for example, remote rural interiors, may decline further. China is a prime example of this phenomenon.

The combination of uneven growth and narrowly targeted assistance to certain poor groups or depressed areas does not result in a level playing field. The benefits of aid are generally limited to selected population groups, types of communities or geographic regions—and even in these cases often prove only transitory.

Community-based programs often yield inspiring results. Regrettably, successful long-term aid projects are not routinely evaluated and replicated and failed projects sometimes go on far too long. For the humanitarian aid system as a whole, "there has been significant under-investment in evaluation and impact analysis."[25]

Despite the best efforts of non-governmental organizations, bilateral aid agencies and multilateral institutions, their resources are "miniscule in relation to the needs for poverty eradication."[26] At the community level, they support what are in effect demonstration programs (though, regrettably, they do not on that account routinely undergo rigorous third-party evaluation).[27]

Community-based programs often show the *potential* for large-scale poverty reduction, but less often the *probability*. Extrapolating from an apparently successful local experience to a full-blown national program does not always yield the expected results. A national program lacks the halo effect of a single local demonstration.

Administrative problems arise from the expansion of clientele, staffing and costs. The energy and commitment of local program administrators are not matched everywhere. Program rules become more complex, governmental oversight more exacting and the potential for fraud and abuse seeping in more ominous. What works in one locale cannot easily be replicated elsewhere without adequate prior preparation and testing.

When governments change hands, the new set of ministers will tend to disavow the initiatives of their predecessors. Absent scientific evaluation of their impact and potential for replicability, community-based programs are vulnerable to this fate. If they continue at all, they may remain dependent on foreign aid and private humanitarian assistance.

The expansion of effective community-based programs into successful national antipoverty programs is the exception rather than the rule. Disillusionment with such programs—and with foreign aid in general—stems from the lack of evidence-based knowledge about what really works to produce progress on the ground.

Past disappointments with antipoverty projects have given rise to skepticism internationally toward new initiatives and a reluctance to risk more failures. Scientifically credible evidence about what does and does not work could serve to counter such skepticism.[28]

Guaranteeing Income

Poverty may decline here and there in consequence of the growth-and-aid combination. However, its eradication across the board requires the permanent redistribution of some of growth's benefits from the haves to the have-nots. Current social protection schemes around the world, which are not designed explicitly for poverty reduction, do not fill the bill.

Among a variety of measures needed to assure human security, there is a need for "a social and economic minimum for all, including the working poor and those not in paid work."[29] In short, the twenty-first century requires a new paradigm, one built on the floor of a guaranteed minimum income for all.

The notion of a guaranteed income, as distinct from targeted social insurance and categorical welfare schemes, has morphed into three distinct approaches—a negative income tax, a universal demogrant and a stakeholder grant.

With a negative income tax, instead of being liable for "positive" taxes, people below a certain income level instead *receive* payments from the government designed to bring their income up to an official minimum. A negative income tax redistributes resources to poor people while doing away with the stigma, cost and administrative complexity of means testing.

An alternative that some find compelling is a basic income in the form of a demogrant, that is, a regular payment of a minimum income to every citizen, regardless of socio-economic status. Its advocates see it as a right of citizenship, a means of narrowing income inequality and a strategy for eliminating poverty. The money comes on top of other after-tax income. The problems associated with "targeting" and take-up rates vanish since the scheme is universal.

The high outlays and corresponding high tax rates required to finance a universal demogrant have hindered its political acceptability. Since the non-poor as well as the poor benefit, under a fixed national budget, the poor will receive less per person than they would under a scheme designed solely for them. The effects of a universal demogrant on labor force participation would be far more profound than a more targeted negative income tax.[30]

More recently, in the tradition of Thomas Paine, the notion of a stakeholder grant has been advocated. Under a proposal by Ackerman and Alstott, upon reaching age twenty-one, every person regardless of income, employment or family status would receive a grant of $80,000 with no restriction on its use. The money could be saved, spent or invested.[31] The scheme would be financed through an annual wealth tax. Like the universal demogrant, it is expensive. While potentially politically feasible in rich countries, it has less immediate appeal for developing and transitional ones.

What to Expect

The three approaches have their advocates (I prefer the first) but a common heritage. They rest on the premise that a guaranteed basic income is the surest path to personal economic security and the general social welfare. The approach I advocate is a variant of the negative income tax. Individual countries would administer their own refundable tax credit plan, with technical support and partial, formula-based reimbursement for costs from the United Nations.

For a participating country, the program would guarantee citizens and residents who are members of income tax filing households a minimum income of PPP$1 a day. The amount of the credit would be based on household income from all sources, not a subset like earned income. On a global scale, I believe, the scheme is administratively more achievable than other options.

The history-based structure of this book may leave the impression that the world community is moving inexorably toward a guaranteed income of some sort. Not so. The future has a way of surprising prognosticators. I do think that the evidence from history and, for that matter, religion and philosophy, establishes the credibility of a global tax credit. Obviously, that does not guarantee its acceptance by the world community.

Throughout this book, I use $ when referring to the value of money within the U.S. economy. US$ will refer to international currency values in current dollar-denominated terms. PPP$ will indicate adjustments in US$ to reflect purchasing power parity (what a dollar or its equivalent in other currencies will buy outside the U.S.).

In this book I say little that has not been said, often more thoroughly and better, elsewhere. My reason for writing is that not all of it has been said in one place.

Upcoming chapters build a case for the global tax credit.

Chapter 2 describes the state of global poverty, while critiquing the flawed yet indispensable poverty estimation methods available to the world community.

Chapter 3 examines the ethical and religious underpinnings of social welfare systems and the reasons why past societies have assumed responsibility for at least some of those in need.

Chapters 4, 5, and 6 respectively identify harbingers of a guaranteed minimum income in Europe, the United States, and elsewhere.

Chapter 7 reviews a succession of global antipoverty strategies in recent decades and finds them wanting.

Chapter 8 sets forth the rationale for a global tax credit, Chapter 9 presents a plan for the design of the program and Chapter 10 addresses its implementation through the United Nations system.

Chapter 11 ventures to predict the likely effects of the program at the individual, national and international level.

Chapter 12 considers many of the inevitable objections to the approach.

Finally, Chapter 13 assesses its geopolitical prospects and discusses elements of a strategy to make it a reality.

And Chapter 1, you ask? That, to set the stage for what follows, is a piece of fiction describing one beneficiary's experience with the global tax credit in the mythical nation of Peñuria. (A second fictional interlude appears in Chapter 11.)

END NOTES

1. To "satisfice" is to achieve an outcome that does not necessarily maximize one's objectives, but is considered good enough. Much public policy decisionmaking is of this sort. The term was introduced by Simon, Herbert A. (1957). For more see Endnote 2, p. 213.
2. This image was introduced by Rawls, John (1988).
3. The Universal Declaration of Human Rights was adopted and proclaimed by General Assembly resolution 217 A (III), December 10, 1948. A rights-based approach to economic development remains more of a vision than a reality.
4. Bardhan, Pranab (2005) 12.
5. This section draws heavily on International Labour Organization (2004b) 30-32.
6. http://www.wto.org/english/res_e/statis_e/its2004_e/its04_longterm_e.pdf
7. Majid, Norman (2003) 25.
8. Stiglitz, Joseph E. (2002) 6.
9. Some 20-25 million farmers in fifty countries of Latin American, Asia and Africa depend on the global coffee market for their livelihoods. In recent years, due largely to a breakdown in the 1989 International Coffee Agreement, the massive overproduction of coffee has led to a collapse in prices, plunging coffee growers worldwide into extreme and chronic poverty. Their governments have no fallback option and the world trading system is not designed to protect the extremely poor against such economic shocks. See Chronic Poverty Research Centre (2004) 46.
10. See http://www.wto.org/english/tratop_e/trips_e/intel2_e.htm
11. International Labour Organization (2004b) 22.
12. Whereas twenty years ago, the correlation between stock market movements in the United States and Europe was 40 percent, today it is twice that. International Labour Organization (2004b) 22.
13. Ibid.: 7.
14. World Bank (2004b) 3.
15. World Bank (2004b) 148.
16. World Bank (2004b) 15. The findings emerge from the World Bank's program of Investment Climate Surveys, initiated in 2001, that cover more than 26,000 firms employing some 4.8 million people in fifty-three countries.
17. Small and medium enterprises play an important role in creating jobs, pioneering new technologies and production processes and changing market conditions. However, recent

maroeconomic evidence "casts doubt on the claim that SMEs are especially important for growth and poverty reduction." World Bank (2004b) 64. The opposite may be truer.

18. World Bank (2004b) 100. The report contrasts an average business startup time of two days in Australia and nine days in Turkey to more than two hundred days in Haiti. Op. cit.: 99.

19. U.S. Central Intelligence Agency (2005).

20. Alarmist sentiments? Not to the government of the United States. Under the National Security Strategy of U.S. President George W. Bush, September 2002, development assistance has been elevated as the third pillar of U.S. national security, along with defense and diplomacy. See U.S. Agency for International Development (2003).

21. U.S. Central Intelligence Agency (2005).

22. Lieberson, Joseph and Jonathan Sleeper (2000) 9.

23. African Development Bank, Asian Development Bank, European Bank for Reconstruction and Development, International Monetary Fund, World Bank (July 2000) i.

24. United States Conference of Catholic Bishops (2003) 15.

25. Overseas Development Institute (2004) 33.

26. International Labour Organization (2004) 79.

27. Fortunately, the impact of nongovernmental organizations goes well beyond their support for limited community-based programs. They have developed into effective advocates in national and international forums for global poverty reduction.

28. The Poverty Action Lab at the Massachusetts Institute of Technology, which evaluates antipoverty projects in various countries using randomized trials is a welcome exception. However, it operates on a small scale relative to the size of its mission.

29. Commission on Human Security (2003) 38. This Commission was an initiative of the Government of Japan. It received support and encouragement from several United Nations entities and financial assistance from the Japanese Ministry of Foreign Affairs, Government of Sweden World Bank, Rockefeller Foundation and Japan Center for International Exchange.

30. For an alternative view, see Frankman, Myron J. (2004), especially Chapter 6 in which he makes a bold case for a planet-wide citizens income, benefiting rich and poor alike. Clearly it would be the least stigmatizing approach and in theory reach all of the world's poorest people. However, he acknowledges that such a scheme "involves higher direct outlays than either targeted grants or a negative income tax" (p. 153). To be sure, these are offset somewhat by reduced administrative costs, but the final bill would still be much higher than the one for more targeted approaches.

31. Ackerman, Bruce and Anne Alstott (1999).

1

Story

First Fictional Interlude: A Taxing Experience[1]

Angel Estrada arrived in Oczuc with his llama in tow at four in the afternoon. His two-day trek over the High Plane had left him weary. At the depot near Oczuc's market, he unloaded bags of coca leaves, turned the llama over to the care of the depot manager and walked across the square to the provincial office of the United Nations.

Mercifully the line inside was short and he was called within the hour. He removed the cap with folding earflaps, brushed back his black hair and straightened his poncho before entering the cubicle. The woman behind the desk eyed a clock on the opposite wall. She had spent the day helping people like Angel prepare and file their tax returns.

With less than two hours left in her workday she was thinking about supper for her husband and their two-year old daughter. After that she would wash clothes, clean the house, rock the baby to sleep, briefly discuss the day's events with her husband and fall into bed. Tomorrow would bring another surge of very low-income tax filers from the villages.

She smiled half-heartedly at the slightly nervous Indian. In the surrounding cubicles, other villagers met with UN representatives. Each of the past three years had been different. The first year the line had stretched around the block and Angel had stood outside for over five hours before his name was called. The refund had been delayed by several months.

The process had become more efficient by the second year but the experience even less pleasant. The UN representative had sneered as he penned in the meager figures Angel gave him. The official obviously viewed people like him as social parasites, tax eaters, possibly even tax cheaters, rather than taxpayers. Apparently other people had complained about their treatment from this official because Angel heard later that the man had been fired.

Last year the process had gone much more smoothly. The UN representative had been the soul of courtesy and the refund delivered on schedule. What would this year bring?

The country had a depressing history of corrupt tax administration. For several years it had been ruled ineligible to participate in the United Nations' Global Tax Credit Program. Reluctantly the government of Peñuria had asked the United Nations to assist with reform of the country's tax system.

UN experts had descended on Peñuria's capital to assist the Ministry of Internal Revenue with that task. It would take another year or so before the reforms were fully implemented and the system certified as meeting international standards. Meanwhile the government had delegated management of the tax credit program to the UN. The world body had opened offices in provincial capitals like Oczuc and recruited native Peñurians as tax credit representatives.

The job announcement drew many more applicants than could be hired. Although seasonal the job paid almost as much as a year-round job. Most of the new employees were conscientious and hard-working. The few who succumbed to bribe-taking, falsification of documents or other acts of dishonesty were dismissed without notice.

Angel and hundreds of other people from his and neighboring villages made their way at this time each year to Oczuc to file their returns. Word about the availability of a refundable tax credit program continued to swell their numbers. To meet the demand the UN had to hire a contingent of new representatives, including the one who sat across from Angel.

The woman sighed, pulled a tax form from the shelf behind her, rested her chin in her left hand and languidly picked up a ballpoint pen. She straightened suddenly as a supervisor walked past the cubicle and momentarily peered in. She proceeded briskly.

Married? Yes, wife Serafina. Children? Four, two boys, two girls. Occupation? Farming, mainly a variety of potatoes that could withstand the cold temperatures, thin air and rocky soil of these mountains. Also, coca leaves. Property? A windowless mud brick house, inherited from my father. Farm tools, a shovel and hoe. Two llamas. Income for the past twelve months? 24,000 soles (PPP$1,200).

His return could be audited, she explained. If the information on it proved false, he would be subject to fines and possible imprisonment. Did he understand these terms? Good. Angel marked an affidavit affirming that to the best of his ability he had provided complete and correct information.

He had brought along a few receipts but, apart from a cursory scan, the woman behind the desk simply wrote down the figures he gave her. The data Angel provided would be cross-checked with other information in the government's databases. Odds were that it would be accepted as is. Within a few minutes, the form was completed and as instructed he placed his mark on the signature line.

The representative counter-signed the form and placed it in an envelope, which she sealed and dropped into an out-box. "Barring any problem with the information you have provided, your check will arrive in this office in three months, señor. Please come by then. Adios."

This was the fourth year for Angel's family to receive the refundable tax credit. The first year, giddy with good fortune, he and his wife had bought a used tractor for their small plot of land. Unfortunately they did not have enough money for gas and repairs. It was slowly turning into a rusting hulk.

The second and third years, they rushed to buy new clothes for the children and new furniture for the house. The second half of last year turned disastrous when the potato crop failed and they had no reserves to make up for lost income. The family hovered on the brink of starvation and the children got sick.

This year, Angel vowed, we will spend only half the money from the refund and save the rest. On a previous trip, he and Serafina had opened an account at the Oczuc National Bank.

The United Nations' Global Tax Credit Program was a joint venture between the United Nations and participating governments. It was designed to eliminate extreme global poverty, defined as per capita income of less than PPP$1 (or in the case of Peñuria, 20 soles) a day.

For Angel's family, the poverty threshold was an annual income of 20 soles times 6 persons times 365 days or 43,800 soles. Subtracting the Estrada family's income of 24,000 soles from that amount left him entitled to a refundable credit of 19,800 soles.

The program was not altogether equitable. Some of Angel's neighbors owned more llamas, larger plots of land and even vehicles like a tractor or pickup truck. The villages had a lively barter economy as well. However, none of that counted toward a family's income.

Self-declaration of income supplemented by minimal records invited dishonesty. Some would earn money from temporary work or from illegal activity in the region's thriving drug trade. None of this income would be reported. Around the country, a tiny percentage of returns were selected for in-depth examination. Occasionally citizens with grievances against their neighbors would report suspected abuses to the program's administrators.

However, during the early years, while investigating informant reports and conducting random audits, the program's administrators relied mainly on the integrity of tax filers. Only the most blatant cases of fraud and misrepresentation were prosecuted. A more extensive system of auditing the returns of the country's poorest people would cost too much, absorb a disproportionate amount of staff time and energy, and yield too small a payoff.

The government subjected the few convicted abusers to severe and widely publicized penalties. The approach aimed more at deterring abuse than uncovering it. This did not satisfy the critics. Cases of proven abuse invariably provoked public outrage followed by shrill demands to "reform the system" or even to abolish the tax credit altogether.

Over time the tax credit system would accrue a body of regulations on all aspects of the system, including countable income, treatment of assets and required record keeping. With UN assistance, the Ministry of Internal Revenue would create a technologically sophisticated system for auditing tax credit claims. The government and the UN would also conduct detailed studies of the tax credit, its administration, costs and economic impact.

For the present, the United Nations determined that administrative simplicity outweighed other considerations. The government of Peñuria concurred. It was most important to get an easily understood and efficient tax credit system up and running. If most filers were honest, it would keep the incidence of abuse within bearable limits.

The hardest part was staffing the system with polite, reliable and well-trained representatives. As awareness of the tax credit program expanded, more and more representatives were needed to process claims. Hiring standards slipped. People were selected without adequate background checks and assigned to their posts after only minimal training.

Supervisors imposed unrealistic quotas on their subordinates for completed tax claims. Claim reviewers spent more and more time correcting errors by the frontline representatives. Complaints by villagers over demeaning treatment by arrogant tax credit representatives mounted. Despite these problems, the system as a whole lumbered forward.

The United Nations and each participating government shared in the cost of the tax credit program. Based on a formula using variables like a country's total population, per capita income, income inequality, and population living on less than PPP$1 a day, Peñuria's share was one-half of total costs.

The United Nations had established a global tax credit fund, to which individuals, private organizations and governments made contributions. The fund sought to replenish the fund by US$100 billion annually.

This was calculated on the following basis. An estimated one billion persons worldwide lived on less than PPP$1 a day; on average their daily per capita income was PPP$.50. Hence the amount to be made up per person also averaged PPP$.50 a day. This worked out to PPP$.50 times 365 days times 1 billion people or PPP$182.5 billion.

On average, participating governments were responsible for half the claimed amount. If every eligible person on the planet received a refund, the United Nations would reimburse these governments for the remaining half, PPP$91.25 billion. Adding in an estimated PPP$8.75 billion for administrative, overhead and transaction costs yielded a total of PPP$100 billion.

In reality the takeup rate was far lower than 100 percent. Not every country with citizens living on less than PPP$1 a day participated. Some governments were unwilling to endure intrusive oversight by the United Nations.

Other governments like Peñuria's very much wanted to implement the program but were not permitted, due to the failure of their internal revenue systems to meet international standards. They could either wait until the systems came into compliance or they could like Peñuria request the UN to administer the program on an interim basis.

Even though countries might participate, many of their eligible households would not, out of ignorance about the program, distrust of government, unease with the tax system or simple inertia. Worldwide, the United Nations estimated that the proportion of individuals benefiting from the program to be about half of those eligible. Consequently, the global tax credit fund was building up a surplus.

The critics disagreed with the United Nations—and with one another. Some said that the proportion of eligibles actually served was more like a fourth. At the other end of the statistical spectrum, some argued that the program was reaching virtually everyone. They claimed that official UN estimates of the population around the world in extreme poverty were highly inflated.

On the outer limits were critics who contended that the program annually overshot its mark. A few beneficiaries might have legitimate claims on the credit but most had resources that exceeded the PPP$1 a day standard. The program essentially was a subsidy that discouraged work effort and stifled capital investment. The building surplus was scandalous.

The Secretary General responded that the amount raised from annual contributions was unpredictable. If the world economy faltered or donors turned their attention elsewhere, the fund would not be sufficiently replenished. This could happen even as participation rates by countries and households increased.

Surpluses would enable the tax credit program to weather lean times. Indeed, in an economic downturn, it was more important than ever for the UN to provide support to the world's poorest. If the size of the world's population in extreme poverty proved to be smaller than the UN's estimate, all the better. The tax credit program would eliminate extreme poverty sooner rather than later.

There was even a distant possibility that, if the fund were assured of regular replenishment and the surplus grew large enough, the tax credit could be extended to persons living on less than $2 a day, a level that surely qualified as severe, if not extreme, poverty.

Indeed, already civil society organizations were pressuring the United Nations to expand the program. Predictably, this sounded the alarm in conservative circles. The tax credit was the stalking horse for a major redistribution of income internationally, they cried. The specter of a socialist world government was raised.

For the moment, however, the goal was to assure the participating governments that, with UN monetary assistance and technical support, the elimination of extreme poverty lay within their grasp.

There was always the chance that not only individuals but governments as well would portray their conditions as more dire than warranted. By lowering the estimate of per capita income and raising the estimated proportion of the population in extreme poverty, a participating government could decrease its share of program costs.

This was a risk particularly in countries with inadequate statistical resources, national survey capabilities and national income and product accounts. The United Nations could not guarantee that it had successfully unmasked these tactics in all cases. More fodder for the critics, ever ready to charge that the program was riddled with waste, corruption and mismanagement.

To improve its poverty estimation capabilities, the United Nations lobbied for more funding so that its statistical units and the participating countries could upgrade their data collection systems.

Still the program appeared for the most part to be reaching its target population, the world's extremely poor people. Despite its shortcomings, real and fancied, it retained a critical mass of support among the member states of the United Nations. For at least another year.

Unaware of these global machinations, three months after filing his return, Angel returned to the local United Nations office, received his refund and handed over some money to his oldest son who was attending the Oczuc Technical School on a government grant but needed to buy his textbooks.

Then Angel was off to the bank. There he learned that in the future he would not be receiving his annual refund as a check. Instead, through a new mechanism called Electronic Benefit Transfer, the refund would be deposited directly into his account. EBT was being used successfully in other provinces.

Angel would be issued something called a "smart card" that he could use for secure deposits and withdrawals. For Angel such technologies were intimidating. As a farmer he knew how to extract the maximum potato yield from thin windswept soil using the simplest of implements.

In other situations his lack of literacy worked against him. More than once he had made his mark on a bank note only to find that the loan came with an exorbitant interest rate that drained his meager savings.

After one such painful experience he made sure that his wife Serafina, a no-nonsense bargainer who had completed elementary school, worked with him on any loan application. She would have left the children with a cousin and come with Angel on this trip if the youngest child had not come down with a fever at the last minute.

For many years the city of Oczuc had offered adult basic education courses free of charge to residents of the province. But the trek from his village to the capital for classes was too demanding and took too much time away from his livelihood.

At the bank, he heard interesting news. On a pilot basis, the city would be sending out basic education instructors to conduct once-a-week classes in each village. If enough villagers showed interest, the capital might assign a full-time instructor. The tax credit refund made it easier to justify taking time off from his labor.

He planned to enroll.

END NOTE

1. Not based on a true story — yet.

2

Poverty

Poverty as Lack of Human Freedom

Human poverty is about more than lack of income or the lack of access to basic consumption needs. It has been conceptualized as capability deprivation or the lack of freedom to pursue one's chosen goals in life.[1] It includes factors like gender equity, social inclusion, and respect for human rights.[2]

The United Nations Development Program employs an index that takes such factors into account. There are two versions of its Human Poverty Index, one for developing countries that emphasizes basic living standards (e.g. access to health services, availability of safe drinking water) and one for industrialized countries that gives greater weight to income and employment.

Under the UNDP's framework, an all-out attack on global poverty would go well beyond making available a minimally adequate income. It would address the essential aspects of human and societal development. My goals in this book are more modest. For global poverty measurement and comparison purposes, I fall back on income or consumption. The tax credit proposal is limited to the income variable.

An all-fronts war on human poverty will need to go on. Still, a minimum income guarantee through the tax system will underpin prospects for the broader development of human capabilities.

This chapter is an excursion into the measurement and estimation of global poverty. Projecting the cost of a global tax credit depends on the number of extremely poor people in the world and their rate of participation in the tax credit scheme. No one knows what those numbers are. And no one disputes the need for scientific consensus on poverty measurement issues and improvements in data quality.

The design and cost estimation of a refundable tax credit would benefit from better data on poverty. Obviously the smaller the actual number of extremely poor people in the world and the lower the participation rate by those eligible, the less costly the credit. And vice versa. The current data limitations need to be understood and acknowledged since they bear on the projected scope and cost of a refundable tax credit.

Global Poverty Estimates

The literature on global poverty reveals a lively, at times even acrimonious, debate on how best to estimate the extent of extreme global poverty. The virtual monopoly on poverty data production and analysis enjoyed for decades by the World Bank has eroded. The World Bank's estimates continue to command respect but not total allegiance among independent researchers.

The World Bank estimates the number of people in extreme poverty in 2000 at nearly 1.1 billion or 21.1 percent of the developing world's population. By 2015, this is expected to fall to 622 million or 12.5 percent.[3] Good news, except for those left in extreme poverty.

Extreme poverty is concentrated in developing countries of Asia, Africa, Latin America and the Caribbean. Three-quarters of the extremely poor live in rural areas, dependent for survival on agriculture or related agro-business activities.[4] Those at greatest risk are "rural households headed by women whose husbands have migrated to urban centers in search of paid employment."[5] India, Bangladesh, Indonesia and China alone account for three-quarters of the world's extremely poor rural people.[6]

Between a quarter and a third (300 million to 420 million) of the world's poorest live in chronic or persistent poverty.[7] They can expect to live for extended periods, if not all their lives, with hunger, illiteracy, unsafe water, lack of access to health care, exploitation and social isolation. They suffer disproportionately from racial, ethnic, gender, or caste discrimination. They are marginalized in labor markets. They are routinely blamed for social ills like crime and disease.

The chronically poor have not chosen their lot and many try hard (but unavailingly) to improve their circumstances. They work for oppressively long hours in dirty and dangerous jobs for little pay.[8] They will most likely pass their poverty on to their children.[9]

Extreme poverty, whether transitional or chronic, disproportionately affects certain demographic subgroups: children, single parents, persons with disabilities, seniors, indigenous peoples, refugees, migrants and internally displaced persons.

The World Bank relies for its estimates primarily on consumption expenditure data from national surveys, particularly a series of Living Standards Measurement Surveys conducted at irregular intervals in a number of countries.[10] Consumption is widely taken as a more valid indicator of one's standard of living than income but consumption data are not always available. Even when there are data, the categories of consumption included in household surveys are not standardized. Income is often taken as a proxy for consumption.

Table 1. People Living on Less Than $1 a Day: 1990, 2001

- People Living on Less Than $1 a Day -

Developing World	Millions (1990)	Percent of Population (1990)	Millions (2001)	Percent of Population (2001)
China	375	33.0	212	16.6
Rest of E. Asia/Pacific	97	21.1	60	10.8
South Asia (incl. India)	462	41.3	431	31.3
E. Europe & Central Asia	2	0.5	17	3.6
Latin America & Caribbean	49	11.3	50	9.5
Middle East & North Africa	6	2.3	7	2.4
Sub-Saharan Africa	227	44.6	313	46.4
Total-1	**1,218**	**27.9[a]**	**1,089**	**21.1[a]**
Total-2	**1,218**	**23.1[b]**	**1,089**	**17.8[b]**

[a]Percent of developing world population.
[b]Percent of total world population (my calculations).
Source: World Bank (2005a) 21.

Within countries, the measurement of poverty is affected by differences in the cost of living between rural and urban areas. Furthermore, what poor households actually consume differs from the non-poor. The poor must concentrate their limited resources on meeting basic needs like food, clothing and shelter. They are far less able to enjoy more modern lifestyle "necessities" like cars, telephones and computers, let alone outright luxuries.

Increasingly levels of consumption from non-market sources (for example, a person's own land) are imputed but the methods by which such consumption is valued vary. The quality of household survey data is not consistent from one survey to another. No one is completely satisfied with the survey data that underpins global poverty estimation.

Individual countries are free to (and do) devise their own official poverty lines. However, for purposes of global poverty estimation, a global metric is required. Toward this end, the World Bank draws first on a set of international prices adjusted to local currencies.

Purchasing Power Parity

Purchasing Power Parity (PPP) exchange rates take into account the cost of a common basket of goods for the compared countries. The data and methods for calculating PPP rates have evolved over several decades to facilitate international comparisons of countries' Gross Domestic Product and other elements of national accounts.

During the 1950s and 1960s, United Nations' teams, under the leadership of Nobel Prize economists Richard Stone and Simon Kuznets, developed a standardized System of National Accounts. Most countries make entries in accordance with the UN system's concepts, definitions, accounting rules and formatting. The data for each country's national accounts come from three main sources: administrative records, national censuses and sample surveys.

Obviously the frequency, mix and quality of these data sources vary from country to country. National accounts provide a comprehensive framework within which national economic data can be gathered and presented in a format suited to economic analysis and policymaking.[11]

The UN's System of National Accounts initially enabled a country to monitor its own economic performance over time but did not permit cross-country comparisons. In 1968, with assistance from the Ford Foundation, the United Nations established the International Comparison Program to foster the development of multilateral comparisons.

Benchmark studies were required that would enable the price data in local currencies for national accounts to be converted into an internationally comparable "currency."[12] In the years following, a number of such studies were conducted with the participation of the United Nations, and since 1980, Eurostat at the European Union, the Organization for Economic Cooperation and Development and UN Regional Commissions.

After 1980, PPP exchange rates were derived from the Penn World Tables, which extended and integrated regional benchmark studies into a global framework. This work, undertaken at the University of Pennsylvania, updated and reconciled data from earlier International Comparison Program rounds. The World Bank has created its own consumption-based adaptation of these tables.

In the 1980s, the International Comparison Program was taken over as a cooperative venture of the United Nations Statistical Office, Eurostat and the Organization of Economic Cooperation and Development.[13] Price surveys are conducted in participating countries every three years. Since 1993, the World Bank has coordinated the International Comparison Program in non-OECD countries. The data set covers about three hundred surveys in ninety countries.

The PPP$1 a Day Standard

PPP exchange rates have been used by the World Bank as a way to compare the incidence of poverty across countries. The PPP$1 a day and PPP$2 a day were adopted as poverty thresholds since they appeared typical of the official poverty lines in very low-income countries. Thus the poverty population is composed of people living below PPP$1 or PPP$2 a day using 1985 international prices (equivalent at 1993 international prices to PPP$1.08 and PPP$2.15 respectively).[14]

By this standard, a person categorized as poor in a developing country must survive each day on what a person in the United States would pay for a cup of coffee.

In theory, at the purchasing power parity rate, PPP$1 has the same purchasing power in any country's domestic economy as it has in the United States. The prices of a common "market basket" of items across different countries are converted into a common standard price. If US$10 were converted to another country's currency and could buy five times as much in the market basket in that country compared to its purchasing power in the United States, the US$10 would equate to PPP$50.

Measuring poverty is as much art as science. Purchasing power parity exchange rates, for example, were developed not to compare poverty rates among countries but to compare aggregates from national accounts. "Thus there is no certainty that an international poverty line measures the same degree of need or deprivation across countries."[15]

Put another way, the local currencies of two countries may have the same purchasing power parity but that does not necessarily mean that the people in both—especially the poorest—have the same standard of living. To ameliorate this problem somewhat, since 1990, instead of using PPP exchange rates for aggregate output, the Work Bank has relied on a separate series of PPP exchange rates for consumption.[16]

Problems with timeliness, consistency and reliability of pricing survey data persist. The World Bank endeavors to provide consistent comparisons over time. When new and better data become available, the World Bank updates its poverty estimates not only for the current period but for prior periods as well.

This approach yields internal consistency across countries and regions over time. It can also produce large revisions in the official poverty estimates for individual countries and regions. With more surveys and better pricing data, Sub-Saharan Africa reveals a larger share of the global poor than previously estimated, offsetting a higher rate of global poverty reduction elsewhere.

However unsettling this may be, "it is hard to argue that we should ignore new data on either the distributions [of poverty] or the PPP exchange rates."[17] For all its widely acknowledged limitations, the PPP approach is, as they say, the only game in town (or on the planet). As the data get better, startling new findings on global poverty may appear abruptly.

Until 1993, the World Bank adjusted the estimates of mean income from surveys to make them accord with income and consumption data from national accounts. However, the testing of data from some twenty countries indicated that, while income data yielded a higher mean than consumption data, it also displayed greater income inequality.

Thus, and paradoxically, income data indicated that the poor had a higher income than indicated by consumption data but at the same time a smaller share of aggregate national income. The difference created by these two disparate effects was not statistically significant. Since they roughly offset each other, the World Bank felt safe in measuring poverty directly from survey data rather than making adjustments to accord with national accounts.[18]

While survey data and national accounts may differ widely and even be diverging over time, survey data may still be the most accurate way to measure poverty (as distinct from income inequality or other variables). Even if the poor had the same incentive as the rich to underreport their incomes or consumption to interviewers, their resources base and hence their margin for "fudging" is much more constricted.

National Poverty Budgets

Instead of the "arbitrary" PPP$1 a day standard, some analysts would prefer to anchor poverty estimates in national budget standards, that is, the baskets of goods and services considered essential by society to satisfy basic needs, participate in societal life or meet some other criteria.

Critics contend that, the claims of the World Bank to the contrary, "the international poverty line does not correspond consistently or closely to the official domestic poverty lines of poor countries."[19] According to these critics, poverty statistics should measure "adequacy not arbitrary thresholds."[20] The PPP$1 a day standard "does not correspond to any single underlying conception of poverty, [such as] human needs or elementary capabilities."[21]

There are additional problems relating to the updating of the PPP$1 a day measure. For example, if a country's currency appreciates relative to the U.S. dollar, its extreme poverty rate falls.

Why? Say a country's currency is denominated in "bolls" and the PPP conversion is ten to one. Hence, one U.S. dollar is equivalent in purchasing power to ten bolls. An annual income of US$365 is equivalent to 3,650 bolls, putting everyone below this income level in extreme poverty.

Suppose the currency strengthens in relation to the dollar and a PPP$1 is worth only five bolls. The income required for extreme poverty status drops to 1,825 bolls and a large chunk of the population is lifted out of extreme poverty. Conversely, if the currency weakens, making PPP$1 equivalent to twenty bolls instead of ten, the number of people in extreme poverty mushrooms.

Critics argue that these kinds of changes are only statistical artifacts, not valid measures of the incidence of poverty. Additionally, it is not possible to tell for any given country what proportion of basic food and shelter needs is covered by the PPP standard. PPP price indices include many items that may be cheap in a developing country but outside the bundle of consumption goods required by the poor.[22]

On such grounds, the purchasing power parity approach is rejected as an unreliable indicator for national poverty analyses. Global measures essentially have "limited, essentially propagandistic rather than analytical, value."[23]

What meeting basic needs means can vary from country to country and, for that matter, within countries. However, so long as the contents of a "basket" of consumption goods are defined in the same way, critics contend, it should be possible to gather comparable international data.

Thus, what is meant by "food" as a basic need is understood everywhere, even if the amount and types of food required to meet standards of nutritional adequacy can vary for different countries, regions of a country or population groups within countries.

Such approaches are regarded by their advocates as more meaningful for policy purposes in that they suggest the types of interventions needed at the national level, where action against poverty actually takes place. Countries of course have their own national definitions and standards to measure progress in their poverty reduction initiatives.

In developed countries, the incomes of the poor are invariably higher than the extreme poverty standard. For the United States in 2003, a single individual is deemed poor if his or her annual income is less than $8,980.[24] This works out to US$24.60 a day or $1 an hour, compared to the international definition of extreme poverty as PPP$1 a day.

The variation in official poverty thresholds established by individual governments militates against a global poverty count. A person who is designated as poor in a rich country might be redesignated as rich by moving to a poor country. And vice versa. Given increased immigration rates within and among countries, this takes on more than academic significance. If extreme poverty were ameliorated throughout a developing country, the pressure to migrate from devastated rural areas to urban centers might diminish, as might the pressure to migrate from developing to developed countries.

The PPP$1 a day standard assuredly identifies people who are poor. Referring back to our bolls example, we see that, even if an appreciating currency artificially lifts some people above the poverty line, those who remain below the new threshold are obviously worse off than those above. In statistical terms, with respect to those in extreme poverty, the proportion of false negatives goes up and the proportion of false positives goes down.

True, if the currency weakens, more people are rendered extremely poor. The number of false positives goes up, false negatives down. Some of the new entrants are legitimately poor under the international standard, since under a weakened currency, it would require more bolls to buy the same amount of goods and services as before. The effect is inflationary and causes prices to rise. The PPP$1 a day standard, however, is so minimalist that it would be hard to deny that the remaining "false positives" are not at least severely poor.

Consider the following admittedly *ad hominem* argument. Suppose you had to live on PPP$365 for a year. Where in the world (literally) and under what circumstances could you do that and regard yourself as non-poor? Granted, the depth of your poverty would vary depending on place and circumstances. But poor you most certainly would be. Even if your income doubled under that standard, you probably would continue to consider yourself poor.

Would countries have an incentive to manipulate their currencies in order to increase the number of extremely poor people and thereby qualify for more assistance? Yes. However, this incentive must be examined in light of its macroeconomic effects. A weakening currency will eventually lower the standard of living for the entire population and retard overall economic growth. Few governments will want to risk that consequence.

For all its defects, in my view, a single cross-cutting measure like PPP$1 or PPP$2 a day says something real about the state of global poverty and provides reasonable grounding for international action.[25] If one does accept the measure, the question arises: how does one go about estimating the number of people in the world who all below the threshold? The international debate over this question is lively and persistent.

Household Surveys and National Accounts

The United Nations, through its Statistics Division, maintains an international System of National Accounts (SNA), to which member states contribute data on economic factors like production, income, household expenditures, capital, financial transactions and assets and liabilities. The system, which has been in place since 1953, permits international comparisons of major economic activity. Many national statistical offices also publish their own SNA-like data series.[26]

The United Nations Conference on Trade and Development has adopted an approach to poverty estimation that is based on national income accounts estimates of consumption rather than household survey data.[27] Retaining the PPP$1 a day standard, UNCTAD has concluded that household survey data underestimate the incidence and depth of poverty in the least developed countries.[28]

Other researchers, notably Xavier Sala-i-Martin and Surjit Bhalla, have relied extensively on national income accounts for their analyses. They conclude that the World Bank's figures considerably overestimate the number of people living on less than PPP$1 a day.[29]

Bhalla makes a number of adjustments that combine survey distributions and national accounts means. In the end, he estimates that in 2000 some 647 million people or 13.1 percent of the world's population were living in extreme poverty. Thus, in his analysis, the Millennium Development Goal of halving the global poverty rate (from 29 percent to 14.5 percent) between 1990 and 2015 has been met fifteen years ahead of time.[30]

In a 2002 study, Sala-i-Martin puts the number at 350 million, not 1.2 billion.[31] He draws on income data from national accounts for his control totals while using the survey data to estimate income distribution. More recently, using more sophisticated econometric methods to estimate world income inequality, he finds the even lower number of 195 million in 2000 (the year of the Millennium Declaration), or one-sixth of the 1.2 billion figure reported by the World Bank and United Nations.[32]

In Bhalla's view, "The past 20 years were a golden period for poor people."[33] Sala-i-Martin concurs: "The world just might be in better shape than many of our leaders believe!"[34] Encouraging words, if true. Whether or not one subscribes to their conclusions, Bhalla and Sala-i-Martin have alerted researchers to deficiencies in the World Bank's survey data. The debate over national accounts versus surveys shows little sign of abating.[35]

Most analysts prefer personal consumption expenditures (and income as a fallback) as the key variable for poverty measurement. However, there is wide divergence between aggregate national consumption as estimated in surveys and as reported in national income and product accounts. The latter approach tends to increase mean income per person and therefore drive down the number of people below the PPP$1 a day threshold.[36] Surveys capture only a fraction of the national account estimates and the divergence grows over time.[37]

One option is to derive the income distribution from surveys, since this is not available in national accounts, and take consumption expenditures from national accounts. Consumption is then allocated among population subgroups (e.g. quintiles) according to their share of the national income. If the poorest quintile has five percent of the income (per the surveys), then it accounts for five percent of total consumption (as taken from national accounts).

However, this approach is not without its own difficulties. For one thing, in surveys higher income households are more likely to underreport consumption; hence, without appropriate adjustments, the share of total consumption assigned to lower income households may be overstated.[38] This in turn overestimates the mean income per person and drives down the number of people below the PPP$1 a day threshold.

National accounts report personal consumption expenditures as well as other such expenditures that benefit households. The latter include expenditures by non-profit organizations like charities, religious organizations, legal aid societies and certain educational institutions that serve low-income people on a free or below cost basis.[39] So one problem is how to aggregate personal consumption at the household level with other consumption spending that benefits the household.

Finally some public spending, say, on health care or subsidized housing, directly benefits the poor as well as some non-poor persons. Other public spending (e.g., for national defense or law enforcement) serves the general population. The challenge is how to allocate shares of these types of expenditures among income groups for purposes of poverty estimation.[40]

On Behalf of Surveys

The findings on poverty from a blend of national accounts and survey data rest on assumptions that are open to challenge. For instance, as Martin Ravallion notes, if surveys cannot be trusted for their consumption data, why should they be trusted for their income distribution data?[41] And why should national accounts be taken as the gold standard for consumption in the first place?

Yes, the nations of the world work with the same categories and international definitions of those categories. They gather national accounts data on a regular basis whereas surveys are conducted episodically. But this does not guarantee the validity and reliability of the national accounts data sources. Everything comes out looking tidy but the accounts may be riddled with errors. What is included in categories like "consumption" varies between surveys and national accounts.[42]

Since it is a residual, consumption will be loaded with the error amounts from other categories that are estimated directly. For many purposes, like estimation of gross domestic product, the errors may cancel each other out. But for poverty measurement, the consequences can be serious. Even if surveys under-estimate consumption, for poverty estimation it may be wrong to adjust on the basis of national accounts and even further to assume that an adjustment is distribution-neutral.

Thus, if the bottom quintile of the income distribution has five percent of the national income, it may be off the mark to assume that their share of any additional consumption not captured in survey estimates is also five percent. It could be as low as zero. A distribution-normal assumption would artificially raise the amount consumed by the lowest quintile, and thereby lead to an undercount of the world's poorest people.

No, the safest course is to ask the poor directly what they consume. Since their resources are minimal, they are unlikely—one might say, unable—to significantly underreport their expenditures. Whatever else may be deficient in surveys, for poverty measurement it is the method of choice.[43] On such grounds, the World Bank defends the survey-only approach and stands by its global poverty population estimates.

No one disagrees that there are problems. Proper sampling using the appropriate sampling frames is challenging. Survey questionnaires may not be updated to reflect new goods and services. Refusal rates can be high and differ significantly among respondent subgroups. With pencil-and-paper methods, there is greater probability of error in recording responses by interviewers and/or subsequent entry of data into survey research databases.

The list goes on. Much needs to be done to improve international survey standards and practice.[44] For example, to test for validity and reliability, income and consumption surveys could be administered to extremely poor people whose income (regardless of source) and assets are known independently. Elaboration of this approach could include a double-blind research design, longitudinal surveys of the same respondents, varied recall periods and sufficiently large samples to permit detailed subgroup analyses.

To the extent that there is a downward bias in survey measures of consumption, there is an upward bias in the World Bank's global poverty estimates.[45] If reliance on national accounts leads to an overestimation of consumption and hence an underestimation of extreme poverty, surveys may lead in the opposite direction. Neither approach serves as a gold standard.

How to adjust for discrepancies between the two approaches, however, is not readily apparent and risks bringing in an unacceptable degree of subjectivity. Should surveys be used to adjust national accounts data or should national accounts data be used to adjust for the lacunae in surveys? Because the data in surveys includes responses directly from the poor, I tend to favor the latter. But that is just one person's opinion. And there is more.

Income, Assets, Spending and Culture

People may be defined as poor under an income standard but may own assets like real property that can be converted into cash. Poverty is not the absence of income so much as the absence of wealth (that is, income plus assets). Additionally, the poor benefit from public spending on "goods" ranging from health care, housing and education to national defense and environmental protection. It is hard to allocate the share of these expenditures that directly benefit the poor in a national context, let alone globally.

The plasticity of poverty as a concept and the absence of valid and reliable poverty data on a global level adversely affect the ability of analysts to estimate its prevalence with much precision. The number of extremely poor people may range from an unlikely low of 195 million to well over one billion. Happily, there is general agreement that global poverty *rates* have declined over time, though not on how much or how fast.

The population living in extreme poverty is not static. People in extreme poverty fall into one of three categories. First, there are those persons whose poverty is transient, due to an adverse event like job loss, divorce, disability, illness or natural disaster. Their poverty tends to be shallow, in the sense that their incomes lie not far from official poverty lines (both above and below).[46] Frequently they recover from such adversities using their own initiative and resources. However, adversity can plunge new cohorts beneath official poverty lines. The cycle repeats itself.

Second, there are those for whom there is no escape from poverty through their own unaided effort. Persons with severe or profound intellectual disabilities fall into this category. Persons lacking literacy or job skills may become permanently unemployed. Their poverty is far deeper, their prospects for overcoming it much dimmer. To survive such persons require income support and social services permanently.

Finally there are those persons in poverty who can escape through a combination of their own efforts, economic opportunity and outside public support. They may be in poverty due to illiteracy, disability, geographic isolation and depressed job markets. Their prospects improve with the expansion of the economy and increased job opportunities, combined with education, skills training, day care (for children), transportation and temporary income subsidies.

Such persons are the intended "target group" for most service-based antipoverty programs. However, identifying them to the exclusion of others in poverty, or, for that matter, non-poor persons who *claim* to be in poverty, is a daunting challenge. Service-based programs try with only mixed success to be target-efficient.

Service providers may lack accurate information for means testing. This can occur because of administrative incapacity (e.g. lack of staff with appropriate skill sets, unreliable data on applicants, inadequate coordination within and across provider organizations) or because the income and assets of applicants come from the informal economy and are simply unverifiable. Even harder is the task of updating information and making re-determinations of eligibility due to *changes* in applicants' status.[47]

Providers may resort to indirect methods, such as targeting selected groups like children, single parents, seniors, or even entire communities. In either case, whether targeting is direct or indirect, some benefits go to those who do not need them, some to those who cannot possibly benefit from them and some (an unknown proportion) to those who can and in many cases do benefit from them. Only through rigorous and controlled evaluation can it be determined whether the recipients would be worse off but for the service intervention.

Current antipoverty strategies emphasize labor-intensive growth strategies with targeted social and sectoral assistance. While there are documented successes along these lines, hundreds of millions of people at a minimum remain mired in income poverty. The pace of progress is unacceptably slow. There is no guarantee that the impressive growth rates in many developing countries over the past several decades are sustainable. Even if they prove to be, there is no guarantee that the extremely poor will benefit significantly, especially if growth exacerbates income inequalities.

More direct action against extreme poverty is needed. A refundable tax credit would lift the permanently poor to a state of "only" severe rather than extreme poverty. It would cushion the transiently poor from personal and economic shocks. It would give a boost to the upwardly mobile poor.

Poverty is often treated as a complex and multi-faceted problem for which no simple solution exists. Yes and no. For income poverty, at least, "it is a matter of simple common sense that...the most direct and obvious way is to put a floor under everyone's income. . . ."[48] The concept of poverty may go beyond income but overcoming the income gap is necessary (if not sufficient) to eliminate poverty.[49] Some developing countries resist the idea of subsidizing income for fear that work effort will be adversely affected and resources will be diverted from capital formation. Point taken.

The goal therefore is to devise a system that insures everyone against the risk of extreme poverty without undermining incentives that are considered essential to economic growth. In this book I set forth a proposal for progressing toward this goal.

Not all who read this book will agree. In that case, I hope they are prepared to offer a more viable alternative. For, if you think, as I do, that no one should have to live on less than PPP$1 a day, there is a compelling case for aggressive action against extreme global poverty.

Certainly the ethical underpinnings are there.

END NOTES

1. Sen, Amartya (1999) 87-110.
2. This view of poverty has been consistently and persuasively advanced by the United Nations Development Program. See www.undp.org.
3. World Bank (2005a) 21-25. As estimation methods have improved (partly in part in response to criticisms by independent outside researchers) and survey data have become more complete and current, the World Bank's estimates of the numbers and proportions of people in extreme poverty for a given year have shown declines in more recent reports compared to its earlier reports. For example, for the year 1996, a 2000 World Bank working paper estimates the number of the world's poorest at 1.191 billion while a subsequent 2004 paper by the same authors arrives at a figure of 1.097 billion, a drop of 94 million. Compare Chen, Shaohua and Martin Ravallion (2004) Table 4 with Chen, Shaohua and Martin Ravallion (2000) Table 2.
4. International Fund for Agricultural Development (2001) iv.

5. Estes, Richard, J. (1997).
6. World Bank (2003b) 105.
7. Chronic Poverty Research Centre (2004) 9.
8. Ibid. 17:
9. Ibid.: 9.
10. The World Bank's database of household surveys has expanded since 1990 when it issued its first estimates of global poverty. The database of 440 household surveys includes 1.1 million randomly sampled households (93 percent of the population of developing countries) from almost one hundred countries. Data quality has improved as well, although problems persist including methods of valuating income (e.g. how to impute profit from the production of non-market goods) and consumption (e.g. estimating the local market value of in-kind consumption). See World Bank (2005b) 286.
11. The initial standardized System of National Accounts was released by the United Nations in 1952. It drew on earlier work by the Organization for European Economic Cooperation, the forerunner of the Organization for Economic Cooperation and Development. The SNA was revised in 1968 and, most recently, in 1993. See Muller, Pierre (2003) 40.
12. United Nations Department of Economic and Social Development: Statistical Division (1992) 2. Also, see pwt.econ.upenn.edu.
13. Maddison, Angus (2002) 171.
14. The $1 a day standard as measure of extreme global poverty was selected since it was seen as being typical of the poverty line in very poor countries. With survey data from eight poor (of 33 total) countries, World Bank researchers observed that their poverty lines averaged about $1.02 a day per person.14 This international poverty line was converted to country currencies using 1985 Purchasing Power Parity exchange rates for consumption. With the greater availability of survey and other relevant data from developing countries, the World Bank updated its findings using the 1993 index. Researchers drew on 265 national surveys from 83 countries as well as more extensive price data for PPP estimates; they also modified their earlier analytical approach (e.g. relying on survey medians rather than simply "eyeballing" country poverty lines). This revised approach netted a $1.08 a day poverty line in 1993 prices, compared to the $1.02 line in 1985 prices. See Clark, Robert F. (2002) 12-13, among others. Bhalla criticizes this adjustment on the grounds that it severely understates the rate of inflation from 1985 to 1993. The difference in the rate of inflation for the two years is not an unrealistically low eight percent (1.08/1.00 minus 1, or roughly one percent a year) but more like 28 percent. If the latter is correct, to maintain 1985's $1 a day standard in 1993 prices would require a poverty line of $1.28. All this would lead one to think that the World Bank's estimates would therefore *understate* the number of extremely poor people in the world. Based on Bhalla's analysis, however, the World Bank significantly *overstates* the number of poor, even with its reduced poverty line. For the $1.08 line, Bhalla finds 559 million poor and for a more "realistic" $1.30 line, 899 million, both well below the World Bank's estimates of 1.1 billion. See Bhalla, Surjit S. (2002) 61-67 and chapter 9.
15. World Bank (2003a) 61.
16. Ravallion, Martin (2001) 150-151.
17. Ravallion, Martin (2001) 151.
18. Ibid.
19. Reddy, Sanjay and Thomas W. Pogge (2002a) 2. Whether domestic poverty lines cluster around the international level depends on the year of the comparison and the type of PPP conversion used. A conversion factor using consumption measures more relevant to the poor (e.g. food) rather than general population consumption measures seems to

increase divergence from the PPP$1 a day line rather than greater clustering around it. Op. cit.: 2-3.

20. Gordon, David, "The International Measurement of Poverty and Anti-Poverty Policies" in Townsend, Peter and David Gordon (2002) 66.

21. Reddy, Sanjay and Thomas Pogge (2002a) 3.

22. Wade, Robert Hunter (2002) 6.

23. Srinivasan, T.N. (2000) 15. He adds that only the "somewhat naïve" believe that policies behind bilateral and multilateral aid to developing countries are "driven by [the developing countries'] levels of poverty."

24. See aspe.hhs.gov/poverty/03poverty.htm.

25. It should be noted that this view is not universally shared. Because it fails to incorporate an explicit poverty bundle that is geared to local currency values, economist T. N. Srinivasan considers the dollar-a-day threshold as essentially "meaningless". Srinivasan, T.N., "The Unsatisfactory State of Global Poverty Estimation" in International Poverty Centre (2004) 4.

26. In a 1993 revision to the original 1968 version, the UN's handbook for the System of National Accounts for the first time specified the relationship among final consumption expenditures and actual final consumption for three sectors: government, Non-Profit Institutions in Service to Households (NPISH) and households. This was a welcome development. The source data come solely from expenditures and hence actual final consumption for the whole economy is exactly equal to final consumption expenditures.

27. United Nations Conference on Trade and Development (2002) 50-51. The national-accounts-consistent approach is not without its own limitations for household poverty estimation. For example it implicitly includes spending by nonprofit groups, not just households. Private consumption is calculated as a residual from other economic aggregates like output, imports, inventory changes and the like. Relying on national income accounts alone has resulted in overestimation of the rate of poverty reduction. For its poverty reduction forecasts, the World Bank generally assumes that household consumption growth rates will equal 87 percent of the private consumption growth rates from the national income accounts. See World Bank (2001a) 40. Hence national income accounts cannot serve uncritically as a "gold standard" for poverty measurement.

28. Why this should occur is not well understood. UNCTAD speculates that the very poor may be underrepresented in national household surveys and that the value assigned to home-produced consumption is inflated. See United Nations Conference on Trade and Development (2002) 50-51. However, the World Bank concludes that in household surveys "higher-income groups tend to underreport consumption." (World Bank (2001a) 45. The debate goes on.

29. Perhaps a clarification is in order. The World Bank does use reported consumption growth rates from national accounts to align its survey data (which come from different countries in different years) in order to generate global poverty estimates. Also, where survey data are lacking, consumption is estimated by multiplying survey income data by the share of aggregate private consumption in national income based on national accounts. See World Bank (2001b) 17.

30. Bhalla, Surjit S. (2002) 139-142.

31. Sala-i-Martin, Xavier (2002).

32. Sala-i-Martin, Xavier (2004) draft paper. For this estimate he applies the $1 a day standard in 2000 prices (or $340 a year), with 1996 as the base year. If other $1 a day poverty lines adjusted of inflation are used, the estimates vary. For example, $365 a year ($1 a day) in 1985 corresponds to $495 a year in 2000 and an extreme poverty headcount of 321.5 million. If the poverty line is adjusted still further upward to $570 a day (to account for survey factors like underreporting of the rich), the headcount estimate rises to

398.4 million. These upwardly adjusted poverty lines continue to yield results that are far lower than those reported by the World Bank.

33. Bhalla, Surjit S. (2002) 8, 200.

34. Sala-i-Martin (2004) 39 (draft paper).

35. For our purposes, the debate has the following consequences. On the positive side, the lower the global poverty estimate, the less potentially costly the refundable tax credit we propose. On the negative, if global poverty headcounts as well as rates are declining dramatically, there will be less incentive to support concerted international action on behalf of those remaining in extreme poverty.

36. United Nations Conference on Trade and Development (2002) 50-51.

37. Bhalla, Surjit S. (2002) 109-111.

38. It is inherently more difficult for the extremely poor to underreport their consumption spending since their resources are so limited.

39. These are labeled in the national accounts as Non-profit Institutions Serving Households (NPISH).

40. See United Nations Conference on Trade and Development (2002) 50-51.

41. Ravallion, Martin (2003) 14.

42. Based on a thorough review of the poverty measurement debate in India, Deaton and Kozel comment that "there is no simple shortcut to better poverty measurements by scaling up the survey data to match the national accounts....[T]he two measures of consumption are not the same thing...[and] there are large errors in the National Accounts...." See Deaton, Angus and Valier Kozel (2005) 31. Surveys have their own problems but national accounts are not the solution. Deaton and Kozel note that if India, with its enviable statistical capacity, has difficulty measuring and monitoring poverty, the situation in the rest of the world is "almost certainly worse" (p. 28).

43. Ravallion, Martin (2003).

44. For a more thorough treatment of this issue, see Deaton, Angus (2001) among others.

45. Deaton, Angus (2004) 41.

46. Adams, Richard H., Jr. (2003) 13.

47. United Nations Millennium Project (2004) 94-95.

48. Smolensky, Eugene (2001) 5.

49. Ibid.: 6.

3

Guideposts

Human poverty has persisted throughout history. Attitudes toward poverty have evolved over time, as have the mechanisms by which societies have sought to overcome or at least diminish the incidence of this ancient evil.

Poverty has persisted even as nations hitherto dependent on traditional agriculture were transformed over the past three centuries by urban industrialization and expanded international trade. Latterly the global impact of forces like information and communications technologies, large-scale capital migration and freer trade are remaking the world economy. These forces have brought upward mobility and even prosperity to billions of people—yet left billions more mired in severe or extreme poverty.

Social and economic forces as well as each individual's initiative and sense of personal responsibility play a role in creating and maintaining poverty conditions. In popular discourse, some (usually among the non-poor) blame the poor for their plight, others (the poor themselves and their advocates) blame society. Few in either camp disagree about the degrading effects of long-term poverty on individuals, families and communities.

The lack of consensus over the causes of poverty and the appropriate remedies has hampered the development of social welfare policy. The extent to which poverty is an inherent consequence of market-based, capital-intensive and technology-driven globalization thrives as a subject for research and debate.

Accepting a degree of societal responsibility for assaulting poverty, some governments seek to distinguish between the deserving poor—those able and willing to work but unable to find jobs or those incapable of working due to age, illness, disability or discrimination—and the non-deserving poor who could on their own initiative improve their condition.

Through elaborate eligibility criteria and detailed administrative procedures, governments seek to direct benefits and services to the former. Such targeting approaches often founder in their implementation. The specific policies and procedures designed to differentiate the deserving from the undeserving can create more problems than they solve.

The targeting of social welfare benefits based on popular moral or ethical criteria invariably rachets up transaction costs, leads to high error rates, and spawns discontent among both providers and beneficiaries.

Global economic growth plays a role in reducing poverty but not in eliminating it. Growth itself can produce economic dislocations that adversely affect different demographic groups and different places on the globe. Taking a decisive step to eliminate global poverty requires more than growth alone. An efficient and effective way of redistributing some of growth's benefits to the world's poorest people is needed. Anything less is an affront to our common humanity.

Wisdom of the Ancients

Historically, human societies have in general recognized a special responsibility to those in need. The reasons for this sense of responsibility vary but in the main spring from a few core values.

Pharaonic Egypt (c. 3000-343 BCE) was operated as a command economy and its people supported the state through their labor and through heavy in-kind taxation. However, ordinary Egyptians also benefited from these levies. To cope with unpredictability in the annual inundations of the Nile, which affected the timing and yield of harvests, grain was stored for distribution in times of famine.

Artisans and builders were employed in public works (e.g. construction of palaces and temples) and were paid from the royal treasury. Temple offerings were used in part to feed the poor. Redistribution benefited the upper classes most but "care was taken not to leave too many people with nothing to lose..."[1] The success of these policies is shown by the country's more than two millennia of relatively peaceful development.

Hammurabi, the Amorite who became king of Babylon in 1792 BCE, unified the city-states of Mesopotamia and made his capital one of the great cities of the ancient world. As king he felt a divinely imposed duty to ensure justice and provide for the general welfare. In 1750 BCE, he had 282 laws (most only a sentence in length) engraved onto an eight-foot stele, using the Akkadian language and cuneiform script.

The Code of Hammurabi makes provision for the upkeep of women and children. In the case of divorce (law 137), for example, the man was required to assign his former wife the usufruct of field or garden, as well as goods, to maintain herself and their children until they grew up. At his death she received a portion of the estate equal to that of one son and was free to marry again.[2]

In Plato's *Republic*, the ideal society is governed by an intellectual elite that has tapped into ultimate truth and reality. For Aristotle (384-322 BCE), "the state is a creation of nature and prior to the individual [who], when isolated, is not self-sufficing; and therefore he is like a part in relation to the whole."[3]

Modern notions of self-sufficient individualism would have sounded strange to both philosophers' ears. The root of social policy is the dependence of the individual on the state and vice versa.

To their discredit, ancient Greek and Roman societies countenanced slavery, an inferior status for women, abortion and infanticide. But more humane impulses also surfaced. For example, in Rome, uncertain harvests, irregular transportation schedules and price gouging periodically triggered famines. During two terms as tribune (123-122 BCE), Gaius Gracchus won popular support for his law enabling Roman citizens to buy grain at a subsidized price. This measure helped maintain regular grain supplies and kept a lid on prices in periods of shortage. Eventually the grain subsidy turned into a free dole.[4]

Among other kinds of support, Greek and Roman societies made provision for poor widows, gave pensions or allowances to people with disabilities and established institutions to care for orphans whose fathers died in battle.[5] If nothing else, ancient societies determined that the alleviation of poverty, or at least some cases of poverty, went beyond the responsibility of the individual and merited governmental intervention.

Religion and Poverty

In the world's great religious traditions, voluntary poverty through self-denial can produce a spiritual payoff. Involuntary poverty is another matter. Religious leaders have decried the material disparities between rich and poor and called on the former to share their bounty.

In Hinduism, there is no dichotomy between material and spiritual well-being. Material goods can sustain and enrich the spirit and the spirit can assure the proper enjoyment of material goods. Greed and selfishness prevent people from experiencing the ultimate reality of Brahman but instead condemn them to a cycle of suffering and rebirth.

Commitment to duty (or dharma), material success and love are integral to Hindu teaching, all with the goal of achieving *moksa* or spiritual freedom. Hinduism stresses both the rights of the individual and the collective welfare of humanity, material and spiritual. All have a right to share in the earth's bounty, which comes through Brahman.

The individual and society are interdependent. The individual is entitled to a secure place in society so that he can both contribute to it and derive support from it. In this context, for example, aid should be given to the poor with no thought of reward. India's caste system was evolved as a societal expression of Hindu values but that expression could take other societal forms as well.[6]

Buddhism, which grew out of Hinduism, also recognizes the interplay between physical and spiritual well-being but stresses the priority of the latter over the former. Siddartha Gautama (ca. 563-ca. 463), revered as the Buddha, placed little value on material riches. By extinguishing desire, one achieves victory over suffering, the lot of mankind. A life of few wants and desires paves the way to the final beatitude of nirvana.

The goal is detachment, not poverty per se. When ordinary people are deprived of basic needs and instead are exploited or marginalized, they tend to resort to violence. A just social order provides for full and productive employment so that all people can live together in harmony, free of social tensions, conflict and war. The quality of life in society is measured not by material abundance but by conditions that foster caring and compassion.

Some Buddhist thinkers oppose Western-style antipoverty programs that in their view promote not only the acquisition of material goods but also greed, selfishness and overly competitive behavior. Such external influences undermine traditional beliefs and values. The eradication of poverty is desirable, provided that "poverty" is properly understood in all its dimensions.[7]

The monotheistic faiths of Judaism, Christianity and Islam share a concern for the common welfare. The ancient Hebrew scriptures known collectively as the Old Testament included commandments to give to the poor.[8] These duties are spelled out in the five books of the Torah (Genesis, Exodus, Leviticus, Numbers and Deuteronomy) and elaborated on in the Talmud and in other authoritative Jewish commentaries.[9]

Christianity not only retained this notion but also extended it through the commandment to love one's enemies and through universalization of the concept of "neighbor". Poverty was seen as a permanent feature of human society. Charity towards all but especially toward the poor was the guiding principle.

Among the five pillars of Islam is the duty to give alms.[10] According to the Koran, "To be charitable in public is good, but to give alms to the poor in private is better and will atone for some of your sins."[11] The Prophet Muhammad (570-632), who had been orphaned as a child and raised by an uncle, always emphasized that widows, orphans and people in poverty deserve help and respect.[12]

More broadly, the Prophet's message stressed social solidarity and compassion. The Koran highlights the virtue of *infaq,* or voluntary spending to benefit the poor. Islamic countries mandate almsgiving by law; in non-Muslim countries, local communities collect alms as voluntary gifts. In both cases alms aid the needy and help with the spread of Islam.

Influence of Humanism[13]

In Western societies, especially since the Renaissance, traditional Judeo-Christian values of love and charity as the response to poverty have ceded ground to more legalistic notions of equity and social justice. With the rise of humanism during the sixteenth century, European thinkers began to tout the duty of government rather than the Church to alleviate poverty.

In *Utopia*, humanist (and Catholic saint) Thomas More (1478-1535) has the fictional Portuguese traveler Rafael Nonsenso recount a conversation involving Rafael, the Most Reverend John Morton, Cardinal Archbishop of Canterbury and Lord Chancellor of England, and a certain lawyer. The lawyer wondered why England continued to be plagued with thieves and robbers, since so many were caught and hung.

Rafael responds that, instead of meting out such severe punishment, it would make more sense "to provide everyone with some means of livelihood, so that nobody's under the frightful necessity of becoming first a thief and then a corpse."[14]

When the lawyer rejoins that many trades are open to those who have instead opted for thievery, Rafael launches into a lengthy indictment of English society. Idle nobles extort exorbitant rents from their tenants. Retainers who lose their positions will not accept more menial jobs and instead turn to violence for their livelihoods.

Nobles, gentlemen and abbots enclose ever more land as sheep pasture, evict small farmers, and drive up the price of wool. Incongruously, wretched poverty is linked with expensive tastes, as all classes of society "are recklessly extravagant about clothes and food." They waste money in brothels and at gaming tables.

Rafael's solution? "Stop the rich from cornering markets and establishing virtual monopolies. Reduce the number of people who are kept doing nothing. Revive agriculture and the wool industry, so that there's plenty of honest, useful work for the great army of unemployed. . . .[15]

This falls short of guaranteeing everyone an income. But it does dictate a responsibility for society to change conditions that induce people to resort to violence and thievery as their means of survival.

Thomas More's friend Johannes Ludovicus Vives (1492-1540) was the first to develop an argument and a detailed plan for a minimum subsistence. Born in Valencia into a family of converted Jews, Vives left Spain in 1509 to escape the Inquisition, studied at the Sorbonne, but spent most of his adult life in Bruges.

During a stay in England in the 1520s, he mingled with people prominent in letters and politics, including Thomas More, and was often a guest at the court of Henry VIII. He was exposed to new theories about the duty of the state to provide for the poor and efforts to outlaw begging as a means of support.

Bad harvests in most of Europe during 1521 and 1522 caused widespread hunger and expanded the population of paupers, beggars and vagrants. The various English poor laws for the administration of relief at the parish level influenced Vives' thinking on how to cope with this crisis.

In a 1526 memo to the mayor of Bruges, titled *De Subventione Pauperum* ("On Assistance to the Poor"), Vives proposed that the municipal government assure a subsistence minimum for all its residents. No one, he contended, not even the most dissolute, should die of hunger.[16]

Why is this a social responsibility? Theologically, God's creation is meant for all His children. Those who appropriate nature's gifts for themselves are "thieves" unless they help those in need. Subsistence aid should be extended only to those truly in need but before they are compelled to request it.

However, the poor must deserve the help they get by being willing to work. Those who have lived lives of dissipation should be given "smaller rations and more irksome tasks" in order to serve as an example to others.[17]

Christ had said that the poor would always be with us. Some actually worried that, if poverty were eliminated, these words would be proven false. In strikingly modern terms, Vives replied that "not only those without money…are poor, but those who lack bodily vitality, physical well-being and mental health and sanity…."[18] These latter poor would remain in abundance.

Mild as they may appear to us in the twenty-first century, Vives' proposals ran into opposition from Church leaders. In Bruges, private religious and parish associations rather than municipal authorities handled poor relief.

Elsewhere in Europe, the situation was changing as cities and other local governments introduced new experiments for poor relief. These included, for example, Nuremberg (1522), Strasbourg (1523-24), Leisnig (1523-24), Zurich (1525), Mons (1525), Ypres (1525), Lille (1527), Oudenarde (1531), and Valenciennes (1531).[19] Bruges amended its municipal relief system in 1556.

Assistance to the poor became more bureaucratic and professionalized, particularly in northern and central Europe. Municipal centralization became the order of the day. Relief revenues were pooled into common chests. Larger towns were subdivided into relief districts. Relief administrators investigated the conditions of needy individuals case by case. Registers were maintained that recorded the "name, profession, birthdate and place, occupation and disability as well as the number of dependants of every pauper."[20]

Drawing on these local plans, a 1531 edict by Emperor Charles V fostered the shift from ecclesiastical to municipal control by regulating the practice of begging in his domains but also mandating provision for the sick and needy out of locally managed central funds.[21] Central governments in the Netherlands (1531), England (1531, 1536) and France (1536, 1566) issued laws and decrees on relief and regulation of the poor.[22]

Vives' memo "moulded educated opinion across Europe," both Catholic and Protestant.[23] Small wonder that some Church leaders viewed Vives' approach as a threat to the status quo. Religious orders like the Franciscans, Dominicans, Augustinians and Carmelites denounced it. Faculties at the Sorbonne condemned the Ypres plan for transferring the administration of poor relief from ecclesiastical to civil authorities. The Bishop of Sarepta declared it heretical and subversive, a product of the Lutheran sect.[24]

Not surprisingly, in Catholic Spain, France and Italy, and in the Catholic towns of Germany, the movement toward secular control was slow and spotty. Relief remained largely decentralized (and often haphazard) through the giving of alms to the poor or through the activities of traditional community-based entities like parishes, confraternities and hospitals.

As a response to extortionate moneylenders, communal pawnshops first organized by Franciscans appeared in central and northern Italy in the fourteenth and fifteenth centuries. As charities, the pawnshops made small loans at low or no interest to the poor against common household objects. Spurred by the reforms of the Catholic Counter-Reformation, these *monti de pietà* proliferated throughout Italy and in parts of France. From the available evidence, they met a real need and proved remarkably durable.[25]

However, the secular genie was also out of its bottle. Although Protestant areas were quicker to adopt the new municipality-oriented approach, the objections in Catholic cities and towns were eventually overcome. While seeking to

preserve the autonomy of Church institutions, the Council of Trent acknowledged a role for civil authorities in poor relief. Christian humanist perspectives
prevailed. In many places both systems of poor relief, civil and ecclesiastical,
continued side by side.

By establishing an enclosure commission (1517), founding a College of Phy-
sicians (1518) and implementing measures to offset the effects of bad harvests
(1521, 1527), statesman and churchman Thomas Cardinal Wolsey (1475-1530)
laid the foundations of English social welfare.[26]

As part of the English Reformation, Henry VIII had closed monasteries, de-
stroyed religious orders and thereby "created a vacuum in social welfare."[27]
Recognition of that vacuum helped pave the way for the poor laws. Poverty was
not a condition to be ignored or reflexively punished; instead, relief for the deserving poor was to be provided by the state at public expense. "No other Protestant country had a welfare apparatus paid for by taxation."[28]

Vives' ideas about the role of the state in providing for the poor espoused
principles that were embodied in the great Elizabethan Poor Law of 1601. That
law consolidated an unwieldy tangle of poor relief legislation developed in Britain over the prior century.

Humanist notions found their way into the country's new colonies on the
eastern seaboard of North America. As pioneered in Connecticut, Massachusetts, Pennsylvania, and Virginia, the American system of poor relief included
almshouses for the deserving poor, workhouses for the able-bodied, prisons for
debtors and public hospitals for sick paupers.[29]

Vives had helped set in motion an antipoverty approach that replaced donor
beneficence and isolated local efforts with more coordinated local and national
plans. However, the goal of public assistance continued to be alleviation of individual need rather than elimination of poverty as a social evil.

During the Age of Enlightenment, French thinkers like Montesquieu,
Diderot, Rousseau and Voltaire attracted followers among the newly educated
middle classes of eighteenth century Europe. While their writings tended to buttress notions of constitutional government, they themselves were not averse to
advising such "enlightened despots" as Frederick the Great in Prussia and Catherine the Great in Russia.

In the latter capacity, these *philosophes* advocated for such reforms as equality before the law and reduction of noble and clerical privileges. They thus lent
support to the emergence of liberal governments in the post-revolutionary era of
the late eighteenth and nineteenth centuries.

In his *L'Esprit des Lois*, the product of twenty years' labor, Montesquieu
(1689-1755) sought to uncover the principles and on-the-ground conditions that
would enable laws to contribute to the happiness of man in society. He examined laws in relation to government, climate, customs, religion and other characteristics of a country.

He observed that "in proportion as luxury gains ground in a republic, the
minds of the people are turned toward their particular interests..." and concluded famously, "Republics end with luxury; monarchies with poverty."[30]

According to the English political philosopher John Locke (1632-1704), "God gave the world to men in common . . . [and] . . . the fruits it naturally produces, and beasts it feeds, belong to mankind in common. . . ." The improvements to the earth made by an individual's labor give rise to the right of private property. "As much land as a man tills, plants, improves, cultivates, and can use the product of, so much is his property." Still, as I read Locke, the right to private property is not absolute, since it should not operate to the "prejudice" of the rest of mankind.[31]

For Thomas Paine, the issue boiled down to a matter of stakeholding.

A Stake in Society

Thomas Paine (1737-1809) is justly celebrated for his authorship of *Common Sense*, a pamphlet issued on January 10, 1776 that powerfully influenced the American movement toward independence.

The Rights of Man, written in defense of the French Revolution and published November 1790, contended that the young, aged and indigent deserved public assistance not as charity but as a right. In Part II of this great work, published in February 1792, Paine attacked the British monarchy, advocated world revolution on behalf of democracy and presented ideas for making wars unnecessary.

In other writings, Paine advocated governmental reform, popular education, poor relief, pensions, and a progressive income tax.[32] For our purposes, his argument and plan for wealth transfer deserve particular note.

There are echoes of Vives in his rationale. Land is the natural inheritance of all people. The privatization of property can result in improvements in the land through cultivation; at the same time, it leaves many of a nation's inhabitants dispossessed of their inheritance, thereby plunging them into poverty. As a matter of right, not charity, they should be indemnified against this loss.

> "[The plan I propose is] to create a national fund, out of which there shall be paid to every person, when arrived at the age of twenty-one, the sum of fifteen pounds sterling, as a compensation in part, for the loss of his or her natural inheritance, by the introduction of the system of landed property...And also, the sum of ten pounds per annum, during life, to every person now living, of the age of fifty years, and to all others as they shall arrive at that age."[33]

Thus, Paine's conception of social justice was "grounded" in land as the common inheritance of humanity, the role and function of privatization notwithstanding. Everyone therefore is entitled to some share in the land's bounty. This contrasts with Aristotle's emphasis on the individual as a component of the social whole, thereby setting up reciprocal obligations between people and the state. For both Aristotle and Paine, the notion of the individual as being in opposition to society would have sounded very strange indeed. The issue is one of finding the appropriate balance between individual autonomy and liberty and the demands the state can make on the individual on behalf of the general welfare.

The French Factor

Concern for the welfare of the poor marked the political rhetoric of the French Revolution, whose leaders depended on the support of the masses. The Swiss banker Jacques Necker (1732-1804), the reform-minded (but ultimately unsuccessful) director general of finance under Louis XVI, saw the elimination of poverty not only as a moral but also a political imperative.

While in prison for his role in the French Revolution, a contemporary of Necker and Paine, the Marquis de Condorcet (1743-1794), journalist, mathematician, and member of the Convention, penned a treatise in which he espoused a system of social insurance.

Employing actuarial and investment analysis methods, he devised a system to benefit older persons, widows, and fatherless children. The basic idea was to distribute the savings of those who died before they could enjoy them. The principles of insurance would be applied not just to individuals or groups but to society at large.[34]

Utopian socialist Charles Fourier (1772-1837) argued that civilization owes the means of subsistence to people unable to meet their basic needs because they are deprived of access to natural resources. Such access included the right to hunt, fish, pick fruit and graze cattle on common lands. Subsistence would take the form of lodging in a sixth class hotel and three meals a day.

For Fourierists, eligibility for subsistence, while not entailing a work test, was nonetheless not unconditional. Rather it was intended as compensation to the poor for being deprived of certain basic rights.[35]

In John Stuart Mill's description of Fourierism, this was changed. Industrial associations would make distribution of a certain minimum of production "for the subsistence of every member of the community, whether capable or not of labour."[36] Thus Mill clearly but mistakenly ascribes to Fourier an unconditioned right to subsistence.

In a book published in 1848, Joseph Charlier (1816-1896), a Brussels lawyer, proposed a scheme under which every citizen would receive quarterly—later changed to monthly—a minimum income payment. Following in the Fourier tradition, Charlier saw the right to a regular guaranteed income as flowing from an equal right of all to ownership of land.

The amount of the payment would be based on the rental value of all real estate. The payments would constitute a monetary equivalent of sharing out equally the common patrimony. He viewed his scheme, labeled variously as "minimum", "revenue garanti", and eventually "dividende territoriale", as a means of ending the domination of capital vis a vis labor. Since the income would truly be minimal, it would not encourage excessive idleness. Anything above the minimum would have to come from paid work.[37]

His contemporary, French professor of philosophy and social theorist François Huet (1814-1869), sought to reconcile the extremes of individualism and communism while integrating Christian concepts with the ideals of the French Revolution: liberty, equality, fraternity.

Instead of a basic income, he endorsed sharing the common patrimony (or divine patrimonium) with individuals through an unconditioned capital endowment.[38] This patrimony includes produced assets as well as the means of production. It would be funded through a one hundred percent inheritance tax.

While the value of uncultivated land might in principle be shared out equally, what about the value of improvements? Or, more broadly, what is the appropriate distribution of net new assets produced from the earth's resources through the investment of capital and labor by individuals and groups? What are the appropriate shares for these producing entities relative to all others? The answers vary from one society to another.

Charlier and Huet appear to have been unaware of each other's work. Both have largely been ignored, despite their standing as progenitors of current debates over the comparative merits of basic income versus stakeholder grant schemes.

The first formal consideration of a negative income tax appears in the writings of the brilliant French economist Augustin Cournot (1801-1877).[39] The concept in more modern garb appears to have been first advanced by the British economist Abba Lerner and subsequently further developed and popularized by the American Milton Friedman.[40]

Social Justice and Religion

In recent centuries, leaders in some religious traditions have worked to improve conditions for the poor as less as a matter of compassion or even moral obligation than as a matter of social justice. The notion of fairness in the distribution of society's burdens and rewards underlies the concept.

Usually the advocates of social justice envision a prominent role for government in assuring a decent quality of life for all citizens. Critics of the concept see it as a cover for social engineering and a threat to individual liberty and enterprise.

In the second half of the twentieth century, the concept of social justice as a religious ideal gained ground over traditional charity and almsgiving. Churches began putting pressure on governments for more aid to the poor and worked to empower poor people and their communities.

A prominent example of this trend is found in Latin America. In the Roman Catholic Church, a new liberation theology promoted by certain bishops and priests contended that one's personal salvation was inseparable from the struggle for social justice. In 1968, at the Second General Conference of the Latin American Bishops in Medellín, Colombia, a "preferential option for the poor" was institutionalized.

In part this stance was a response to the inroads by Protestant sects and socialist movements, in part dissatisfaction with traditional Catholicism, which was seen as tied too closely with the wealthier classes and insufficiently sensitive to the poverty of Latin America's masses.

Before long, more traditional forces in the Catholic Church reasserted themselves. The Vatican silenced left-leaning bishops and replaced those who retired or died with conservatives. At the Fourth General Conference of the Latin American Bishops, held in Santo Domingo in 1992, the emphasis was on personal holiness, not social activism. Even so, another genie had escaped from its bottle. Some new conservative bishops who faced the reality of extreme poverty and other social evils have come to support social activism and lay initiatives in their dioceses.[41]

For a number of religious traditions, a fundamental moral measure of any economy is how the poor and vulnerable are faring. In the United States, for example, Catholic bishops asserted: "If persons are to be recognized as members of the human community, then the community has an obligation to help fulfill these basic needs unless an absolute scarcity of resources makes this strictly impossible."[42]

Members of other Christian traditions have interpreted their religious beliefs as warrants for the pursuit of social justice. In essence they argue that, in order to be able to live in decency and dignity, the poor have a basic (that is God-given) right to some share of society's resources. Across the spectrum of Christian beliefs, religious groups have come together to push for an end to global poverty. They are pressuring world leaders to be more vigorous in pursuing the Millennium Development Goals, one of which is to halve extreme global poverty by 2015.

Rawlsian Justice

In the secular world of the twentieth century, liberal-egalitarian notions of social justice predominated among western theorists, among whom philosopher and social theorist John Rawls (1921-2002) stands out. Rawls conceived justice as fairness, a condition in which there is "social cooperation among equals for mutual advantage."[43] The implicit notion of reciprocity has been drawn on in arguments for and against a guaranteed basic income.

Rawls was concerned among other things with the just distribution of "primary goods", that is, universally desired resources (like rights, liberty, freedom, income, assets) that enable one to pursue his conception of the good. He postulated a hypothetical "original position" in which members of society, who start out as rough equals, agree on the principles of fairness without knowing how they as individuals will be affected as a result.

Thus, for a case like income distribution, they will not know where on the socio-economic pecking order they will end up. Society is predicated not in the equality of results but in the equality of basic rights and duties.

For Rawls, social and economic inequalities are tolerable in a just society so long as "they result in compensating benefits for everyone, and in particular for the least advantaged members of society."[44] This difference principle, as it is known, has attracted critics from the right, who resist redistribution, and the left, who cannot countenance inequality. The former refuse to acknowledge a shared human patrimony and the latter minimize the connection between inequality and incentives for self-improvement.[45]

Given the Rawlsian emphasis on rights and duties, which suggests reciprocity among the members of society, some use the difference principle to advocate societal assistance only for those who are incapable of supporting themselves.

Society is a cooperative enterprise and only the cooperators share its benefits. Critics reject the notion of subsidizing people able but unwilling to work or, to put it differently, the voluntarily disadvantaged. Others, however, expand the notion of reciprocity beyond the metric of paid work. It is taken as embracing all aspects of life—work, leisure, parenting, hobbies, volunteerism, self-improvement, etc.—and the whole of society, not just its members individually.

Seen through this lens, the principle of reciprocity can justify providing a minimum measure of security for all as a way of stimulating the release of latent human capabilities. That, of course, is the approach parents take with their children. Some free riders (the legendary "Malibu surfer") may abuse the privilege but in the long run and on the whole society will gain more than it loses.[46]

Thus, in the context of a guaranteed basic income for all, the Rawlsian concept of justice cuts both ways. Writing as an American, Rawls tended to view society in terms of the nuclear family and the autonomous nation-state. Others will determine how well his core ideas can be applied to the emerging global village.[47] For instance, it remains to be seen whether and if so the extent to which the difference principle should govern relations among nation-states.

Some Basic Propositions

The arguments for minimum levels of support for the poorest boil down to a few propositions. Whether or not conceived as God-given, we share a common humanity. We naturally organize ourselves into human societies. This creates rights and responsibilities for the individual on one side and for the social units to which he or she belongs on the other.

The relative weight assigned to these four factors—individual rights, individual responsibilities, societal rights, societal responsibilities—varies from one social unit to another. The state is the overriding social unit and can make the largest claims on the individual. At the same time it is responsible for assuring the welfare of its individual members.

The earth's resources are a common trust. Whoever exploits these resources has an obligation to share at least some of the benefits with the larger society. For the world's great religious traditions, that implies a special responsibility for those in the greatest need.

However, overcoming material poverty must not in turn create poverty of the spirit. The goal is individual happiness and social harmony. The acquisition of material goods is desirable only so long as it contributes to that fundamental goal. The state is the ultimate guarantor that the earth's resources are used for the benefit of all.

Despite some progress over the past decades, the persistence of extreme poverty is testimony to the failure of the "state"—in this case, the world community—to serve as that guarantor.

END NOTES

1. See nefertiti.iwebland.com/economy. Informative website maintained by a self-professed non-specialist in Egyptology.
2. Hammurabi's code may be found at several websites. One of the best is at Yale, www.yale.edu/lawweb/avalon/medieval/hamframe.htm.
3. Aristotle (1885).
4. The *lex frumentaria* permitted citizens to buy grain from the government at 6 2/3 sesterces per modius (or "bushel"). Citizens would buy on the private market so long as prices remained below that level but, if prices rose above it, they had an alternative, providing they could endure long lines. See www.barca.fsnet.co.uk/gracchus-gaius.htm
5. Trattner, Walter I. (1999) 1-2.
6. www.btinternet.com/~aurelia/povertyandhinduism.htm. India's hierarchical caste system, which has shaped its history for several thousand years, evolved from earlier Vedic society that was divided into four classes, Brahmans, Nobles or Warriors, Commoners and Serfs. For more, see inter alia Radhakrishnan, S. (1989) 371.
7. Premasiri, P.D. (1999).
8. Consider, for example: "When reaping the harvest in your field, if you have overlooked a sheaf in that field, do not go back for it. Leave it for the stranger, the orphan and the widow, so that Yahweh your God may bless you in all your undertakings." (Deuteronomy, 24:19). *The Jerusalem Bible: Reader's Edition.* Garden City, New York: Doubleday & Company, 1968.
9. The entire Hebrew Bible often goes by the relatively modern term Tanak, which is an acronym drawn from its three main divisions: Law (Torah), Nevi'im (Prophets) and Writings (Ketuvim). Its canon largely overlaps but diverges in places from the Old Testaments of Protestants and Catholics. Peters, F.E. (2003) 4, 18-19.
10. The other four are to: (1) confess faith in God and Muhammad as his prophet, (2) perform ritual prayers, (3) perform the fast at Ramadan, and (4) make a pilgrimage to Mecca.
11. Surah 2: 267 ("The Cow"), from the translation by Dawood, N.J. (1999).
12. Nasr, Seyyed Hossein (2002) 171.
13. This section draws heavily on Van Parijs, Philippe (2001a) and Vives, Juan Luis (1526).
14. More, Sir Thomas (1516), Penguin Books edition (1965) 44-49.
15. Ibid.
16. According to Jütte, although Vives dedicated his work to the magistrates of Bruges, he "cannot be credited with prompting the welfare reforms," since the city had already "embarked on a new social policy." See Jütte, Robert (1994) 113. An alternative interpretation is provided by Tobriner, who contends that Bruges did not adopt the principle of municipal administration along Vives' lines until 1556, after the bitterness of Catholic-Protestant controversies and the Council of Trent's condemnation of giving civil authorities the primary role in poor relief. See Vives, Juan Luis (1526) 15 and Endnote 23 below.
17. Vives, Juan Luis (1526) 40.
18. Vives, Juan Luis (1526) 51.
19. These were not the first civil initiatives to regulate assistance to the poor. In the fourteenth century, a municipal ordinance in Nuremburg aimed at limiting the number of beggars to those genuinely in need. In 1522, Nuremburg centralized its aid to the poor, followed a year later by Strasbourg. See Gerembek, Bronislaw (1997) 46, 121.
20. Jütte, Robert (1994) 102.

21. Geremek, Bronislaw (1997) 144.
22. Slack, Paul (1988) 8-9. He emphasizes that the list is not exhaustive, but enough to show that this was a "European phenomenon."
23. Slack, Paul (1988) 9.
24. Vives, Juan Luis (1526) 18. Alice Tobriner, SNJM, a Catholic sister who in 1999 published an English translation of Vives' work, also provided an introduction and commentary from which this account of Church leaders' reaction is derived.
25. Jütte, Robert (1994) 131-132.
26. Slack, Paul (1988) 116. Hostility from the nobility and his failure to obtain papal approval of King Henry VIII's divorce from Catherine of Aragon led to Wolsey's fall from power and ushered in the English Reformation.
27. Slack, Paul (1988) 206.
28. Ibid.
29. Vives, Juan Luis (1526) 25-28.
30. Montesquieu (1748, as translated in Carrithers, David Wallace, 1977) 165-166.
31. Locke, John (1690). Quotes are taken from Chapter 5, "Of Property", Sections 25-51. See inter alia Hwww.constitution.org/jl/2ndtr05.htmH.
32. Most prominently, in Part II of *The Rights of Man*, published in London in February 1792. See Foner, Philip S., editor (1999) xxix-xxx and, for the pamphlet itself, 345-458.
33. Foner, Philip S., editor (1999) 611-613. The plan is included in Thomas Paine's last great pamphlet titled *Agrarian Justice*, which was published in the winter of 1795-96 and is reproduced in Foner (1999) 605-623.
34. Condorcet, Marie Jean Antoine Nicolas Caritat, Marquis de (1988) 273-74.
35. Fourier, Charles (1967) 491-492. More background is found in the history of basic income found at www.bien.be/BI/HistoryBI.htm. This website is indispensable for anyone interested in a universal basic income.
36. Mill, John Stuart (1909) Book II, Chapter I.
37. He expounded his plan in several works, including: 1) *Solution du Problème Social ou Constitution Humanitaire: Basée sur La Loi Naturelle, et Précédée de L'exposé de Motifs*, Bruxelles: Chez Tous les Libraires du Royaume, 1848 and *La Question Sociale Résolue, Précédée du Testament Philosophique d'un Penseur*, Bruxelles: Weissenbruch, 1894. My description draws on *Basic Income* — 32, Spring 1999 (Newsletter of the Basic Income European Network), which is found at www.estes.ucl.ac.be/BIENbackup. Also see Cunliffe, John and Guido Erreygers (2000).
38. Cunliffe, John and Guido Erreygers (2000) 7-9.
39. "Bounties [subsidies]...are the opposite of taxes. To use an algebraic expression, they are a negative tax, so that the same analytical formulas are applicable to taxation and bounties." Cournot, Augustin (1838) 69. See bibliography for information on English edition.
40. Lerner, Abba P. (1947). Friedman, Milton (1962).
41. Swatos, Jr., William H., editor (1998). The discussion of the Catholic Church in Latin America draws on the encyclopedia's web version's entry on "Preferential Option for the Poor".
42. United States Conference of Catholic Bishops (1986) Introduction.
43. Rawls, John (1999) 13.
44. Ibid.
45. Political systems like socialism and communism of course exemplify the extreme leftist perspective. On the far right, we have libertarianism, which advocates maximum individual liberty within a minimalist state. Libertarian philosopher Robert Nozick, a critic of Rawls' difference principle, argues on libertarian grounds that the principle of redistributive justice cannot be used to warrant an individual's (or a group's) entitlement

to a portion of society's collective assets. Hence, on this principle, a more extensive state is not called for to achieve a more "equitable" distribution of society's resources. However, he does introduce what he calls the "principle of rectification". Past injustices may have left their victims — and their victims' descendants — worse off than they otherwise would have been. (One thinks of the history of slavery and racial discrimination in the United States as a case in point.) A more extensive state might be required "in the short run" to compensate for past injustices through, e.g., "a scheme of transfer payments". More broadly, to address past injustices, he offers as a *"rough* rule of thumb" that society could organize itself "so as to maximize the position of...[the] least well off in society." Nozick, Robert (1974) 231. Thus do the musings of philosophers at times collide with social and historical realities.

46. The Malibu surfer image, a staple in debates over a guaranteed basic income, was first employed by Rawls.

47. Nussbaum, Martha (2001).

4

Europe

Social Welfare in Europe

The relationship of welfare to work has thrived as a subtext of European social welfare history. Attitudes toward poverty evolved over time. Perceived as having a special place in God's eyes, the medieval poor as individuals were objects of Christian charity.

The poor as a class were a different story. They were associated with dirt, disease, idleness and contagion. In medieval Europe, poverty scythed through large swaths of society. It was driven by factors like war, periodic food crises, demographic growth, new economic forces and the effects of the Black Death. Such factors led to the proliferation of begging and vagrancy—which were regarded as a scourge by both ecclesiastical and secular authorities.

Such economic security as existed was grounded in the feudal system. Serfs were obligated to perform manual labor and pay taxes to their lord. According to custom, lords protected their serfs from hunger, abject poverty and invasion.

That system began to break down during the thirteenth and fourteenth centuries due to a number of factors, including the proliferation of small farms, an emerging market economy, the wider use of money, destructive wars (for example, the Hundred Years War), epidemics like the Black Plague and social polarization.[1]

Under Church law, the wealthy had an obligation in both justice and charity to share their resources with the less fortunate. The aged, persons with disabilities, widows and others outside the labor force relied on family members and relatives for support. In the medieval period, assistance to the poor was also provided through the vast network of monasteries, dioceses and parishes.

In the eyes of the Church, poverty took on two forms: voluntary and material. Voluntary poverty was embedded in Church teaching and life as a way to link man with God. It had spiritual value. The clergy and members of religious orders vowed to live in poverty, chastity and obedience. Some holy people chose lives of poverty as a form of protest against the power and wealth of their Church.

Material poverty characterized those who, for one reason or another, could not provide for their basic needs. Toward these latter, medieval society had ambivalent attitudes. On the one hand, poverty was seen as a shameful and degrading condition. The poor were looked down on with pity or disdain.[2]

On the other hand, Christians were taught to see Christ in the faces of the poor. The poor had inherent dignity in the eyes of God and deserved assistance. In practical terms, priority was given to those who had no means of supporting themselves over those who were capable of work but instead chose idleness, thievery, vagrancy and begging.

Charitable assistance was not designed primarily to alleviate poverty as a social condition but rather to enable the giver to earn spiritual merit. The scale of almsgiving was enormous in some places.[3] Such charity aimed at alleviating the material plight (hunger, disease, and the like) of poor individuals while emphasizing to them the values of work and moral reform.

Charity took on an institutional form under the aegis of the Church. While the modern hospital specializes in medical care, medieval hospitals were often multi-functional. Besides treating the sick, they might care for orphans and those too old or too disabled to work, take in wayfarers and strangers, serve as hostels for pilgrims, or shelter lepers in segregated facilities. Some of these facilities were attached to monasteries, others had their own endowments.[4]

At the end of the Middle Ages, efforts to centralize aid to the poor were undertaken in Italy. In 1406 Milan established an organization composed of both clergy and lay persons to control aid. In the 1440s, Brescia, Milan and Bergamo created centrally administered general hospitals. Church and secular authorities cooperated in these endeavors.[5]

New Social Structures and the Exacerbation of Poverty

As cities and villages grew and economic relationships became more complex, new types of organizations emerged outside the rural manorial environment and the structures of the Church. From the tenth to the fifteenth centuries, there arose a variety of mutual aid associations of craftsmen or merchants called guilds. The guilds set prices and standards of quality, trained apprentices and protected their interests in society. Eventually there were religious guilds, moneylender guilds, burial guilds and guilds of teachers and students.

The guilds provided a range of benefits to their members that included financial assistance in times of poverty or illness and contributions to help defray the expenses when a member died.[6]

Other factors affected the response of society to the needs of the impoverished—the Protestant Reformation, the Council of Trent and the gradual emergence of the nation-state.

While theological and religious issues were central, the Protestant Reformation of the fifteenth and sixteenth centuries had widespread political and economic consequences. It shattered the religious unity of European society while simultaneously unleashing new forces of social renewal and reconstruction. With the rejection of traditional Catholic doctrine came an expansion of the humanist perspectives espoused by the Dutch scholar Desiderius Erasmus (c. 1466-1536) and emphasis on a simpler, more Biblical piety.

Cities in central and southern Germany and Switzerland were the first to usher in the new order. Despite rejecting a hierarchical priesthood and monasticism, reformer Martin Luther (1483-1546) realized that parishes had to be maintained and "[t]he needs of education and charity had to be met."[7]

Luther influenced the systems of poor relief organized by German towns (beginning in Wittenberg) between 1522 and 1530. He composed the poor ordinance for the Saxonian town of Leisnig. This included establishment of a common chest (a kind of trust fund), of which part was for the benefit of the poor. The common chest was financed by taxation of nobles, townsmen and peasants.[8]

Huldrych Zwingli (1484-1531) in Zurich and John Calvin (1509-1564) in Geneva also confronted not only questions of Christian doctrine and religious practice but also the problems of political governance. In Zurich, under Zwingli's leadership, poor relief was centralized in a single agency.

Although not its founder, Calvin supported the Geneva General Hospital, a lay-managed multi-purpose facility that replaced a number of different and competing institutions. Under a 1541 ordinance, the hospital's lay governors were recognized as deacons and had the duty of ministering to the poor out of Church revenues. Calvinistic principles of poor relief were adopted in the Netherlands near the end of the century.[9]

During the sixteenth century, the religious focus on mysticism, monastic life and holy virginity ceded ground to secular concerns around marriage, family life, social issues, even war.[10] "The dissolution of monasteries, chantries, religious gilds, and fraternities in the 1530s and 1540s radically reduced existing sources of charity."[11] This paved the way for new secular interventions.

As a response to the Protestant Reformation, the Council of Trent (1545-1563) sought to codify and systematize Catholic doctrine and reform the life of the Church to overcome widespread abuses. The Council integrated aid to the poor more clearly into Catholic doctrine and decreed a larger, more central role for bishops in the administration of charitable hospitals.[12]

At the same time, in Rome, the Church under several successive Popes, notably Pius IV (1559-1565), Pius V (1566-1572), Gregory XIII (1572-1585) and Sixtus V (1585-1590), endeavored to eliminate the "infestation" of begging on Roman streets. Thus, while Church aid to the poor was systematized to some degree, beggars were subjected to harsh treatment that included harassment, social isolation, confinement to designated areas and imprisonment. Other countries of Catholic Europe emulated the papal example.[13]

Both Catholic and Protestant societies categorized the poor as either deserving or undeserving. The latter, presented as vagabonds and beggars, were identified with idleness, contagion and immorality. They represented a danger to society. They were to be distinguished from needy widows, orphans and victims of fire or theft.[14] Gradually, societies uncovered a third category of poor people, those who sought work but could not find it or who found work but were paid too little to support their families.[15]

With national state structures emerging throughout Europe, secular authorities sought more control over organized aid to the poor. As already noted, humanist perspectives influenced some governments to assume responsibility for poor relief from church parishes and monasteries.

Within the feudal system, declining revenues led to an economic bifurcation: "refeudalization" (that is, a renewed emphasis on serfdom and feudal farming practices) in some countries, agrarian modernization in others.[16]

As the modern state took shape, relief for people in poverty moved beyond unorganized almsgiving and church-sponsored institutions to more systematic means of providing public assistance. At the same time, secular authorities emphasized the obligation of the able-bodied poor to work. "Labour became the new medicine for poverty."[17]

England provides a distinctive example of the new attitudes. During the sixteenth century, in order to increase revenue, rich landowners enclosed common pasture and arable land, expropriated tracts of peasant land, and shifted to animal husbandry (notably, sheep) and the raising of more profitable crops.

This process of modernization reduced the need for agricultural labor, squeezed out small peasant farmers, induced the migration of unemployed workers to villages and cities and exacerbated rural and urban poverty.[18] The impact of bad harvests, fluctuations in the demand for English industrial goods, unemployment and rising prices focused attention on the needs of the poor. Initially relief measures were adopted by local jurisdictions.

In the last three decades of the sixteenth century, the king and the Privy Council began to develop a more general system for addressing the needs of the poor. In part government's interest was aimed at controlling the spread of begging, especially by the able-bodied, while assistance to the poor continued to rest with their neighbors and communities.[19]

The Elizabethan Poor Laws

In the 1590s, a combination of poor harvests, grain speculation and continuing abuses in the enclosure system in England led to a more activist governmental role. The Elizabethan poor laws marked a decisive shift in the nation's approach to dealing with poverty and vagrancy.[20] Not a "blueprint for social reconstruction," the poor laws were parish-based, "applicable to small rural communities as well as major cities."[21]

The Poor Relief Act of 1598 assigned churchwardens and parish overseers the role of administering relief assistance for the poor. Local poor rates were defined. Though there was preference for assisting people in their own homes ("outdoor relief"), the law allowed for the establishment of workhouses in urban areas. Essentially it codified many existing local experiences into national social policy.

The 1598 act and a further act of 1601 remained England's only provision for the poor until the Poor Law Amendment Act of 1834.[22] By the end of the seventeenth century, financing of relief though poor rates had become universal throughout England.[23] The amount of relief assistance varied not only from parish to parish but also on individuals' social status and moral worth. Impoverished widows tended to receive more than unemployed male laborers.[24]

The Industrial Revolution had led to the expansion of cities and towns, growth of the population and cycles of unemployment. The 1834 amendment provided that workers had higher priority for assistance than paupers. As an alternative to relief payments or food assistance to people in their own homes, local governments turned increasingly to a system of workhouses. Through these establishments, the authorities pursued a couple of aims.

They sought to save money by confining the poor in centralized locations and to eliminate begging and vagrancy by requiring able-bodied individuals to work in return for room and board.

Workhouses also sheltered poor women, children, seniors, and persons with disabilities or illnesses. Those capable of work were given hard labor. In some places, children could learn trades as apprentices in specialized workshops maintained by craft guilds.

Workhouse life and conditions varied as reform efforts waxed and waned. At its worst, the system was harsh and repressive, rife with abuse. Social tensions were inevitable when poor people of very different backgrounds including domestic servants, military veterans, vagrants, beggars and thieves were thrown together.[25]

Their diet was typically a watery porridge called gruel. Corporal punishment (e.g. flogging) was meted out routinely. Private contractors exploited the labor of residents including children to boost profits.[26]

The poor laws did not meet all needs and private giving expanded. In the sixteenth century, out of the guild tradition, friendly societies appeared in England; these associations provided members with protection against illness and misfortune. They evolved into fraternal organizations, which were the forerunners of the modern trade union movement.[27]

Wealthy individual donors provided for the poor not only in their bequests but also through gifts while alive. The latter approach grew in scale and sophistication. In the seventeenth and eighteenth centuries, charitable enterprises such as schools and hospitals were funded in England through "associated philanthropy", which entailed subscriptions from a large number of benefactors. This approach began to predominate over charitable endowments through wills.[28]

Not all the poor entitled to benefits under the poor laws chose to do so, preferring self-help to the stigma of the dole or workhouse. Politically, in view of the role of self-help, friendly societies and organized philanthropies, there were calls for reducing the poor rates and relying more on private initiatives.

Poor relief, to some eighteenth century critics, impaired work incentives and lowered productivity. According to an 1832 report of a Royal Commission, the system perpetuated poverty "by subsidising early marriage, large families and low wages."[29] While no doubt true in some cases, the validity of this as an indictment of the system as a whole is still debated. (Much the same could be said about present-day systems of social protection.)

In any event, it seems fair to conclude with British economic historian Paul Slack that the poor laws did help many people in adverse circumstances to maintain a decent standard of living and, perhaps more importantly, inculcated expectations in society of what that standard should be.[30]

In the village of Speen, the principle was given a new twist.

To Speenhamland and Beyond[31]

During its wars with France from 1793 to 1815, Britain had difficulty importing foodstuffs from the Continent. This plus a series of poor harvests increased the price of bread and created food shortages. This led to a variant of the poor laws approach.

On May 6, 1795, the magistrates of the Berkshire village of Speen decided to institute a system whereby a worker could have his income raised to a subsistence level based on the price of bread and the number of children in his family.

The Speenhamland system with some local variations spread throughout the south of England between 1795 and 1834 and is credited with saving many families from starvation. The subsidy was withdrawn altogether once a family's income exceeded a certain threshold. In other words, above the income floor, the benefit reduction rate was an abrupt one hundred percent.

By assisting all needy families, Speenhamland differed from the Elizabethan poor laws, which provided relief only to those who could not find work. The system was financed by poor rates levied in village parishes. It provided benefits equal to or better than the wages of some low-paid workers at menial jobs.

In time the Speenhamland system came to be seen as undermining the work ethic. The view that people under a social assistance scheme should not be better off than people who are working full-time for minimum wages came to underpin British social policy.

While the workhouse system was developed most fully in England, other countries had similar institutions, notably Holland, Belgium, Germany, France, Norway, and Denmark. By the end of the eighteenth century, efforts to reduce poverty through forced labor and harsh punishments had proven ineffective.

During the nineteenth century, local governments in England and Wales were mainly responsible for the administration of the poor laws. In the twentieth century, however, British society as a whole became more attuned to the problems of poverty and unemployment. There was increased emphasis on understanding how large-scale poverty manifested itself in a modernizing industrial economy with boom-and-bust cycles. This in turn gave birth to (or rather midwifed) contemporary systems of social welfare.

The Twentieth Century in England

In 1920, Dennis Milner proposed a scheme under which the government would provide a minimum income to all, regardless of employment or other status.

Under the scheme, one-fifth of national income would constitute the pool from which minimum incomes would be paid out. In the manner of a national dividend, the actual amount would vary from year to year according to the level of national production. The incentive to work would not in general diminish, since everyone shared in the increased benefits from higher production.[32]

The scheme was subsequently rejected by the Labour Party at its annual conferences in 1920 and 1921. The British economist and Fabian Society leader G.D.H. Cole later described this kind of approach a "social dividend."[33] Although not embraced, the notion of jobless income had nonetheless entered the social welfare policy space.

In England, the workhouse system was officially abolished in 1930, though at the local level many old buildings were turned into institutions that housed the elderly, sick persons, unmarried mothers and vagrants.[34] World War II (1939-1945) in particular accelerated the government's efforts to meet pressing social needs. Beyond the familiar arguments for underwriting security and opportunity, the government sought to reward the British people for their sacrifices and steadfastness in confronting Nazi Germany.

The Beveridge Report of 1942, produced under the leadership of economist and theorist Sir William Beveridge, was especially instrumental in the creation of a British welfare state, which was grounded in the principles of social insurance. The report advocated such measures as a National Health Service, Children's Allowances, Industrial Injuries Scheme and training for the unemployed.

While Beveridge proposed national minimum standards for pension and welfare benefits, he was equally forceful in arguing that social security should not "stifle incentive, opportunity, responsibility."[35] Beyond the minimum, people should provide for themselves.

As an alternative to the Beveridge plan, the economist Lady Juliet Rhys-Williams (1898-1964) proposed a "social dividend," which would be paid to people who worked, sought work or did housekeeping. In addition to reducing poverty, this would have highlighted the value of unpaid work by giving wives a source of income apart from their husband's. While her proposal was not adopted, it foreshadowed later calls for income independent of one's paid work status.

The Beveridge Report served as the blueprint for the post-war British Labour government, which passed social security (1946), national health service (1946) and welfare services (1948) legislation, with a joint effective date for all three of June 7, 1948.

Until 1975, this National Insurance scheme was financed on a pay-as-you-go basis through flat-rate worker contributions that were collected by their employers for the government. After that, the National Insurance Contributions (NIC) system grew more complex. In 1975, contributions were linked to income, with higher income earners paying more into the system. In the 1980s, cost-cutting measures were introduced. Increases in benefit levels, for example, were decoupled from average earnings growth and tied instead to inflation rates.

While the Pay As You Earn (PAYE) system for income tax remained relatively straightforward, the more complicated National Insurance Contributions system proved increasingly nettlesome and costly for business, especially small business, to administer.[36] The business community has begun pressing for reforms that would align, and possibly over time, merge the PAYE and NIC systems.[37]

During the 1946-1975 period, the Treasury controlled social welfare expenditures centrally by allocating resources to social service departments, which in turn provided benefits and services within overall spending constraints. The 1980s and 1990s witnessed a degree of administrative decentralization, with government health and social agencies gaining more flexibility (and accountability) in the purchasing and delivery of services.

At the same time, responsibility for income transfer payments has shifted increasingly to the Department of Inland Revenue. Like the United States, the United Kingdom has adopted tax credits as a major element in attacking poverty among the working poor. Effective April 2003, the government implemented a Child Tax Credit and a Working Tax Credit.

Tax credit awards are based on the taxable income received in a tax year by the filer, whether an individual or a couple. For purposes of calculating the amount of the credit, income is not limited to earnings from employment, but includes income from savings, investments, property, foreign sources, pensions and certain student grants.

These two new tax credits replaced the Children's Tax Credit, Working Families Tax Credit, Disabled Person's Tax Credit, child elements of Income Support and child elements of the United Kingdom's unemployment benefit, the Jobseeker's Allowance.

The Working Tax Credit provides for payments to low-income households (not just "families") whether or not they have children. In its current form, the Working Tax Credit is designed for people sixteen years and above with a disability or with dependent children and working at least sixteen hours a week and for people aged twenty-five and above working at least thirty hours a week.

The size of the payment is adjusted according to whether claimants are couples, single parents, persons working thirty or more hours a week, persons with a disability, or persons aged fifty and above going back to work after a period of receiving benefits. The payment is also increased to help cover child care costs. For full-time workers aged twenty-five and above without a disability and without children, the credit guarantees an income of 183 pounds a week for couples and 154 pounds a week for single individuals.

The Child Tax Credit streamlines the prior systems of income support for children by making a payment directly to the person primarily responsible for a child's care.[38] These new tax credits move the United Kingdom further down the road toward providing a guaranteed minimum income for all, independent of work status, marital status, age or source of income.

The country in western Europe that first sought to protect its citizens from extreme social and economic need through a state-sponsored system of social insurance and welfare benefits was Germany. Its social welfare policies and programs are implemented through a decentralized network of voluntary agencies.

Bismarck's Foresight

Prior to late in the nineteenth century, Germany existed as a region with a common general culture but also with territories that had varying degrees of independence and historical uniqueness.

For many centuries, Germany was synonymous with the Holy Roman Empire, a large but ambiguous political entity whose dominant state was Austria. The legislative body was the Reichstag, divided into three groups or "councils"—electors, princes (secular and ecclesiastical) and imperial cities.

In 1871, the members of the North German Confederation united to form a Prussian-dominated nation-state called the German Empire, which excluded Austria. Wilhelm I, king of Prussia, was named the first emperor.

Under Otto von Bismarck (1815-1898), who served as German Chancellor from 1862-1890, the Reichstag received an imperial message, November 17, 1871, to the effect that advancing the well-being of workers was needed to cure social ills. Bismarck was motivated by a desire to keep the economy at maximum efficiency and to stave off calls for more radical socialist alternatives.

At Bismarck's urging, the idea of social security was proposed in an 1881 letter to the Reichstag, in which Emperor William the First contended that "those who are disabled from work by age and invalidity have a well-grounded claim to care from the state."[39]

In the years following, Germany enacted legislation providing health insurance for workers (1883, with expanded coverage in 1892), accident or "sickness" insurance (1884, expanded in 1887) and "Invalidity and Old Age Insurance" or social security (1889).[40] The latter anticipated the structure of many contemporary social security systems.

The German social security system provided both retirement and disability benefits. The scheme was financed by mandatory contributions from employees, employers and the government. Coupled with prior legislation, this gave Germans broad income security coverage under the principles of social insurance. The system was completed with the addition of unemployment insurance in 1927.[41]

Due to the comprehensive nature of social insurance and various tax-supported benefits (unemployment insurance, child allowance, housing allowance, and the like), both means-tested and non-means-tested, a last-resort benefit, Sozialhilfe (Social Assistance), has traditionally played a relatively marginal role, though in recent years its importance has been growing.[42]

Social Protection in Other Selected Countries

Throughout Europe, from the end of the medieval period, the view of the poor as objects of Christian charity gradually gave way to the notion that human beings enjoyed certain basic rights. During the French Revolution, this was made explicit in the *Declaration of the Rights of Man and the Citizen,* issued August 26,

1789 by the National Assembly of France.[43] These rights extended to the poor, who had a claim on the state.

In the 1890s, Denmark, then Australia and New Zealand, established fully state-subsidized pension systems. Instead of employer and employee contributions, means and character tests were used to determine eligibility for benefits. By the time the United States enacted the Social Security Act of 1935, thirty-four European nations had already followed the lead of Germany by adopting their own forms of social insurance.

European social insurance and welfare systems tend to be more comprehensive and generous than their U.S. counterparts. For example, in most member states, health care is universally available either for free or at affordable and refundable prices. Social protection schemes provide a wide range of other assistance:

(a) income support for persons with disabilities;
(b) pensions, food and services for older persons;
(c) survivors' pensions;
(d) cash or in-kind support for children and families;
(e) income maintenance and cash support for unemployed persons;
(f) various forms of assistance with housing; and
(e) cash or in-kind benefits to combat social exclusion.[44]

In 1999, social protection absorbed 27.5 percent of the European Union's gross domestic product. Old-age pensions and health care accounted for about two-thirds of total social protection expenditures. This is due in large part to the aging of Europe's population.

Poverty and social exclusion persist as issues of major concern within the European Union.[45] The risk of social exclusion has risen due to a number of factors, including structural changes in labor markets; expansion of information and communications technologies; greater longevity coupled with falling birth rates; mobility within and migration to the European Union; greater ethnic, cultural and religious diversity; and changes in family and household composition.

Social inclusion policies in EU member states are geared to expanding access to labor markets and jobs, guaranteeing adequate income, providing educational and training opportunities, preserving families and protecting children, and insuring access to needed services.

A number of countries that either are members of the European Union or included in the European Economic Area provide a minimum income to certain persons. In Belgium it is called the Minimum de Moyens d'Existence, in France the Revenu Minimum d'Insertion, in Germany Sozialhilfe, in Ireland the Supplementary Welfare Allowance, in the Netherlands the Algemene Bijstand and in Sweden Socialbidrag.[46]

Portugal's Minimum Guaranteed Income, which was instituted in 1996, was designed for the most extreme cases of poverty. Even though the scheme covers only the poorest fifth of the poverty population, fully a quarter of these beneficiaries held jobs. The fact that they qualified for the benefit points to the low level of wages and the precarious nature of their employment.[47]

While the operational characteristics vary from country to country, in general a minimum income is provided to those who cannot support themselves or their children by other means.

Typically (but not universally) the amount provided is the difference between a national minimum and what is already available to the recipient. Recipients in most countries must seek work and accept suitable employment. Claims to other benefits must be exhausted. A minimum income is social assistance of the last resort.[48]

Some European governments are pursuing less conditioned approaches. The inability of market-based economies to assure full employment and to share more equitably the benefits of economic growth is one incentive. The inability of existing social welfare systems to eliminate poverty is another.

Few European countries are content any more with passive income-support programs. In the face of aging populations, high unemployment rates, increasing welfare expenditures and burgeoning national deficits, the emphasis has shifted toward more work-oriented policies. To counter dependency among recipients, countries are promoting "activation" measures that include skill training, work incentives and job placement and support.

It is in this context that European countries like Austria, Belgium, Ireland, the Netherlands, to name only some, have been examining the potential effects, both positive and negative, of a guaranteed basic income, particularly with respect to work disincentives. The notion of jobless income for able-bodied individuals, it is fair to say, has so far lacked political traction.

A Note on Ireland

High levels of growth and employment in Ireland in the 1990s focused the government's attention on poverty.[49] Despite growing prosperity, Ireland was 17th out of 18 industrialized countries on the 2000 United Nations Human Development Report's Poverty Index.[50]

Since 1997, Ireland has had a national anti-poverty strategy, developed as part of the country's commitments at the 1995 United Nations World Summit in Copenhagen. The government seeks to maintain high growth rates and global competitiveness while building a fair and inclusive society.

To combat poverty and exclusion, Ireland administers a familiar array of social services, employment assistance and income support programs. With prodding from groups like the Conference of Religious of Ireland, the country has engaged in a debate over a tax-based minimum income plan. Following many years of analysis, in 2002 the Irish government issued a green paper (or discussion document as opposed to statement of policy).

The green paper asserted that "achievement of social justice and an adequate income for all requires a high employment, high value-added society [with] adequate social protection . . . for those who cannot work (due to e.g. age, disability, illness). . . ."[A]ll policies impacting on income levels in the community [should] provide sufficient income for a person to move out of poverty and live in a manner compatible with human dignity."[51]

The paper outlines a scheme under which existing social welfare and income tax systems would be replaced by a universal payment to all adults and a lesser amount for children. The plan included elements like a Social Solidarity Fund to compensate beneficiaries who would end up with less than they had before under the existing social welfare systems. It sought to distribute the tax burden through a flat tax.

Critics fastened on these elements to argue that the scheme was not so simple as advertised. Determining eligibility for assistance from the Social Solidarity Fund could prove administratively nettlesome. A flat tax would prove ultimately regressive.

The Irish experience shows that the more complex the plan for a guaranteed income and, in particular, the more such a plan demands broader social welfare and fiscal reforms, the greater its risk of failing in the political marketplace. Public sentiment in Ireland and elsewhere remains more disposed toward separate targeted antipoverty approaches in health, housing, education, employment and the like.

Still, the government has invested resources into examination of a basic income scheme in the Irish context. The idea has not gone away.

Challenges of a New Century

As the twentieth century drew to a close, European countries wrestled with reform of their social assistance and minimum income schemes. Broadly conceived, these schemes aimed at overcoming hardship, social exclusion and marginalization of their poorest people.

With the collapse of communism, member states of the former Union of Soviet Socialist Republics (USSR) could no longer provide cradle-to-grave social protection to their citizens. This highlighted the need for safety net programs to help cushion the countries' transition from socialist to market economies.

During the 1990s, high unemployment rates and increases in economic poverty contributed to growth in the number of social assistance recipients. These and other factors (e.g. economic recession, aging populations) placed major strains on national social welfare spending.

Europeans sought ways of preventing long-term dependency on social assistance, mainly through activation policies that emphasized paid employment over government support. Thus the relationship between benefit levels and work incentives came to dominate the social assistance policy debate.

In practice, activation packages vary from country to country, as well as from recipient to recipient, but in general incorporate such elements as information, training, counseling, subsidized job placement with public or private employers, child care and other ongoing support for families. Concerns were expressed that the jobs would pay little and involve marginal work. Once off social assistance, the former recipients would hold no further interest to the social welfare authorities, even though their new jobs might not pay much or last long.

A more basic question facing European policymakers is whether to continue refining their systems of selected benefits aimed at particular subgroups of poor people or instead to move to universal benefits that leave no one behind.

END NOTES

1. Geremek, Bronislaw (1997) 59, 60 79-80. Also see Wresinski, Joseph (1994) 42
2. Geremek, Bronislaw (1997) 24-25.
3. As described in Geremek, Bronislaw (1997) 37-38, at the monastery of Cluny in France, at least ten thousand poor people a year were fed at table during celebrations in honor of deceased monks. The wills of some wealthy townsmen provided for alms to be distributed to thousands of poor people.
4. Trattner, Walter I. (1999) 3-6.
5. Geremek, Bronislaw (1997) 207-208.
6. For more, see www.ssa.gov/history/early.html.
7. Collinson, Patrick (1992) 260.
8. Jütte, Robert (1994) 107, 211. Though innovative, the experiment was not a great success.
9. Jütte, Robert (1994) 110-111, 205.
10. Collinson, Patrick (1992) 259-260.
11. Slack, Paul (1988) 13.
12. Geremek, Bronislaw (1997) 208-209.
13. Geremek, Bronislaw (1997) 210-215.
14. Slack, Paul (1988) 23.
15. Slack, Paul (1988) 27.
16. Geremek, Bronislaw (1997) 60, 92-94. In his analysis, agrarian modernization occurred mainly in Europe's northern area (England, the Netherlands, parts of France and Germany) and refeudalization predominated in central and Eastern Europe. Both approaches could be identified in the Iberian and Italian peninsulas. Southwest Europe developed its own specific agrarian model.
17. Jütte, Robert (1994) 198.
18. Geremek, Bronislaw (1997) 107-108.
19. Slack, Paul (1995) 10.
20. Geremek, Bronislaw (1997) 163-167.
21. Slack, Paul (1995) 12.
22. See www.bbc.co.uk/history/timelines/britain/tud_poorrelief.shtml.
23. Slack, Paul (1995) 18. Initially the poor rate was a type of progressive local income tax; eventually it developed into a property tax based on the value of real estate. Generally, tenants rather than owners paid the poor rate. For more on this topic, see http://users.ox.ac.uk/~peter/workhouse.
24. Slack, Paul (1995) 19.
25. Geremek, Bronislaw (1997) 217.
26. See http://users.ox.ac.uk/~peter/workhouse.
27. In the United States, a number of familiar contemporary fraternal organizations made an early appearance: Freemasons (1730), Odd Fellows (1819), Benevolent and Protective Order of Elks (1868), Loyal Order of Moose (1888), and Fraternal Order of Eagles (1898).
28. Slack, Paul (1995) 42.
29. Slack, Paul (1995) 46. The preceding paragraphs also draw on his account.
30. Slack, Paul (1995) 47.

31. Adapted from Canada, Government of (1994) 27. Also, see article by Bloy, Marjie at www.victorianweb.org/history/poorlaw/speen.html.

32. Milner, Dennis (1920). The proposed scheme was universal because for Milner it was clear that "existing devices for supplying food to unsuccessful or unfortunate persons are costly and subversive of freedom." (p. 17) Milner and his wife were Quakers and members of a group that promoted a State Bonus Scheme. See "A Most Neglected Movement" by John Tomlinson, www.basicincome.qut.edu.au/docs/most_neglected.doc.

33. Cole, G.D.H. (1935) 234. Milner's scheme may be seen as foreshadowing the Alaska Permanent Fund, about which more in the next chapter.

34. Over the past quarter of a century, many remaining buildings have been either demolished or converted for use as office buildings and, ironically, luxury accommodations. Again see http://users.ox.ac.uk/~peter/workhouse.

35. Beveridge, Sir William (1942) 6.

36. British Chambers of Congress (2004).

37. Ibid.

38. Information on the Working Tax Credit and Children's Tax Credit was derived from www.inlandrevenue.gov.uk/taxcredits. The information bulletins at the website from the UK's Inland Revenue Department are models of clarity and succinctness.

39. Quote as shown at www.ssa.gov/history/ottob.html.

40. www.eurofound.eu.int/emire/GERMANY/SOCIALSECURITY-DE.html.

41. www.ssa.gov/history/ottob.html

42. Heikkilä, Matti and Elsa Keskitalo, editors (2001) 19.

43. See Hwww.yale.edu/lawweb/avalon/rightsof.htmH for an English translation of the Declaration.

44. European Commission (2002a) 20.

45. Ibid. 16.

46. See http://europa.eu.int/comm/employment_social/index_en.htm.

47. da Costa, Alfredo Bruto, "Minimum Guaranteed Income and Basic Income in Portugal", Chapter 5 in Standing, Guy, editor (2003) 79, 84.

48. Ibid.

49. "Between 1997 and 2001, real GDP in Ireland rose at an average rate of 9.7% per year compared to an average of 2.6% in the EU over the same period." Long term unemployment fell from 5.2 percent in 1997 to 1.2 percent in 2001. See Ireland, Government of, Department of the Taoiseach (2002)

50. European Anti-Poverty Network (2002) 70.

51. Ireland, Government of, Department of the Taoiseach (2002).

5

U.S.A.

American Poverty[1]

In the first three decades of the twentieth century, economic growth in the United States fueled a general optimism, including a belief that poverty could be prevented or overcome. The economy appeared to absorb easily an increasing number of workers. Yet poverty persisted, especially among the elderly, persons with disabilities, children in female-headed families, black sharecroppers and tenant farmers in the South, and displaced workers in depressed areas or trades.

Public attitudes toward the poor varied. The Charity Organization Societies of the 1880s and 1890s had sought to differentiate between "the deserving poor...and the lazybones who would not work."[2] Beginning with Illinois in 1911 states began to offer programs of public aid to mothers with dependent children. The prevailing attitude was that advancement depended on work and aid was a last resort.

In contrast to the organized charities, the settlement house movement tried to avoid stereotyping the poor. Settlement houses, like Jane Addams' Hull House in Chicago, offered educational and cultural opportunities as the means to prevent or overcome poverty.

Some settlement house workers favored major social reforms like a minimum wage, abolition of child labor, unemployment insurance and racial equality. They however lacked the resources to effect such reforms. During the 1920s the organized charities, which increasingly relied on trained social workers, again assumed the more prominent role.

During the Great Depression of the 1930s, poverty expanded from the margins of society toward the middle class center. The Roosevelt Administration's New Deal met with mixed reviews. Conversations in polite society spawned endless jokes about the alleged malingering of workers in projects of the Federal

Emergency Relief Administration (FERA), the Civil Works Administration, the Works Progress Administration (WPA), its offshoot the National Youth Administration, and the Civilian Conservation Corps.

Stereotypes of the poor as shiftless prevailed in the middle class. The morale of participants in these programs suffered. The idea of work relief faced mounting resistance by the end of the 1930s.

President Franklin D. Roosevelt (1882-1945) had more success with his programs for categorical welfare assistance and social insurance. In 1935 the Congress passed the Social Security Act under which the government provided aid to needy persons aged sixty-five and over, blind persons and dependent children.

The Aid to Dependent Children (later renamed Aid to Families with Dependent Children or AFDC) welfare program in particular reinforced the notion of a federal responsibility for needy groups based on income rather than work status. No one could hold children responsible for their poverty.

The public pension scheme took the form of the Old Age, Survivors and Disability Insurance (OASDI) program. A major selling factor was the portrayal of the program as "insurance" rather than welfare. Employers and workers both made "contributions" to the system (though in the form of payroll taxes rather than premiums).

However, unlike private insurance, there was no hard and fast relationship between contributions and the level of benefits. The decisions about each were ultimately political. Nevertheless the portrayal of Social Security as insurance enabled people to claim that they had earned the benefits in contrast to traditional welfare handouts.

The Great Depression left a legacy. People became more security-conscious. Poverty was seen more as a product of economic conditions rather than ethnic and cultural norms. Organized constituencies arose to lobby for reform. And the role and responsibility of the federal government became a large, even dominating, factor in the agenda of the reformers.

Massive government spending during World War II (1941-45) ignited a return to prosperity. While poverty declined, the composition of the population in poverty changed, largely due to technological advances in agriculture.

For instance, sharecroppers and tenant farmers in the South were increasingly displaced by technological advances such as mechanical cotton pickers. Overall economic growth absorbed only a fraction of these displaced workers. From the beginning of World War II to 1950, over 1.4 million black Americans migrated from the South into northern centers of industrial and political power.[3]

Such large numbers began to swell the unemployment rolls in the big cities. Poverty was becoming an ever more urban phenomenon. For African American communities, burdened with pervasive racial discrimination, broken families and widespread poverty, the situation had grown intolerable.

In the early 1960s, a group of writers produced critical analyses of the American economy and the subculture of poverty. Gabriel Kolko showed that statistical evaluations of income failed to "tell all there was to say about poverty."[4] Michael Harrington's celebrated book *The Other America* portrayed poverty in understandable human terms and the poor as victims of their environment.[5]

While campaigning in the West Virginia primary in 1960, President John F. Kennedy (1917-63) had grown acutely aware of chronic unemployment and depressed areas even in a period of overall prosperity. He had charged the Eisenhower Administration with indifference to the plight of West Virginia's one hundred thousand unemployed.[6]

During the spring and summer of 1963 President Kennedy devoted his attention to the national problem of poverty. In that year, Walter Heller, who chaired the President's Council of Economic Advisers, updated an earlier analysis by Robert J. Lampman of the University of Wisconsin on trends in poverty.

Lampman had noted a slowdown in the rate at which the economy was moving people out of poverty; between 1956 and 1961, the number of families with annual incomes under $3,000 had actually increased.[7] The Cabinet devoted its June 1963 meeting to the issue of black unemployment.

The March on Washington in August 1963 dramatized the social and economic crisis of America's African-American community. Dr. Martin Luther King shared his prophetic "dream" before 200,000 marchers. The reality was disturbingly different.

Chapter Two of the Economic Report of the President, which was transmitted to the Congress in January 1964, provided an authoritative national profile of poverty. This was the first instance in which the President's Council of Economic Advisers "employed an income-based poverty measure and related it to proposed macroeconomic policies."[8]

Unemployment among non-whites was at least double that of whites. Racial discrimination pervaded a society in which minorities lacked the vote and basic civil rights protections. In spite of general prosperity, the rate at which people were escaping poverty was dropping.

President Kennedy's assassination on November 22, 1963 halted progress on his domestic agenda, which had already run into trouble with the Congress. His successor, Lyndon B. Johnson (1908-1973), seized this period of national crisis to reinvigorate that agenda and give it his personal stamp.

In his First State of the Union Address, January 8, 1964, President Johnson declared war on poverty. On January 31, 1964, the President announced the appointment of R. Sargent Shriver to serve as his special assistant in mapping out the War on Poverty.

Shriver's Task Force in the War Against Poverty worked at a feverish pace to design a national antipoverty program and submit legislative language to Congress. On August 20, 1964, President Lyndon B. Johnson signed into law the Economic Opportunity Act of 1964 (P.L. 88-452). This launched the U.S. War on Poverty, which was a critical component of what evolved as the President's vision of a Great Society.

The U.S. Office of Economic Opportunity, which was the lead agency, pushed the issue of poverty to the forefront of the federal domestic policy agenda. The new agency mounted a series of antipoverty programs like Community Action, Head Start, Job Corps and Volunteers in Service to America (VISTA).

The Office of Economic Opportunity also developed an enviable research and demonstration capacity. The new agency supported several carefully designed and rigorously evaluated social experiments. First off the mark was the test of a negative income tax.

On October 20, 1965, R. Sargent Shriver, named first OEO director, submitted a memorandum to the President proposing a National Anti-Poverty Plan. Its goal was to achieve "a permanent increase in opportunity and productivity." It set forth a three-legged stool strategy, in the form of jobs, social programs and transfer payments.

The jobs portion included public as well as private employment with emphasis on skill training and entry-level positions in teaching, social work, and public works (roads, parks and the like). The social programs component emphasized community action, which was seen as the means to empower the poor and increase their influence on laws, regulatory practices and institutions.

After reviewing various options for transfer payments, the Plan came down on the side of a negative income tax.[9] Everyone would file a tax return. If household income fell below a designated threshold, there would be no tax liability. Instead, the Internal Revenue Service would send the filer a check to make up the difference.

In 1966, the agency's research arm produced a more detailed National Anti-Poverty Plan, which took as its goal the elimination of poverty by 1976, the nation's bicentennial year. On the whole, however, the Plan relied on economic growth and opportunity programs to achieve its goals.[10]

An income maintenance program was among the instruments proposed for people who could not be assisted out of poverty by other means. Once again this took the form of a negative income tax in place of the traditional welfare system.

The National Antipoverty Plan was never implemented, having fallen victim to the nation's growing involvement in the Vietnam War and domestic controversies around the community action program. However the idea of testing the negative income tax continued to percolate in government and academic circles.[11]

Negative Income Taxation

The issue of work incentives has always dominated discussions around the feasibility and desirability of a guaranteed basic income. Between 1967 and 1972, the Office of Economic Opportunity conducted a large-scale experiment to examine the effect of a negative income tax scheme on work incentives.

Under an OEO grant, the Institute for Research on Poverty at the University of Wisconsin and Mathematica Policy Research, Inc., a well regarded consulting firm, carried out the experiment. The basic idea was to use the tax system to establish a minimum income guarantee for very poor families. These families might not only pay little or nothing in taxes but they might also be entitled to a payment *from* the government to bring them to the guaranteed minimum.

To illustrate the basic idea, consider a very stark hypothetical plan. Imagine that a household of four persons is guaranteed a minimum income of say $4,000 a year. A household with zero income would file a tax return, pay no tax and receive a payment of $4,000 from the government. A household *with* income would be subject to positive taxation. For purposes of illustration, let us put its tax rate at a grossly unrealistic 50 percent.

The household would file a tax return owing a tax of 50 percent on its income. On income between $1 and $7,999, the household would end up with its after-tax income (namely, half of its pre-tax income) plus whatever else it took to reach the $4,000 minimum. The "whatever else" would include retention of some or all of the taxes owed plus, if necessary, a payment from the government.

Thus a 50 percent tax rate on income of $2,000 would leave the household initially with an after-tax income of $1,000. Under a negative income tax, it would keep the $1,000 in owed taxes and receive an additional $2,000 from the IRS. Take another example. A 50 percent tax on income of $6,000 would amount to $3,000. To reach the $4,000 minimum income guarantee, the household would simply pay $2,000 (not the full $3,000) to the IRS.

The break-even point would be reached at a pre-tax household income level of $8,000 a year, since its net income would be exactly $4,000. Income above $8,000 would be liable solely for positive taxes, that is taxes with no expectation of a refundable tax credit. For instance, an income of $9,000 taxed at the 50 percent rate would leave the household with $4,500, which is $500 above our hypothetical guaranteed minimum.

Up to the break-even point, there is a reduction of one dollar in the refundable credit for every dollar of other income. In short, our hypothetical plan incorporates a 100 percent benefit reduction rate. Tax filers with positive income under $8,000 would end up with the same net income as those with zero income. This constitutes a severe work disincentive.

However, the benefit reduction rate need not be 100 percent (or a dollar reduction in the credit for every dollar of income). It could be less, for example, a dollar reduction for every two dollars of income. While the tax structure may prevent a filer's income from falling below the minimum income guarantee, it can permit a combination of income and the tax credit to exceed the minimum. (With a 25 percent tax rate, for example, the break-even point is $5,333.)[12]

The goal under these more complex designs is to establish a floor under a household's income while minimizing work disincentives. The tax credit is phased out gradually with graduated benefit reduction rates for different income categories and with a much higher final break-even point.

The New Jersey Experiment

In the design of an actual (as opposed to our hypothetical) negative income tax program, many factors come into play. These include the tax filer's resources (earned income? other income? assets? allowable deductions and exemptions?) to be counted in computing the benefit, the amount of the benefit or minimum income guarantee and the benefit reduction rate. A lot of economic analyses, related technical considerations and political tradeoffs go into the result.

Eligibility for the actual negative income tax experiment carried out in New Jersey was limited to male-headed families whose income did not exceed 150 percent of the official poverty line. Over a three year period, 1,357 intact husband-and-wife families were assigned to either experimental or control groups, which were located at three urban sites in New Jersey and one in Scranton, Pennsylvania.

The New Jersey experiment tested four different income guarantee levels to measure their effect on work effort—.50, .75, 1.00 and 1.25 of the poverty line. While families in the experimental group received cash payments ranging from 50 to 125 percent of poverty line income, they also paid taxes of 30 to 50 percent of family income.

The experiment cost $8 million. A mass of statistical and other information was collected and generated a rash of research reports, books and articles. The basic finding was that male heads of families who received negative income tax payments reduced their average hours worked by five to six percent.[13] This was equivalent to a reduction of about 100 hours (2.5 weeks) from 2,000 hours or 50 weeks of full-time work in a year.

The New Jersey negative income tax demonstrated the administrative feasibility of a negative income tax, the desirability being left to political authorities. It raised questions—largely unanswerable within the scope of the experiment—about economic, social and psychological effects beyond labor supply and workforce attachment. Additionally the New Jersey experiment boosted controlled social experimentation as a component of federal government policymaking.

Seattle, Denver, Gary, North Carolina, Iowa and Manitoba

The New Jersey experiment itself came to be compromised. The state had been selected among other reasons because it did not at the inception of the experiment offer state-sponsored welfare benefits for unemployed parents.[14] This made for a purer treatment-control comparison.

However, after the experiment began, New Jersey instituted a comparatively generous unemployed parent program. Indeed, many people in the experimental group began receiving welfare benefits that exceeded the negative tax payments. For critics, this raised questions about the experiment's findings on work effort.[15]

To deal with these questions, the U.S. Department of Health Education and Welfare mounted Income Maintenance Experiments in Seattle and Denver (SIME-DIME) that offered more generous negative income tax benefits and were linked more closely with welfare programs.[16]

Income guarantees for a family of four were set at .95, 1.20 and 1.40 of the poverty line (but, interestingly, not at 1.0, or the poverty line itself).[17] The *maximum* benefit for those with no other income was about 115 percent of the poverty line with an effective marginal tax rate of about 50 percent.

The break-even level (above which no benefits were paid) was above 150 percent of the poverty line for about 88 percent of two-parent families and 83 percent of single-parent families.

The experiments ran from 1971 to 1982 and enrolled 4,800 families (including control group members). Again, there were reductions in hours worked, ranging from nine percent for husbands to 18 percent for wives. Other negative income tax experiments conducted in Gary, Indiana (1971-74, 1,780 families) and in rural areas of North Carolina and Iowa (1969-73, 807 families) showed similar results.[18]

The data on non-labor force effects were more limited and the analyses less detailed. However, the available data suggested that the effects of the experiments in several areas were positive.

Relative to controls, in the treatment group, school attendance improved, grade point averages and test scores rose. The incidence of low birth weight babies declined and household nutrition adequacy improved. Treatment group families were more likely to upgrade their living arrangements through home purchase, higher rent payments or movement from public to private housing.

One unexpected set of findings proved controversial and ultimately undermined the political appeal of the negative income tax approach. In theory, increases in family income should tend to stabilize marriages (an *income* effect); however, a program providing financial alternatives to marriage for low-income women could also destabilize marriage (an *independence* effect). Which effect was stronger?

Early analyses suggested that the SIME-DIME experiments contributed to marital dissolution rather than marital stability.[19] Marital dissolution rates were one-third higher among couples who received negative tax payments than those who did not. Interestingly, the dissolution rates were highest among those receiving the smallest payments (and lowest among those receiving the highest), suggesting that stability might "kick in" at a certain threshold.

Although the effect on labor supply was the principal focus of the experiments, marital issues came to dominate the academic and political debate. Welfare critics quickly read broad causal connections into the findings. Remedying poverty through direct income support was portrayed as counterproductive to family stability.

Subsequent analyses by other researchers called the initial findings into question. Debate on the issue persists in the academic literature. The size and direction of the impact of a guaranteed income on marital stability, and the degree to which the amount of the guarantee plays a role, remain unanswered questions.[20]

Since the negative income experiments ended, enormous changes have taken place in U.S. society. Among those changes, divorce, separation and women's labor force participation have all increased markedly. In today's world, of course, the independence of women is a shared value and abusive relationships are less tolerated. If such had been the environment in the 1970s, the initial findings on marital stability from the SIME-DIME experiments, complex and ambiguous enough in their own right, would probably have created much less of a stir and been less susceptible to being used in the political arena to discredit a guaranteed income approach.

In Canada a similar experiment called the Manitoba Basic Annual Income Experiment or Mincome was attempted in Manitoba from 1974 to 1979. The data from the experiment remain largely unanalyzed but preliminary findings showed work reductions of one percent for husbands, three percent for wives and five percent for single women.[21] In this respect the findings were consistent with the U.S. experiments.

Attitudes toward welfare have shifted, as summed up in the dictum: "Work first." Income support, education, skill training—all take a back seat to the imperative of placing welfare recipients in wage-paying jobs. In the United States, these values are embodied in the Temporary Aid to Needy Families (TANF) program, which is the nation's principal cash assistance program for poor families with children under the age of eighteen.[22]

Even so, the findings from the negative income tax experiments continue to inform U.S. and, for that matter, other countries' welfare policy processes. The notion of placing a floor under income has had a habit of showing at unexpected times and places.

Family Assistance Plan

On August 8, 1969, President Richard M. Nixon (1913-1994) announced a plan to radically reform the nation's public welfare system. In place of the 35-year old Aid to Families with Dependent Children (AFDC) program, he proposed the Family Assistance Plan, which would guarantee an annual income of $1,600 (later raised to $2,400) for a family of four. The Plan included work requirements as a condition of eligibility for benefits.

The plan was bold. That a Republican president with conservative leanings and an aversion to domestic policy would propose it was astonishing. The Family Assistance Plan was the brainchild of Daniel P. Moynihan, a liberal social scientist (and later Democratic Senator from New York) who had unexpectedly become assistant to the president for urban affairs.

The Plan was intended to serve several purposes. It would simplify a complex and (to many observers) counterproductive welfare system. It would help shrink an expanding network of bureaucrats, social workers, community organizers and other activists spawned by the Great Society initiatives of Nixon's predecessor, Lyndon B. Johnson. Politically, it would pre-empt any potentially more liberal reform efforts by Democrats who controlled Congress.[23]

The House of Representatives passed Nixon's Family Assistance Plan on April 16, 1970, by a 243 to 155 vote.[24] Polls showed that most Americans favored the plan, as did editorial opinion in major newspapers. Opponents denounced the proposed benefit levels as inadequate. Some seemed motivated as much by their dislike of the president and his co-opting of "their" issue.

George Wiley of the National Welfare Rights Organization objected to the Plan's combining of stringent work requirements with low benefit levels. The result in his organization's view was a form of penal servitude for welfare recipients.

This latter charge was overstated. Of the 9.6 million persons on Aid to Families with Dependent Children, the vast majority would have been exempted under the Family Assistance Plan's work requirements due to their status as children, mothers of pre-school children, elderly, blind or disabled.

The Family Assistance Plan would have eliminated state variation in welfare eligibility rules and payment levels. It would have shifted the burden of payments from states and localities to the federal government. Such was not to be. On October 8, 1970, the Family Assistance Plan was effectively killed by a 14-1 vote in the Senate Finance Committee.[25]

However inadequate, a guaranteed annual income would have "constituted a major step forward in meeting current and especially future needs. . . ."[26] For women and children on welfare, Congress' failure to enact it into law in effect threw the baby out with the bath water.

Supplemental Security Income

Interestingly, a few years after low-income women and children were denied a guaranteed income, the opposite became true for low-income seniors, blind persons and persons with disabilities. Under Public Law 92-603, enacted October 30, 1972, there was established the Supplemental Security Income (SSI) program.

The U.S. Social Security Administration administers the SSI program, which became effective January 1, 1974. It amalgamated three separate state-administered programs for these populations. Payments are made to persons who establish eligibility based on age, blindness or disability and whose income and other resources fall below certain levels.

From its inception in 1974 to 2000, the SSI caseload more than doubled, from 3.2 million to 6.6 million persons. In 2000, the average federally administered monthly payment was $379, ranging from an average of $463 for beneficiaries under age 18 to $303 for those aged 65 or over.[27] The program was a landmark in that, for the first time in American history, it entitled eligible beneficiaries to a guaranteed annual income.

Three States in Particular

(A) Minnesota's Investment in Families

In the early 1990s, the state of Minnesota set out to reform its welfare system. In 1994, the state initiated a demonstration called the Minnesota Family Investment Program in seven counties, three urban and four rural. The demonstration mandated that long-term welfare recipients participate in employment and training services while it increased the amount of welfare benefits that those who found work could retain.

Evaluation was carried out by the Manpower Development Research Corporation. More than 14,000 families in these counties were assigned randomly to either the MFIP program or the traditional Aid to Families with Dependent Children. The demonstration ran from April 1994 to June 1998.

Compared to persons in the traditional program, single-parent long-term welfare families in the Minnesota Family Investment Program treatment group increased their likelihood of employment by 35 percent and their earnings by 25 percent. The combination of increased earnings and retained welfare benefits lifted a number of families out of poverty.

Additionally, the incidence of domestic abuse dropped, marriage rates increased, and behavioral problems among children declined while their school performance improved. The positive effects were not only large but also long-lasting, extending into the third year of followup.

The gains came at a price, in part due to more relaxed eligibility rules and greater retention of welfare benefits by working families. Minnesota Family Investment Program costs were approximately $2000 more per family each year than were AFDC costs. [28]

The Minnesota experience is valuable in light of welfare reforms mandated by the federal government's 1996 Personal Responsibility and Work Opportunities Reconciliation Act (PRWORA). This legislation scrapped the traditional Aid to Families with Dependent Children program, established strict work requirements (a "work first" approach), set a five year limit on the receipt of federal welfare assistance and gave states unprecedented flexibility in the design of their welfare systems.

On January 1, 1998, the state government expanded the Minnesota Family Investment Program, converting it into the operational heart of the state's welfare reform initiative. Working families have access to subsidized child care, health insurance in which premiums are based on income, and state tax credits that complement the federal Earned Income Tax Credit. [29]

The state has grappled with the potential conflict between two elements in its program, namely, financial inducements that enable (and motivate) working families to receive welfare payments longer and the federal five year time limit on receipt of assistance. [30]

(B) New Hope in Wisconsin

In Wisconsin, a community-based nonprofit organization called New Hope Project, Inc. initiated a work-based demonstration that ran from 1994 to 1998 in two Milwaukee inner-city areas. Although the state's economy was robust, the two areas had high unemployment rates and low levels of education.

Applicants had to be at least eighteen years old, live in one of the target areas, have incomes at or below 150 percent of the official poverty line, and be willing and able to work at least thirty hours a week. For people unable to find full-time work, the New Hope program made referrals to community service jobs.

Participation in the New Hope demonstration was voluntary and applicants were randomly assigned to a treatment or control group. The final sample consisted of 1,357 adult applicants, 43 percent of whom lacked a high school diploma or GED equivalent.

The benefits for participants included subsidies for health insurance and child care plus an earnings supplement that lifted their income above the poverty line. This approach contrasted sharply with traditional welfare rules in which benefits were reduced by nearly a dollar for every dollar earned.

At the same time the policy context was characterized by ever greater insistence on work requirements and welfare time limits, culminating in the 1996 federal PRWORA legislation. Even before PRWORA, Wisconsin had been in the forefront of state-led efforts to reform welfare, through a combination of work requirements and work supports.

The New Hope demonstration offered a single package of benefits and services aimed, as in Minnesota, at overcoming poverty and reliance on public assistance through a work-oriented approach. Parents in the treatment group worked more and earned more than their counterparts in the control group.

The availability of community service jobs was a major reason; 30 percent of the treatment group worked in these jobs. The employment and income effects diminished after the third followup year when the demonstration ended and the supplemental payments ceased.[31]

For the five-year followup period, poverty rates in the treatment group were more greatly reduced. Parents reported fewer signs of depression and better health overall. Their children spent more time in center-based child care and after-school programs. Children also performed better on several measures of reading and math achievement.

The program was not inexpensive, costing an average of $5,300 a year per family. The long-term effects of an operational program in an environment of state budgetary pressures and economic downturn are harder to predict. The demonstration did encourage parents to work and enhanced the well-being of their children. It reinforced the idea of providing work requirements coupled with a customizable menu of work supports to families on welfare as a pathway to self-sufficiency.[32]

(C) Alaska Permanent Fund

The program in the United States that has attracted the greatest attention of basic income proponents nationally and internationally is the Alaska Permanent Fund.

In 1968, Atlantic Richfield pumped oil from an oil field in Prudhoe Bay on the North Slope of the Brooks Range in Alaska. It turned out to be the largest oil field ever discovered in North America. It also happened to lie on state-owned land. As a result, the state received royalty payments from the sale of oil leases.

In May 1977, the 800-mile long trans-Alaska pipeline was completed; oil began moving through it to the terminal in Valdez in the following month. Realizing that oil was a non-renewable resource, Alaskans wanted to make sure that their new wealth would benefit future generations. There was also concern that politicians would spend the royalty income on wasteful projects.[33]

The Alaska Permanent Fund was established under a constitutional amendment approved by voters in November 1976. The amendment and subsequent statutes set aside at least 25 percent of certain mineral revenues paid to the State. These revenues have been deposited into a public savings account that is invested for the benefit of the current and future generations of Alaskans.

A dividend has been paid annually to each of the state's permanent residents. In 2002 it was $1540.76. The dividend is not guaranteed, since it must be paid out of earnings. According to the state's constitution, the principal cannot be touched. The 1980 Permanent Fund Act is the basis for current management of the Fund. It placed the Fund's management under the Alaska Permanent Fund Corporation, an independent entity.

Oil prices rise and fall and the returns on the Fund's diversified portfolio of stocks, bonds and real estate vary. Hence the total value of the Fund and the size of the dividend can fluctuate from year to year. Legislative appropriations are also used to supplement the Fund and offset the adverse impact of inflation.

As of June 30, 2002, the Fund had net earned income of $23.6 billion since receiving its first deposit in February 1977. It has become one of the one hundred largest investment funds in the world. In recent years the annual dividend has amounted to about $1 billion.

In some years the Permanent Fund has shown a surplus while the state's general fund is in deficit. However, Alaskans have resisted using the Permanent Fund as a way to offset pressure on other government programs. There has been little systematic research on the effects of the Fund on household expenditures, labor supply, migration, wage rates, government spending and overall growth.[34]

The Permanent Fund came into being as a practical and political response to the state's unexpected windfall of oil wealth. At the same time, and despite its limitations as a social welfare model, it embodies better than most other approaches the idea of treating the earth's resources as a common trust.

Earned Income Tax Credit[35]

The negative income tax notion can be recast as a refundable tax credit. In this guise it has worked its way in a modified form into U.S. social policy. The history of the Earned Income Tax Credit is especially salutary for the kind of global tax credit I advocate in this book.

Disbursing $40 billion a year, it has "become the biggest single transfer mechanism in the world."[36] Essentially a subsidy to low-income earners, it has become a key feature of labor market and social welfare policy in the United States. Several European countries have emulated the scheme. Yet surprisingly the EITC has been "scarcely noticed by commentators around the world."[37]

In 1971, Russell Long (Democrat, Louisiana), Chairman of the Senate Finance Committee, was among those persuaded that the Family Assistance Plan would penalize work and reward idleness. He conceived an alternative in which earners in low-income families would be eligible for a "work bonus" in the form of a tax credit.

Although his plan failed to pass in Congress in 1972, and again in 1973 and 1974, the Chairman persisted. And interest in some version of a negative income tax continued unabated among policy analysts. In 1975, the United States enacted a temporary "Earned Income Credit" as part of the Tax Reduction Act of 1975 (P.L. 94-12). The Act, introduced by President Gerald Ford, sought to counter the effect of an economic recession through the stimulative impact of tax cuts.

The tax credit was included under the rationale that it would help alleviate the impact of payroll taxes for low-income working Americans.[38] Unlike a purer form of a negative income tax, the credit was conditioned on paid work.[39] Non-workers need not apply. As envisioned by Senator Long, the credit would help move people off the welfare rolls and into paid work.

After several extensions, the Earned Income Tax Credit was made permanent by the Revenue Act of 1978 (P.L. 95-600). It has enjoyed bipartisan support over the succeeding decades, with legislative expansions in 1986, 1990, 1993 and 1996.

Embraced originally as a source of tax relief with work incentives, the EITC has metamorphosed into an antipoverty program for low-income earners. Despite distressingly high error rates, conservatives have continued to view it as a remedy for unfair tax burdens on the poor and liberals as an acceptable alternative to welfare payments and social services.

With the support of a highly conservative President, Ronald Reagan, the EITC was strengthened as part of the Tax Reform Act of 1986 (P.L. 99-514).[40] Its phase-out point was extended and its benefit raised. To forestall future erosion in the value of the credit, it was also indexed to keep pace with inflation.

Available only to households with earnings, the EITC is as already noted a refundable tax credit. "It is the only federal cash aid available to all working poor families with children."[41] If the amount of the credit exceeds the household's tax liability, the Internal Revenue Service mails the household a check for the difference.

Initially as earnings increase, the amount of the credit rises. At a certain point, it levels off over a specified income range, then drops gradually as earned income increases until it reduces to zero (the break-even point). In 2001, for example, families with two or more children and with incomes in the range of $10,000 to $13,100 received a credit up to the maximum amount of $4,008. For families with two or more children, the credit began to phase out at a certain level of earned income, reaching zero when the income exceeded $31,152.

The Earned Income Tax Credit has functioned effectively as an antipoverty program. In 2000, 19.3 million tax filers, about 80-85 percent of all those eligible, claimed the Earned Income Tax Credit, at a cost of $32.3 billion. The number of returns qualifying for a refund was 16.1 million and the amount refunded was $27.8 billion.

The average adjusted gross income for EITC tax filers was $13,360. Tax filers with annual adjusted gross incomes of less that $16,000 comprised 67.1 percent of those receiving a refund and received 72.7 percent of the amount re-funded.[42]

The Earned Income Tax Credit motivates non-working low-income individuals to enter the labor market, since earnings plus the credit increase total income. This is called the substitution effect. However, the "stage" of the credit in which a household finds itself—full subsidy, flat range or phaseout—can serve to a greater or lesser degree as an incentive to reduce time spent at work.[43]

The Earned Income Tax Credit appears to have two contradictory effects, namely, increased labor force participation rates among low-income individuals but reductions in hours worked per low-income participant. Arguably the former effect is more important than the latter.

The Earned Income Tax Credit is appealing in that its recipients are not stigmatized as welfare recipients. It is reasonably target efficient, reaching low-income people through the income tax system. It is politically popular because it appears to reward work. Persons without earned income are not eligible for the credit.

Its sheer size and increasing visibility have attracted greater scrutiny. Conservative critics charged that the program was growing out control, leading to high error rates and work disincentives. It was welfare in tax clothing. Indeed, the structure of subsidies under the EITC has grown more complex over time. The credit in its present form can encourage fraud, abuse or just plain administrative error. Of $31.3 billion in claims for EITC benefits for tax year 1999, the U.S. Internal Revenue Service placed the amount of overpayments in the $8.5-$9.9 billion range.[44]

Some faulted the IRS analysis on methodological grounds and claimed that the magnitude of overpayment was overstated. However, there is consensus that, whatever the true amount, it is substantial.[45] At the same time, the rules may deter eligible families from applying for the Earned Income Tax Credit, either because they are unaware of it or because they are put off by its complexity.[46]

Also not well understood is the extent to which recipients would have worked absent the credit.[47] More research is needed to fully document the program's effects. Even so, as noted by one highly respected U.S. economist, "the Earned Income Tax Credit is the best and most effective response this country has made to the changing economic situation for less-skilled workers."[48]

So far congressional remedies for the program's flaws have been geared toward mending it, not ending it. As testimony to its popularity, eleven states have enacted their own versions of the credit.[49] A number of member countries in the Organization for Economic Cooperation and Development have instituted their own versions of an EITC. These come under the heading of Make Work Pay (MWP) policies.[50]

For our purposes, one interesting aspect of the U.S. experience is the abiding support for a refundable tax credit approach on both sides of the political divide. Liberals endorse the redistributionist features of such schemes while conservatives like the emphasis on paid work. "The EITC represented the perfect policy solution to a set of social problems, and a welfare reform consensus that favored pro-work, pro-growth, low-cost alternatives."[51]

The income tax system in the United States is well developed and taxpayer compliance is high. Hence, "[c]ompared with alternative delivery mechanisms [like Food Stamps and Temporary Aid to Needy Families or TANF], the EITC is inexpensive to administer."[52] The main problem is that the very poorest people do not usually have earned income and cannot benefit directly from the credit.

And there you have it. The re-discovery of poverty in the United States. War on Poverty. Negative Income Tax experiments. Welfare reform. Defeat of the Family Assistance Plan. A small, temporary "Earned Income Credit". A permanent Earned Income Tax Credit. Bipartisan support for EITC expansions. Significant poverty reduction through the income tax system.

Change "Earned" to "Low", make the appropriate adjustments, implement the approach globally, and, voilá, you have a global refundable tax credit as an assault on extreme global poverty.

Other Tax Credits

The U.S. tax code has evolved so that it provides other subsidies for low-income families through tax credits. The Child Tax Credit was created by the Taxpayer Relief Act of 1997. It began in 1998 as a maximum credit of $400 per qualifying child. To qualify, a child must be under age seventeen, be a citizen or resident of the United States, and be claimed as the taxpayer's dependent.

Interestingly, an Additional Child Tax Credit is available for individuals who get less than the full amount of the Child Tax Credit because their tax is too low. The Additional Child Tax Credit may result in a refund even if the person does not owe any tax. In other words, the refundable portion of the tax credit may exceed a household's tax liability.

Thus, tax filers may receive back an amount equal to ten percent of earnings in excess of $10,000 (indexed for inflation), up to the maximum credit per child. The refundability percentage is scheduled to rise to 15 percent in 2005.[53]

Separately, the Child and Dependent Care Tax Credit covers a portion of a family's work-related expenses for the care of children under thirteen or for a spouse or other dependent who is unable to care for him/herself. The maximum allowable credit (35 percent in 2003) is available only to low-income tax filers with an adjusted gross income from earnings of $15,000 a year or less.[54]

Some states offer additional tax benefits for low and moderate income families. Wisconsin, for example, has its own earned income tax credit, child tax credit and homestead tax credit.

Summary

Currently, income support in the United States is provided through a large array of welfare, social insurance and tax credit programs.

Welfare includes such programs as Temporary Assistance for Needy Families (TANF), food stamps, Medicaid, Special Supplemental Food and Nutrition

Program for Women, Infants and Children (WIC), Section 8 (subsidized private rent), and public housing.

Social insurance includes Old Age, Survivors and Disability Insurance (OASDI, or Social Security), Supplemental Security Income, Medicare, Workmen's Compensation, unemployment insurance and related private employee benefits.[55]

The tax code is increasingly serving as the main vehicle of support for low-income households. It exemplifies a trend toward the fiscalization of social welfare policy. If middle and upper income groups can enjoy favorable treatment under various provisions of the tax code, then why should not the working poor?

Applicants for programs like TANF and food stamps must visit a welfare office and fill out detailed application forms. By contrast, those claiming the Earned Income Tax Credit simply file a tax return, something they would most likely do anyway. Consequently, the Earned Income Tax Credit now reaches more eligible families than TANF and food stamps combined. However, it is, perhaps because it is so easy to claim, more prone to abuse and administrative error.[56]

It seems that the United States, the world's main purveyor of neoliberal doctrine, is relying increasingly on refundable tax credits for its assault on domestic poverty. The Earned Income Tax Credit is "the nation's largest program of income-tested cash benefits for families with children."[57] In the United States and in other countries where the approach has been tried, there is bipartisan political support.

For the global community, and especially for developing countries, there is a message in that.

END NOTES

1. Forgive the disproportionate attention I pay to developments in the United States. In part it is because this country's approaches to poverty and development have such a large influence in global affairs. In part it is because the audience for this book will be mainly American. And in part it is because I know the situation here best.
2. Patterson, James t. (1994) 21.
3. Marris, Peter and Rein, Martin (1982).
4. Kolko, Gabriel (1962.
5. Harrington, Michael (1962).
6. Johnston, R.J. H., "Kennedy Hailed in Mining Region/ Crowds in West Virginia Are Large and Enthusiastic — He Stresses Job Losses", *New York Times*, April 27, 1960.
7. Sundquist, James (1969):19-20.
8. Haveman, Robert H., editor (1974) 4.
9. In the U.S., Milton Friedman is often credited with first proposing the notion of a negative income tax. He seems to have been anticipated in that by George Stigler (1946) although Friedman certainly helped disseminate the concept widely. In the federal government, University of Wisconsin economist Robert J. Lampman was clearly the first who, in February 1965, brought the idea to the attention of Joseph A Kershaw, first director of the Office of Economic Opportunity's Office of Research, Plans, Programs and Evaluation. Kershaw presented it to R. Sargent Shriver, the OEO director, who, despite being preoccupied with more immediate program and policy concerns, endorsed it.

10. U.S. Office of Economic Opportunity, The Office of Economic Opportunity During the Administration of President Lyndon B. Johnson: November 1963-January 1969. Volume I - Administrative History (November 1963 - January 1969) and Volume II — Documentary Supplement. Director: H. Kramer. Writers: B. Schiff (ed.), S. Goodell. Assistants: J. Donnelly, M.J. Kelly. Unpublished manuscript. Copies are at the National Archives and Records Administration in College Park, Maryland and in the LBJ Library, Austin, Texas. Washington DC: OEO, 1969:II-12.

11. The suggestion that the negative income tax be subjected to rigorous experimental conditions as a means of assessing is effects on work effort came from Heather Ross, a graduate student in economics who in the summer of 1965 served as an intern with the President's Council of Economic Advisers. See Pechman, Joseph A. and P. Michael Timpane, editors (1975) 17.

12. If BE is the break-even income point where the tax refund is 0, MI the minimum income guarantee, INC the gross income and TR the tax rate, then BE=0=MI-[INC(1-TR)]. Rearrange, so that INC=MI/(1-TR). So for a MI of $4,000, and a tax rate of 50%, the BE is $8,000. For a 25% tax rate, it is $4,000/(1-.25)=$5333.33.

13. Pechman, Joseph A. and P. Michael Timpane, editors (1975) vii, 1-14. Three problems created concern about the definitiveness of this and other findings. Changes in the New Jersey welfare system after the experiment began had an effect on the income guarantees and tax rates "in a haphazard way." The time limit of the experiment was too short to estimate the effects of a permanent program. And the differences by racial and ethnic minority (reduced work effort occurred only among white males) were both startling and puzzling. Ibid.: 4-6. In retrospect the failure to include single parent families, especially those with female heads, is regrettable.

14. The unemployed parent benefit served as a complement to the federal Aid to Families with Dependent Children (AFDC) program, which was geared to female-headed single parent households.

15. Allen, Jodie T. (2002)

16. The Cabinet-level Department of Health, Education and Welfare came into existence under President Eisenhower on April 11, 1953. In 1979, during the Carter Administration, a separate Department of Education was created by statute. HEW became the Department of Health and Human Services, effective May 4, 1980. See www.hhs.gov/about/hhshist.html.

17. In 1971, the official poverty line for a family of four was $4,000 a year. The .95/1.2/1.4 relationship to the poverty line was maintained throughout the experiment by adjusting the dollar guarantee levels according to increases in the Consumer Price Index, which is used to update the poverty line itself. See U.S. Department of Health and Human Services/Office of the Assistant Secretary for Planning and Evaluation (1983).

18. U.S. Department of Health and Human Services/Office of the Assistant Secretary for Planning and Evaluation (1983). Also, Chadwick, Laura and Jürgen Volkert (2003) 8.

19. U.S. Department of Health and Human Services, Office of the Assistant Secretary for Planning and Evaluation (1983). Note: (1) Legal marriage was not a condition of eligibility for the negative income tax experiments. (2) Following the source of this information, USDHHS/OASPE, I use the phrase "marital dissolution" as shorthand for the separation of a couple, whether or not legally married. (3) With respect to subgroups, the marital dissolution rates were fairly substantial for black and white families, but minimal for Chicano families.

20. For the initial findings of marital dissolution, see Hannan, Michael, Nancy Brandon Tuma and Lyle P. Groeneveld (1977). A subsequent reanalysis reported by Cain, Glen G. and Douglas A. Wissoker (1990) found that, contrary to Hannan et al., there was no in-

crease in the incidence of marital dissolution, though perhaps some change in the timing. That was duly followed by a rejoinder by Hannan and Tuma (1990). Differences in model specification, study populations and analysis variables may account for the discrepant findings in the two SIME-DIME analyses. The issue had political as well as academic repercussions. Senator Daniel Moynihan (Democrat - New York), who was convinced that family instability was a root cause of poverty, was sufficiently disturbed by the Hannan et al. findings that he withdrew his support for a guaranteed income. The view that guaranteed income programs adversely affected family stability became the conventional wisdom. Subsequent analyses showing no negative marital effects of an income guarantee have largely been dismissed as elements of academic squabbling and hence have had diminished impact politically.

21. Hum, Derek and Wayne Simpson (2001) 80.

22. TANF was established by the Personal Responsibility and Work Opportunity Act of 1996 (P.L. 104-193).

23. In November 1969, the President's Commission on Income Maintenance (or Heineman Commission), which had been appointed by President Johnson in January 1968, released its report, in which it advocated a universal income supplement program that was more generous than President Nixon's and dropped work requirements as a condition of assistance. See Trattner, Walter I. (1999) 343.

24. Collins, Mick (2000) 100.

25. Ibid. 103.

26. Trattner, Walter I. (1999) 341.

27. See www.ssa.gov/policy/docs/chartbooks/fast_facts/2001/overview.html

28. See Knox, Virginia, Cynthia Miller, Lisa A Gennetian (2000).

29. For more see www.dhs.state.mn.us/ECS/Program/mfip.htm.

30. Miller, Cynthia, Virginia Knox, Lisa A. Gennetian, Martey Dodoo, Jo Anna Hunter and Cindy Redcross (2000) ES-8.

31. The fadeout of program impact on employment, income and use of welfare after earnings supplements ended was also found in a Canadian welfare reform experiment. See Charles Michalopoulos, Doug Tattrie, Cynthia Miller, Philip K. Robins, Pamela Morris, David Gyarmati, Cindy Redcross, Kelly Foley, and Reuben Ford (2002) ES-3.

32. The preceding section on New Hope draws on Huston, Aletha C., Cynthia Miller, Lashawn Richburg-Hayes, Greg C. Duncan, Carolyn A. Eldred, Thomas S. Weisner, Edward Lowe, Danielle A. Crosby, Marika N. Ripke, and Cindy Redcross (2003).

33. In a 1969 speech before the Alaska Chamber of Commerce, a member of the investment banking firm Kidder, Peabody and Company, Robert Krantz, introduced the concept of a perpetual fund. Goldsmith, Scott (2002) 1-2 and Rural Research Agency (1997).

34. Goldsmith, Scott (2002). Also see www.apfc.org.

35. This section draws on the description in Chadwick, Laura and Jürgen Volkert (2003) 8-10.

36. International Labour Organization (2004b) 78.

37. Ibid.

38. See Congressional Research Service (2000) CRS-1. Also, for a clear and detailed reconstruction of the politics leading up to the Earned Income Tax Credit, see Ventry, Dennis J., Jr. (2001).

39. A ten percent refundable credit was given for earnings up to $4,000. For higher earnings, the credit phased out gradually, disappearing altogether at earnings of $8,000. See Ventry, Dennis J., Jr. (2001) 17.

40. In his remarks on signing the tax reform act into law, October 22, 1986, President Reagan famously hailed the EITC as "the best anti-poverty, the best pro-family, the best

job creation measure to come out of Congress." For the full text of the President's remarks, see www.reagan.utexas.edu/resource/speeches/1986/102286a.htm.

41. Congressional Research Service (2000) CRS-1.

42. Campbell, David and Michael Parisi (2002) 13. Percentages are my calculations using data on Table 4, p. 41.

43. The subsidy is the amount by which the credit lowers taxes owed. The flat range is the range of income where the amount of the subsidy stays constant, e.g. in 2001, it stayed at $4008 for incomes between $10,020 and $13,090. The credit begins to phase out above the latter amount, being reduced by 21.06 cents for every dollar earned.

44. U.S. Department of the Treasury, Internal Revenue Service (2003) 3.

45. See Greenstein, Robert (2003) 1. Also, see Holtzblatt, Janet and Janet McCubbin (2003).

46. In fact, the rules governing the EITC "are so complex that nearly three-quarters of those claiming it hire a tax preparer." President's Advisory Panel on Federal Tax Reform (2005) 3. Thus for claimants, typically families with incomes under $35,000 a year, the cost of paying a tax preparer can offset the value of the credit itself. As the Tax Reform panel notes, "This makes little sense. . . ." Op. cit.: 3.

47. For more discussion of these issues, see Blank, Rebecca M. (1996) 192-95. Among households eligible for the credit, an estimated 15-25 percent do not apply, due to the complexity of the eligibility rules and methods of computing the amount of the credit. See President's Advisory Panel on Federal Tax Reform (2005) 68. The Panel recommended adoption of a new and simpler Work Credit that would consolidate the EITC and Refundable Child Tax Credit and would be coordinated with a recommended new Family Credit. Op. cit.: 62-69.

48. Blank, Rebecca M. (1997) 261.

49. Ventry, Dennis J., Jr. (2001) 42.

50. Owens, Jeffrey (2004) 9. Table 13 (p. 13) lists the following countries with in-work credits in 2001: Belgium, Canada (Quebec), Finland, France, Ireland, Netherlands, New Zealand, United Kingdom and United States. Canada does not have a federal Make Work Pay program but most provinces have schemes similar to Quebec's.

51. Ventry, Dennis J., Jr. (2001) 51.

52. Hotz, V. Joseph and John Karl Scholz (2000) 30.

53. Lee, Andrew and Robert Greenstein (2003).

54. U.S. Department of the Treasury, Internal Revenue Service (2003).

55. See the U.S. National Academy of Social Insurance, www.nasi.org.

56. Burman, Leonard E. and Deborah I. Kobes. 2003.

57. Congressional Research Service (2003) CRS-7.

6

Elsewhere

In this chapter we embark on a selective "tour d'horizon" for harbingers of a guaranteed minimum income in parts of the world outside Europe and the United States. Some interesting and innovative approaches show up in both familiar and unexpected places.

Canada's social security system, which developed along European lines, is an example of the former. Australia and New Zealand fit here as well.

Given their history of gross income inequality, several Latin American nations have proven to be unexpected innovators. They have introduced conditional cash transfer programs, under which benefits are provided so long as their low-income recipients comply with certain conditions like attending school regularly or keeping medical appointments. Brazil has moved closest to providing a minimum income without behavioral conditions.

There has been less movement along these lines in most of Asia and the Pacific Region, Africa and the Middle East. But in South Africa, basic income notions, while falling short of full political acceptance, have become an overt part of public policy debate.

Canada[1]

In 1943, Canadian civil servant Leonard Marsh introduced into his country the concept of a comprehensive social security system with three essential elements: a) social insurance for the unemployed, retirees, sick persons and persons with disabilities; b) universal family allowances for child support; and c) means-tested assistance for others in need.

Marsh's approach, which emphasized the priority of wages over subsistence support, influenced Canada's subsequent social security program. In the 1960s contributory, earnings-related pension plans were introduced, the age of eligibility for the Old Age Pension was reduced from 70 to 65, and the Canada Assistance Plan was adopted to help rationalize provincial and territorial assistance programs and expand unemployment insurance.

In the 1970s, a Guaranteed Income Supplement was grafted on to the Old Age Pension. Far from raising concerns about work disincentives, it was seen in part as a form of encouragement to seniors to leave the labor force and open up job opportunities for younger workers.

Through cost-sharing incentives, the Canada Assistance Plan encouraged provinces and territories to collaborate with the federal government in building a comprehensive safety net system. However, since many programs involved means testing, they carried a "welfare stigma" not associated with unemployment insurance or the Guaranteed Income Supplement.

Efforts in the 1970s to implement universal income guarantees proved generally unsuccessful, except for Manitoba's Mincome experiment.[2] Benefits were augmented through devices like a sales tax credit and a refundable child tax credit. They added to rather than consolidating existing programs.

In the 1980s, guaranteed income proposals shifted from an emphasis on minimizing work disincentives to designing a simpler, federally-administered system that would scale back or eliminate many existing programs like the Guaranteed Income Supplement for seniors and unemployment insurance. In 1985, the MacDonald Commission on the Canadian Economy proposed a complex scheme for implementing a Universal Income Security Program.

The Commission's proposals were not adopted. Incremental reforms continued to be the norm. In the provinces, between 1986 and 1993, Ontario moved to increase the real value of benefits, while Quebec sought to harmonize tax and transfer payments and improve work incentives.

While considerable progress has been made, the goal of eliminating income poverty altogether continues to run up against familiar concerns about work disincentives, administrative costs, impact on existing programs and appropriate adjustments to changing economic conditions.

Latin America and the Caribbean[3]

Income inequality in Latin America is deeply rooted and historically persistent. According to a World Bank Study, "[T]he richest 10 percent of individuals receive between 40 and 47 percent of total income in most Latin American countries while the poorest 20 percent receive only 1-4 percent."[4] This, despite major macroeconomic policy changes in the region in recent decades.

Latin American inequality is much higher than that found in members of the Organization for Economic Cooperation and Development, Eastern Europe and most of Asia.[5] Such severe inequality means that the poor are prevented from fully developing their skills and knowledge base. That in turn can have adverse consequences for growth.

Throughout their history, the forty-four nations of Latin America and the Caribbean have been subjected to frequent macroeconomic shocks. These result from factors like crushing external debt burdens, overvalued currencies, high current account deficits, volatile capital flows, declining commodity prices and natural disasters. In the wake of each such shock, the poor are those most adversely affected.

Even in more stable times, the poor suffer the worst consequences of illness, physical or intellectual disability, aging, obsolescent skills, job displacement, and structural unemployment. They lack sufficient savings, access to credit or health insurance to cope with setbacks. Illiteracy and the unavailability of technology hamper their ability to obtain information and assistance. They suffer from discrimination in access to services, the civil and criminal justice systems and political power.

The working poor are found mainly in the informal sector of the economy. Being self-employed or unpaid family workers, they cannot produce documented work histories. Hence they are often excluded from formal social insurance systems. When job loss occurs, they are not eligible for severance packages or unemployment benefits.

Weak public sectors inhibit appropriate targeting and effective administration of social protection schemes. A number of countries have faced these problems head on and addressed them within the context of overall social and economic policy.

Some countries in the region have devised ways to supplement individual and household incomes as part of larger social goals while staying within national budget constraints. While no country has adopted a national minimum income scheme, there are signs of movement in that direction.

Several countries have introduced conditional cash transfer programs, that is, programs where eligible beneficiaries receive cash assistance (often in the form of vouchers) if they meet certain conditions. We highlight a few illustrative cases.

Oportunidades in Mexico[6]

Mexico has pioneered the use of minimum income support schemes to overcome poverty and foster development. Its best known program was designed by Mexico's deputy finance minister, Santiago Levy, and launched in 1998 under the name Programa de Educación, Salud y Alimentación (Education, Health and Nutrition Program), better known as PROGRESA.

The program was designed to improve education, health and economic conditions for some 4.7 million poor rural families. In 2002, the name was changed to the Programa de Desarrollo Humano Oportunidades (Opportunities for Human Development Program) or, popularly, Oportunidades.

Eligible families receive education stipends and food supplement assistance. In return, children must attend 85 percent or more of their classes during the school year. In return, the family receives monthly payments from the time the child enters the third year of elementary school through the third year of secondary school. Interestingly, the monthly value of the stipend or scholarship rises as the child progresses, ranging from 79.05 pesos at the start of eligibility to 305.04 pesos by the end.[7]

The value is raised even higher, by 20-25 percent, for girls in secondary school to compensate for their higher dropout rate. The total monthly benefit to a family is capped at 744 pesos. The average grant per month per family is 251.10 pesos, rising to 372 pesos on average for families with school-age children.

In addition to the monthly stipend per eligible child, the family receives additional assistance with school materials, food and health care needs. An included health care plan provides for scheduled health clinic visits by families. All participating families receive a monthly food grant of $122 pesos; those with undernourished children between four months and two years of age are given priority for food supplements, as are women in difficult pregnancies.

An eligible family may participate in Oportunidades for a three-year period, which may be extended for an additional three years, depending on the results of a socio-economic needs assessment. In 2002, the Progresa program benefited over 4.2 million families in 2,354 Mexican municipalities, 70,520 localities and all of Mexico's 32 states.[8]

Brazil's Universal Basic Income Agenda

With a population of 180 million people, Brazil is the largest country in Latin America and has the largest economy. It also has one of the world's most unequal income distributions; the richest quintile receives about thirty times the income of the poorest quintile.[9] Brazil's initiatives in attempting to provide a basic income support system for all its people have attracted widespread interest.

In 1991, Senator (and economist) Eduardo Suplicy of the Labor Party introduced a guaranteed minimum income bill to the Brazilian National Congress. Under the plan Brazilian adults over age 25 with a monthly per capita family income of less than 240 reales (US$141) would receive a monthly stipend, the amount fixed at 30 percent of the difference between actual income and the R$240 threshold.

While never enacted into law the plan did stimulate an analogous effort. Economist José Márcio Camargo contended that education was a *sine qua non* for permanent self-sufficiency. Raising educational levels would help generate higher future earnings and a higher standard of living. Therefore, a guaranteed minimum income program should target families with school-age children. Under his plan, regardless of other income, a monthly stipend equivalent to one minimum wage would be paid to each family whose children were enrolled in the primary school system.[10]

The school grant (Bolsa Escola) program was piloted in Brasilia under Federal District Governor Cristóvam Buarque beginning in 1994. To forestall the immigration of poor families, the program excluded those who had lived in Brasilia for less than five years. By the end of 1998, the program covered 26,000 families or 80 percent of its target population. Evaluation findings were positive. The school dropout rate fell to zero percent among participating families. The rate of grade repetition was below the national average. The program improved the targeting of other social programs, as poor families made greater use of services and benefits for which they were eligible.[11]

Subsequently, one hundred municipalities implemented similar programs but in general with less success. Because of large-scale poverty and local budget constraints, coverage has been spotty, thereby exacerbating inequality among the poor. The grant amounts have been smaller and their duration shorter. They have not always been coordinated with other social programs.

In 1998, the Ministry of Education mounted a nationwide program that reinforced mandatory school attendance. By December 1999, "504,000 families in one-fifth of the Brazilian municipalities (mostly situated in rural areas) were receiving a monthly stipend...estimated on average at R$37 (US$20)."[12] However there were obstacles. The signing of agreements between the Ministry of Education and the municipalities got bogged down in red tape. Poor municipalities could not manage the 50 percent match rate. And the overall budget for the program was inadequate.

On February 13, 2001, the Brazilian government established the National Minimum-Income Program linked to education.[13] The Bolsa Escola Federal assumed full costs of the benefits and expanded the age range of beneficiaries from 7 to 14 years to 6 to 15 years. Under the program, the child's mother (or other adult responsible for the child) received a Bolsa Escola Card for use in withdrawing funds from a branch of the Caixa Econômica Federal, a large federal bank or other bank-accredited outlets. The program pays families R$15 (US$6) a month per child up to three children or a maximum of R$45.

By the end of 2001, the program was operational in 98 percent of Brazil's 5,561 municipalities and was providing cash benefits to over 8.2 million children in 4.8 million families.[14]

In late 2003, the Brazilian government took steps to combine Bolsa Escola with several other income support programs into a single cash transfer program called Bolsa Familia. The other three programs are the Minimum Income Program Related to Nutrition or Bolsa Alimentação; the National Program of Access to Food or Cartão Alimentação, related to the Zero Hunger Program; and the Auxílio Gás Program (Gas Help Program).[15] By October 2005, Bolsa Familia had reached over eight million households in Brazil.[16]

The evolution of income support strategies has gone still further. Due in large measure to the long-term dedication of Senator Eduardo Suplicy, the Brazilian Congress committed the nation to pursuit of an unconditional basic income for all citizens. On January 4, 2004, Brazil's President Luiz Inacio Lula da Silva signed a law stipulating that basic citizenship income "will be realized in steps, at the discretion of the Executive, giving priority to the neediest layers of the population."[17]

The emphasis on gradualism and lack of a clear implementation plan means that achievement of the goal is by no means assured. However, if nothing else, the law will induce existing social welfare programs to become more integrated with one another and with the social insurance and income tax systems. Furthermore, to the extent that progress is made toward realizing a basic income for all, the long time horizon will permit full airing of the inevitable objections and the orderly phasing down of more targeted and means-tested programs.[18]

Bono Solidario in Ecuador

After a recession in the prior decade, Ecuador initiated a series of market-based reforms in the early 1990s to promote economic recovery. The reforms, which included restrictive fiscal and monetary policies, favored capital-intensive sectors like agriculture and petroleum while adversely affecting manufacturing, where jobs were more concentrated. This led to increased unemployment and by extension diminished demand for tradeable goods.

The economy was roiled further by a series of shocks that included El Niño, collapsing oil prices, declines in foreign capital investment, a destabilized banking sector, interest rate hikes and the freezing of assets. By 1999, the unemployment rate had reached 14.4 percent and the inflation rate had climbed to 60.7 percent. The proportion of households living below a consumption-based poverty line rose from 34 percent in 1995 to 56 percent in 1999.[19]

The most serious economic crisis in modern Ecuador's history generated social and political unrest. In 2000, the government replaced the *sucre* with the dollar as the nation's currency. Currency exchange rates and inflation fell in line with international levels but at the same time were tied more to trends in the U.S. economy than internal business cycles.

The government also stepped in to assist low-income households who were the most adversely affected by the economic downturn. Bono Solidario, which absorbs two-thirds of Ecuador's spending in social assistance, is a program that provides direct cash assistance to mothers raising children and to seniors and persons with disabilities whose incomes fall below $2.00 per capita per day.

Introduced nationwide in September 1998, it was designed initially to counter the loss of subsidies for gas, gasoline and electricity. It has continued as a major antipoverty program of the Ecuadorian government. The program covers about 1.3 million persons. Four-fifths of the beneficiaries are mothers, virtually one-fifth are seniors and the remainder persons with disabilities. In 2001, mothers received monthly benefits of $11.50 while seniors and persons with disabilities received $7.00.[20]

The program was designed by the Council for Modernization of the State, administered initially by the Ministry of Finance and Public Credit, and transferred in 2000 to the Ministry of Social Welfare. Payments are made through BANRED, a national banking network.

Catholic and evangelical churches determine eligibility based on income as sworn to by applicants or their proxies. The data, which have proven inconsistently reliable, is now cross-checked with other sources like the social security administration, banks and transportation administration.

Based on 1998-99 survey data, the program needs to improve its target efficiency. About half (48.1 percent) of eligible persons did not receive Bono Solidario payments. Undercoverage appears to be particularly high in rural areas with limited availability of financial institutions.

Conversely, of the 1.34 million who received payments, close to two-thirds (63.3 percent) did not meet the eligibility criteria. A mirror image of undercoverage, this leakage phenomenon occurs mainly in urban areas, where banking outlets are concentrated.[21] The government is undertaking efforts to improve targeting and to link the program more closely to other social goals like primary education, job training and access to microcredit.

Family Allowances in Honduras

Since 1990, Honduras, the third poorest nation in the western hemisphere, has operated the Programa de Asignación Familiar (Family Allowance Program). Under the program, families receive school grants, infant maternal grants and elderly grants. The program has shifted its emphasis from compensating for lost income to increasing human capital among the extremely poor through education, health care and adequate nutrition.

In U.S. dollar equivalents, the education grants amount to $3 per child per month for up to three children per family for the ten-month school year. The infant maternal grants are $3 a month for pregnant women, each child under three years, and each child with a disability up to twelve years. Elderly grants of $3 a month go to seniors aged sixty or over who are in extreme poverty.

As conditions of assistance, children must attend school with a maximum of seven days absence over a three-month period and parents must comply with the required frequency of visits to clinics.[22] In 2002, the education grant assisted approximately 115,000 beneficiaries, the health grant 69,000 and the elderly grant 11,000.[23] The program covers forty of Honduras' 297 municipalities.[24]

Nicaragua's Social Safety Net

In 2000, with financial support from the Inter-American Development Bank and the Central American Bank for Economic Integration, the government of Nicaragua initiated a program called Red de Protección Social (Social Safety Net). The Program is administered by the Ministry of the Family. Phase I ended in 2002 and Phase II is ongoing.[25] It is modeled on Mexico's PROGRESA program and is targeted to the country's poor rural households.

Under RPS, poor rural households receive transfers conditional on their meeting certain requirements. For example, they receive a bimonthly food voucher ("bono alimentario") for up to three years, provided they attend educational workshops and bring their under-five children to medical appointments.

A school voucher ("bono escolar") is provided contingent on school enrollment and regular attendance. For each eligible child, households also receive a school supplies voucher ("mochila escolar"). Additionally there is a small cash transfer, the teacher voucher ("bono a la oferta"), which a family gives to the teacher. The teacher keeps half and uses the rest for more school supplies.

On a per year basis, in U.S. dollar equivalents, the food voucher is worth $224, the school voucher $112, the school supplies voucher $21 and the teacher voucher $5. By July, 2004, nearly twenty-two thousand rural households had received assistance under the program. An evaluation is being carried out by the International Food Policy Research Institute.[26]

Asia and the Pacific Region

The conventional wisdom is that social protection is not a high priority for Asian and Pacific Region nations. However, the region's most advanced economies have integrated social protection into their modernization processes. Countries like Japan, Republic of Korea, China and Singapore have invested in medical care, housing subsidies, social assistance, pension and disability benefits, and education.[27]

As far back as 1922, Japan's Diet passed its first health insurance law, which was patterned after the German sickness funds. Local societies, eventually numbering some ten thousand, provided primary care and formed the backbone of the Japanese national health scheme. By the start of the twenty-first century, Japan enjoyed the world's lowest infant mortality rate and highest life expectancy.[28]

In principle, social protection schemes are crafted to ameliorate risks to the well-being of society as a whole. To be sure, the poor, with their greater vulnerability to such risks, benefit disproportionately. At the same time, social protections like publicly financed pensions or minimum wage requirements keep many people from falling into poverty.

In the region, social protection schemes include one or more of five components: labor market policies and programs designed to increase skills and foster employment; social insurance to offset the adverse impact of factors like unemployment, disability and retirement; social assistance and welfare services for the most vulnerable; micro- and area based support (such as health care microinsurance); and child protection.[29]

The developing member countries of the Asian Development Bank are characterized by a total population that is young (40 percent under age 19), rural (60 percent) and poor (30 percent).[30] The region's nearly 700 million poor constitute 63 percent of the world's poor.[31] The poor consist largely of unemployed persons, landless laborers, small-scale fishermen and low-wage earners.

The region's population is growing rapidly. Poverty and unemployment among the region's youth remains a threat to social stability. Migrants, ethnic minorities, older persons, persons with HIV/AIDS, children and persons with severe and permanent disabilities are at high risk of extreme poverty.

The poor tend to rely on the support of family members plus religious and charitable organizations rather than the state. Throughout Asia, as elsewhere, these informal safety nets are eroding due to factors like urbanization, migration and changing family structures. Although generalizations are risky, formal social protection in the region appears by and large to be underdeveloped and underfinanced. This is said without prejudice to the high degree of variation within the region and among specific areas and vulnerable subgroups.

South Asian countries like Bangladesh, India, Pakistan and Sri Lanka suffer from extreme poverty, economic shocks and natural disasters. Formal social protection schemes reach only a tiny fraction of their people. Social protection is even less in evidence in the Pacific nations, where half the population is under age 19 and unemployment is a major challenge.

In Central and East Asian countries where social protection schemes are more comprehensive, they lack full coverage and adequate budgets.[32] Developing countries in the region typically have formal protection systems that fall short of meeting the needs of their people. The main obstacles are limited coverage, insufficient funding, mistargeting, and legal and administrative barriers. Program models from developed countries are not always adapted to the particular needy populations and circumstances of a developing country.[33]

Australia and New Zealand

Though situated in Asia, Australia and New Zealand have held on to their European roots in their approaches to social protection. During the 1970s, a Commission of Inquiry into Poverty recommended a type of guaranteed minimum income for Australia. At the same time, another group, the Priorities Review Staff, proposed a tax credit scheme.

In advocating general income guarantees, both groups pursued similar objectives, namely to rationalize existing categorical payment systems, integrate income taxation and Social Security, and reach those receiving little or no assistance. While the groups' proposals were not implemented, Australia's governmental income support system expanded during the 1980s.

The political mood grew more conservative in the 1990s. While the social safety net stayed in place, prominence was given to the distinction between the "needy" and the "greedy." People should not receive assistance from society without giving something back to society. There has also been a shift toward greater privatization of income support, education and health care.[34]

While generous by many standards, the Australian social welfare system remains largely categorical, with separate eligibility and payment criteria for different classes of beneficiaries (pensioners, veterans, persons with disabilities, etc.). The debate between universal and categorical approaches goes on with its traditional liveliness.

In 1975, the Values Party of New Zealand included versions of a guaranteed minimum income and negative income in its policy prescriptions. During the 1980s, support for the idea diminished, especially after the Values Party was absorbed into the new Green Party. During the 1990s, there was a resurgence of interest in a guaranteed minimum approach that included more focused research and advocacy, and notions like a Partial Basic Income as an intermediate stage toward full implementation.[35]

Middle East and North Africa[36]

While the nations that make up the Middle East and North Africa (MENA) region share common characteristics—notably the Arabic language and a predominantly Islamic culture—they also differ greatly. While more than half the

countries possess significant oil reserves, others like Jordan lack natural resources. There are major differences in political systems, ethnic makeup, economic development and social patterns.[37]

Cash transfer programs play a small role in the social protection schemes of
these nations, ranging from 0.2 percent to about 1.0 percent of Gross Domestic
Product. Transfers are targeted to the categorically poor, that is, persons who are
unable to support themselves due to age or disability.

Among the common problems are overstaffing, low pay, complex eligibility
rules, overlap between group-based and need-based approaches, lack of updating, mistargeting and high administrative costs.[38] Essentially, the countries rely
on extended family relationships and other informal mechanisms to cope with
poverty. The future impact of factors like globalization, natural disasters, aging
populations, and conflicts will put stress on these mechanisms.

Average per capita income in the MENA region is higher than elsewhere in
the developing world. The countries have taken advantage of this factor to provide universal and publicly financed access to education. "In 1996, MENA
countries devoted 5.1 % of their GNP to education."[39] This was higher than most
other regions of the developing world.

There is some question as to whether this investment is preparing the future
labor force to deal adequately with globalization and structural changes in domestic economies. Oil and mineral resources are nonrenewable. Agricultural and
other raw commodities bring low returns and are subject to abrupt price swings.

Over time the region will become more explicitly dependent on its human resources for development, while making provision for those at the greatest risk of
extreme poverty.

Tunisia's National Solidarity Fund (commonly called the 26-26 Fund after
its postal address) finances small-scale projects in poor or "shadow" areas.
Aimed at the hard-core poor who are unable to support themselves, the projects
help with electricity, roads, schools and health care. It served as the model for
the UN General Assembly's 2002 endorsement of a World Solidarity Fund to
attack poverty on a global scale.[40]

Tunisia's Ministry of Social Affairs also provides direct cash assistance to
families needing income support. The program has significant flaws like high
administrative costs, lack of updated eligibility lists and inadequate coverage in
the poorest areas, notably the country's northwest and center-west.[41] However, it
does reach over one hundred thousand of the country's neediest families and
complements the country's other antipoverty initiatives. Other countries with
very small to modest cash transfer programs in the region include Algeria,
Egypt, Jordan, and the Republic of Yemen.[42]

Elsewhere in Africa

In Africa's 53 countries, poverty presents a daunting challenge. Half the African
population lives on less than PPP$1 a day. In Nigeria the proportion reaches 66
percent and in Madagascar and Zambia 70 percent. Yet there are signs of progress, though the trend is not uniform across the continent. The incidence of

poverty appears to have declined in Ethiopia, Ghana, Mauritania and Uganda. It has risen in Nigeria and Zimbabwe and remained more or less stable in Madagascar and Zambia.[43]

In oil-rich Nigeria, revenues from oil, which amounted to US$33 per capita in 1965, rose to US$325 per capita in 2000. However, per capita gross domestic product remained stuck at around US$245. The country appeared victimized by the natural resource curse, a condition in which abundant resources like oil or minerals generate not an improved standard of living, but instead productivity declines, institutional waste, public and private corruption, greater income inequality, and deepening poverty.[44] How could this happen?

The conventional explanation is that, under the phenomenon known as the "Dutch disease," oil exports brought in foreign exchange windfalls, which were converted into the country's currency. These revenues were spent largely on local non-traded goods and services (such as retail outlets and domestic construction). Investment flowed into oil production and these non-traded sectors at the expense of agriculture and manufacturing. Currency appreciation created by so much foreign exchange meant that the price of oil on international markets effectively rose. Consequently exports dropped. A boom and bust cycle was set in motion. With little diversification and so much riding on oil revenues, the whole economy suffered.

However, there is some evidence that waste and corruption in the oil sector may account for Nigeria's dismal economic performance even more fully than Dutch disease. This has led two prominent economists to propose that oil revenues be distributed directly to Nigerian citizens rather than being appropriated by the government. From the government's perspective, this would convert an oil economy into a virtual non-oil economy. That in turn would stimulate good governance and greater investment in other sectors besides oil. It would also raise per capita income and reduce the incidence of extreme poverty.[45]

While corruption and leakage would inevitably persist under such a system, their incidence would diminish compared to more incremental reforms. That is because households who are denied their fair share would have a legal, preferably constitutional, right to seek redress.[46]

As elsewhere in the world, poverty in Africa is a transitory rather than a permanent condition for the majority of the poor. According to one study of selected countries, less than a quarter of the population is always poor and 60 percent move in and out of poverty.[47] Still, in varying degree, African countries remain vulnerable to risks from the AIDS crisis, uncertain international markets, deterioration in public services, drought and related climactic disasters, civil wars, endemic ethnic conflicts and localized food shortages.[48]

Efforts to address the needs of Africa's poor through social protection schemes are hindered by inadequate growth rates, lack of institutional and administrative capacity and fiscal shortfalls. Social risk management in this context requires a broad-based system of income support for the extremely poor financed by African countries with international assistance.

Africa generally and Sub-Saharan Africa in particular have had a distressing record in recent decades of weak growth and high rates of extreme poverty. In

2001, the number of people in Sub-Saharan Africa living on less than PPP$1 a day is estimated at 313 million, an increase of 38 percent over the figure for 1990. Contributing to the economic woes and social polarization in many countries is the legacy of colonialism and neocolonialism. African governments are subject to the vagaries of international capital flows and investment patterns. African political and commercial elites benefit from their links to global markets while millions of ordinary people remain economically marginalized.

Overcoming extreme poverty depends, yes, on Africans themselves, but also on the larger global community that bears its share of responsibility for conditions in the African continent. The magnitude and persistence of poverty in many countries are a continuing threat to the region's stability.

A Note on South Africa

Despite its transition to democracy in 1994 and a relatively strong economy, the legacy of South Africa's colonial and apartheid past persists in the form of severe poverty and income inequality.

If one adopts a minimum living level standard appropriate for South Africa, approximately 20.5 million South Africans or 46 percent of the population lived in poverty in 2000.[49] Ninety-six percent of the South African poor are black African; 70 percent live in rural areas. Households in poverty are more than twice as likely to be headed by women.[50]

Between 1995 and 2002, the unemployment rate rose from 16 percent to 29 percent. In 2002, a government-sponsored Committee of Inquiry concluded that South Africa faces a "labour surplus economy with a high skills' deficit at the lower end."[51] Several civil society organizations, notably the Congress of South African Trade Unions (COSATU) and Black Sash, a long-standing human rights organization, gathered around the banner of a Basic Income Grant.

The notion of a universal Basic Income Grant (BIG) emerged as a policy alternative during a Presidential Jobs Summit in October 1998. It has been included in proposals submitted by COSATU. In November 2000, the South African Council of Churches, COSATU, and South African Non-Governmental Coalition jointly launched the People's Budget Campaign. The campaign seeks to stimulate public debate on economic and social policy with emphasis on fighting poverty and unemployment.

A key initiative of the People's Budget is a universal income support grant of no less than one hundred rands (about US$8.70) per month payable to all South Africans and progressively recovered in part through the tax system. The grant amount would be indexed to inflation.

Following the 1998 Presidential Summit, the BIG was investigated and eventually endorsed in 2002 in a report by the Taylor Committee. As part of its proposal for comprehensive social security reform, the Committee of Inquiry recommended implementation of a basic income grant scheme along the lines stipulated in the People's Budget and endorsed by a broad alliance of civil society organizations.

The Basic Income Grant would be phased in over several years, gradually replacing the current patchwork of income support measures inherited from the apartheid era.

Critics like the Treasury considered the proposal fiscally unsustainable. The government as a whole and even the African National Congress rejected the notion of "handouts" and favored workfare (e.g. expanded public works programs and child support grants) over basic income approaches.[52]

While a Basic Income Grant has yet to become a reality in South Africa, the debate around it has underscored the role of expanded social assistance in the alleviation of extreme poverty.

END NOTES

1. This section draws heavily on Canada, Government of (1994) 27-41.

2. For example, Quebec's Castonguay-Nepveu Commission proposed a three-tiered approach: negative income tax, social insurance programs and income-tested family allowances. See Canada, Government of (1994) 31.

3. This section draws considerably on Inter-American Development Bank (2000), which is recommended for those who seek more detailed coverage of social protection policies and programs in the region. Although not all are recognized everywhere as independent, the forty-four countries, large and small, are for present purposes: Antigua and Barbuda, Argentina, Aruba, Bahamas, Barbados, Belize, Bermuda, Bolivia, Brazil, Chile, Colombia, Costa Rica, Cuba, Dominica, Dominican Republic, Ecuador, El Salvador, Falkland Islands, Grenada, Guadeloupe, Guatemala, Guyana, Guyana (Fr.), Haiti, Honduras, Jamaica, Martinique, Mexico, Netherlands Antilles, Nicaragua, Panama, Paraguay, Peru, Puerto Rico, St. Kitts Nevis, St. Lucia, St. Pierre and Miquelon, St. Vincent, Trinidad and Tobago, Suriname, Turks and Caicos Islands, Uruguay, Venezuela and Virgin Islands.

4. World Bank (2004) Summary-2.

5. Ibid.

6. This section draws heavily on International Labour Organization and United Nations Conference on Trade and Development (2001) 5-7. Based on the pioneering programs of Brazil and Mexico, the ILO and UNCTAD have jointly proposed piloting the minimum-income-for-school-attendance approach in several of Africa's least developed countries.

7. $8.50 and $32.80, respectively, based on a January 2000 exchange rate of 9.3 pesos to the dollar. See International Labour Organization and United Nations Conference on Trade and Development (2001) 5.

8. See www.progresa.gob.mx/informacion_general. The emphasis on rigorous evaluation of the program's outcomes and the availability of public use data files for additional studies have contributed to the widespread influence of the program in the development community.

9. http://www.infoplease.com/ipa/A0908770.html.

10. RS$130 or US$76.

11. Lavinas, Lena; Maria Lígia Barbosa; and Octávio Tourinho (2001) 1-3.

12. Ibid.:3

13. Executive Order 2140, signed by President Fernando Henrique Cardoso and Education Minister Paulo Renato Souza. The Brazilian Congress quickly passed the executive order into law, which became effective April 11, 2001.

14. Brazil Ministry of Education (2002). Program expansion was accomplished in large part through a partnership with the Children's Pastorate, a group linked to the National Conference of Brazilian Bishops and active in some 3,400 municipalities.

15. See www.bien.be/Archive/NationalDebates.htm.

16. De Janvry, Alain; Frederico Finan; Elisabeth Sadoulet; Donald Nelson; Kathy Lindert; Bénédicte de la Brière; and Peter Lanjouw (2005) 7.

17. Basic Income European Network (2004).

18. Ibid. These concluding observations are drawn from Philippe van Parijs' article in the NewsFlash. Earlier, on January 8, 2004, Van Parijs delivered an address in Brasilia's Presidential Palace to commemorate the promulgation of the new law.

19. Velásquez Pinto, Mario D. (2003) 1-2.

20. Ibid.: 4.

21. Ibid.: 7.

22. Rawlings, Laura B. (2004) 33.

23. Ayala Consulting Company (2003).

24. Coady, David; Margaret Grosh; and John Hoddinott (2003) 39.

25. www.redsocial.gob.ni.

26. For more see Hwww.ifpri.org/themes/mp18/nicaraguarps.htmH and the website of the government of Nicaragua, www.redsocial.gob.ni.

27. Ibid.:57-58.

28. Ibid.: 631.

29. Asian Development Bank (2001) 41.

30. Ibid.:42.

31. Ibid.:49. The poverty figure is based on the $1 a day standard and reflects the World Bank's estimate for 2000. See World Bank (2003b) 46.

32. Ibid.: 619. Other South Asian countries are Bhutan, Maldives, and Nepal. The Pacific nations are Fiji Islands, Guam, Kiribati, Marshall Islands, Micronesia, New Caledonia, Papua New Guinea, Samoa, Solomon Islands, and Vanuatau. Central Asian countries include Azerbaijan, Kazakstan, Kyrgyz Republic, Mongolia, Tajikstan, Turkmenistan, and Uzbekistan. East Asian countries include Cambodia, Indonesia, Lao People's Democratic Republic, Malaysia, People's Republic of China, the Philippines, Thailand, and Viet Nam.

33. Ibid.: 617.

34. Tomlinson, John (2001) Chapter 1, "Introduction — Income Insecurity".

35. Stanley-Clarke, Nicola (1996)

36. For a more complete treatment of the region's social protection programs, see Handoussa, Heba and Zafiris Tzannatos, editors (2002). The countries under consideration are: Algeria, Bahrain, Egypt, Iran, Iraq, Jordan, Kuwait, Lebanon, Morocco, Oman, Qatar, Saudi Arabia, Sudan, Syria, Tunisia, Turkey, United Arab Emirates, West Bank-Gaza, Yemen.

37. Billeh, Victor, "Matching Education to Demand for Labor in the MENA Region," Chapter 1 in Handoussa, Heba and Zafiris Tzannatos, editors (2002) 2.

38. Tzannatos, Zafiris, "Social Protection in the Middle East and North Africa", Chapter 5 in Handoussa, Heba and Zafiris Tzannatos, editors (2002) 153-55.

39. Billeh, Victor, op. cit.: 3.

40. See www.fonds-solidarite.org/eng/.

41. World Bank, Social Protection Group (2002) 80.

42. World Bank, Social Protection Group (2002) Appendix 6.

43. Christiaensen, Luc; Lionel Demery; and Stefano Paternostro (2002) 13-16.

44. Sala-i-Martin, Xavier and Arvind Subramanian (2003) 4.

45. Sala-i-Martin, Xavier and Arvind Subramanian (2003) 17-26.

46. Ibid.

47. United Nations Economic Commission for Africa (2003) 46.

48. World Bank, Africa Region (2002) 61. The report notes that HIV/AIDS infects some 28 million Africans. In some countries plagued by AIDS or civil conflict, the percentage of children who are orphans has risen from 2 percent to 18 percent.

49. Landman, J.P., coordinator (2003) 4-5. The standard on which these figures are based is 871 rands a month for an urban household of four. Based on United Nations and World Bank data, the percentage of South Africans living in extreme poverty (less than PPP$1 a day) is less than two percent. See United Nations Development Program (2003) 200.

50. South African Council of Churches, Congress of South African Trade Unions, and South African Non-Governmental Coalition (2002) 13.

51. South Africa, Government of (2002) 17.

52. For a much more detailed recapitulation of this history, see Makino, Kumiko (2004) 14-24. Also see Taylor Committee (2002). Note: The Committee, whose formal title was Committee of Inquiry into a Comprehensive System of Social Security for South Africa, was chaired by Professor Viviene Taylor of the University of Cape Town's Department of Social Development.

7

Shortfalls

On January 2, 2002, President George W. Bush signed into law a reauthorization of the Elementary and Secondary Education Act of 1965 (P.L. 107-110), better known as the No Child Left Behind Act. The legislation aimed at closing gaps in U.S. student performance and achievement in elementary and secondary schools. There have been complaints that various provisions of the legislation are underfunded. The Act's emphasis on math and reading test scores as measures of progress has proven controversial.

Even though they quarreled with the means and the amount of resources provided, the Act's severest critics lauded its goal. And one can extrapolate from that particular national goal in the field of education to the world stage and the impact of globalization. Extreme poverty has no rightful place in a prospering world. The international community could do worse than adopt the goal of No Person Left Behind.

In the Millennium Declaration, the General Assembly of the United Nations declared: "We will spare no effort to free our fellow men, women and children from the abject and dehumanizing conditions of extreme poverty."[1] The good intentions expressed in the Declaration have so far outpaced performance on the ground. Over the past half-century or so, the international community's strategies for coping with global poverty have evolved through several stages. Each retains its partisans. Taken singly or together they have fallen short of eliminating extreme global poverty.

In stylized fashion, we can for convenience review these strategies under the following headings: (1) Growth Alone, (2) Growth and Infrastructure, (3) Growth, Infrastructure, and Jobs, (4) Growth, Infrastructure, Jobs, and Services, (5) Growth, Infrastructure, Jobs, Services, and Transfers.[2] Each in its own way has advanced the agenda of reducing extreme global poverty. But insufficiently.

Growth Alone

In the 1950s and 1960s, Growth Alone was the prevailing view. A rising tide would lift all boats. For developing countries the key was capital investment, industrial development, urbanization, and periodic infusions of foreign aid and foreign advice. Developing countries adopted a variety of growth strategies built around low interest rates, favorable currency exchange rates, and trade policies—notably, in the case of the latter, import substitution—to foster domestic industrialization and promote internal capital investment.

The expectation was that industrialization would attract and eventually absorb rural labor forces into higher paid and more productive urban employment. This scenario "failed to materialize in most developing countries."[3]

It was accepted that rural areas, where most of the world's poor were concentrated, could suffer disproportionately for a while as a country industrialized and urbanized. Women, children, seniors and various racial and ethnic population subgroups might lag behind for a time in the general exodus from poverty. But not to worry. Over time, the benefits would work their way down to those at the bottom of the income ladder. So sayeth Kuznets.[4]

Is Growth Alone sufficient to reduce global poverty? The neoliberal view is unequivocal. "Growth is sufficient, period."[5] And growth is best achieved by open markets, elimination of government deficits and reduced welfare expenditures. The needs of the poor are best met through the efforts of individuals, families and private sector organizations.

Others have begged to differ. Factors like high fertility rates, landlessness and illiteracy kept hundreds of millions of people ensnared in poverty. Impressive growth rates only accentuated the shortage of skills and appropriate technology in developing countries, thereby widening the gap between rich and poor. Private voluntary efforts to overcome these conditions fell dramatically short.

Growth tended to expand the pool of unemployed and unskilled members of the labor force. Alarmingly, the young made up a high proportion of this structurally unemployed group. Thus, even under conditions of strong economic growth and declining poverty rates, such as occurred in the 1980s, the number of people in poverty could continue to rise. The very factors contributing to the growth in society's resources hindered the absorption of the least skilled groups into the world of work or adequate distribution of new wealth to society's poorest.

Growth and Infrastructure

Whatever the trends statistically, for antipoverty advocates, the absolute number of extremely poor people would remain unacceptably high for the indefinite future. The benefits of globalization failed to trickle down to the least advantaged, at least on any acceptable timetable. Policy planners decided that something more was needed to accelerate the process.

The answer was Growth and Infrastructure. Deprived urban and, more especially, remote rural communities needed the underpinnings of growth in the form of roads, bridges, power plants, schools and hospitals. So these were built. "Between fiscal years 1961 and 1965, 76.8 percent of all [World] Bank lending was for electric power or transportation."[6]

Much good was done. Roads made it possible for poor villagers to travel to markets. They also made it possible for marketers to travel to poor villages. School enrollment and use of health care facilities went up. Rural electrification fostered business startups. Rural water systems brought potable water and improved overall sanitation to remote communities.

In some cases, the new infrastructures sat until they deteriorated. The money for road maintenance and the managerial and technical skills for running power plants were lacking. New funding tended to go toward new roads and power plants rather than maintenance of the existing ones. Those with entrepreneurial and other skills profited. Those without the requisite education and skill base stayed on the sidelines. Doctors, nurses and teachers—all were in short supply.

In other cases, communities benefited overall but the benefits bypassed their poorest and most isolated members. A road serves no useful purpose if the poor cannot afford the means of transportation. Wells and other rural water systems located close to the houses of wealthier and more politically influential households work to the detriment of their poorer neighbors.

Questions about the target efficiency of Growth and Infrastructure as an antipoverty strategy began to surface. For example, investments in agricultural infrastructure disproportionately favored big landowners over the peasantry. Agricultural marketing boards squeezed the profit margins of small farmers in order to lower food prices for urban residents. Subsidized mechanization raised yields but reduced the demand for labor.[7]

As rural areas began to enjoy some of the benefits of globalization, the extremely poor continued to suffer from their lack of two critical assets, land and education. Weak governance structures opened the door in some areas to corruption, unwise local investments and neglect of maintenance. Once again the few benefited but the many remained marginalized.

Perhaps something more than unalloyed growth was needed. Perhaps that something had to do with enabling people to tap into the benefits of growth through their own economic activity. Perhaps it was time to expand the scope of the world's antipoverty agenda.

Growth, Infrastructure, and Jobs

For policymakers, the problem was that Growth and infrastructure did not routinely expand employment opportunities on a large enough scale to alleviate poverty significantly.

High fertility rates diminished the average size of landholdings in countries operating on the principle of equal inheritance. Hence, marginal farms (less than one hectare) grew as a percentage of all farms. Job creation in both rural and urban areas fell behind expanding labor forces. From 1966 to 1992, for instance, the economic growth rate in India exceeded the rate of population increase, yet the number of unemployed seems to have risen.[8]

The solution? Growth, Infrastructure, and Jobs. Or, if you prefer, labor-intensive growth. In the 1970s, the International Labour Organization launched an initiative called the World Employment Program. This focused on making growth work for the benefit of all, regardless of race, ethnicity, gender, or other characteristics.

The International Labour Organization differentiated among people willing to work at prevailing wages but unable to obtain jobs, younger people holding out for jobs more commensurate with their education and training, and the working poor—those whose earnings were insufficient to lift them out of poverty.

The notion of poverty as a function of unemployment shifted policy discussion from growth alone to job creation. Indeed it was argued that employment should supersede growth as a primary development objective. The ILO has advocated, for example, that large infrastructure projects like road building be carried out using labor-intensive methods that provide employment to the poor.[9]

Development was increasingly seen as having a social as well as an economic dimension. One major cause of global poverty is gender-based discrimination in many societies and particularly in their labor markets. Women find it more difficult to get jobs, especially well paying jobs with career prospects.

Similar discriminatory attitudes diminish economic opportunities for racial and ethnic minorities, as well as indigenous peoples who in some countries are the majority. Some five thousand indigenous and tribal groups are spread among seventy countries.

"The world's highest infant mortality rates, lowest income levels, most widespread illiteracy and slimmest access to health and social services are to be found among the world's 300 million indigenous people, half of whom live in Asia."[10]

A labor-intensive approach to growth was intended to address these problems. The International Labour Organization highlighted the role of the informal sector, the network of small enterprises and ad hoc job creation that developed among rural migrants living at the urban margins. It emphasized the critical importance of education as an economic investment. It advocated "appropriate" technologies that accommodated the scarcity of capital but the abundance of labor in many developing countries.

The World Employment Program was embraced by other elements of the United Nations system. For its Second Development Decade, the United Nations emphasized rural development as a key to combating poverty and narrowing the income gap between rural and urban families.

It promoted labor-intensive growth through the establishment of employment targets and absorption of more of the labor force into modern non-agricultural jobs. Large-scale industrial and infrastructure projects should make way for small-scale job-creation projects.

Developed and developing countries alike have used public employment programs to counter widespread poverty and unemployment. The idea is that poor people, otherwise unemployed, can do socially useful work like road building, construction of public facilities (schools, hospitals, clinics), ditch digging and park maintenance. While targeted on the extremely poor, the evidence indicates that they are as likely to reach less vulnerable households as the most vulnerable.[11]

Public employment programs have been criticized as stigmatizing, administratively costly, and prone to political corruption. Since the jobs often entail heavy manual labor, participation rates are higher among men than women. Extremely poor people find it hard to take part due to associated costs like child or elder care and transportation. For advocates of unrestricted private sector expansion, public employment programs drain away scarce resources for low productivity work.[12]

With respect to growth strategies, developing countries had to decide whether to invest in creating a large number of less skilled, lower paying (and shakier) jobs or a smaller number of more skilled and higher-paying jobs geared to emerging technologies.

The former would increase employment and reduce poverty in the short run. This was attractive to countries with few resources and high population growth rates. However, labor-intensive growth strategies might work to their long-run disadvantage. To remain competitive, "[m]any companies in third-world countries have been forced to invest heavily in automated technologies."[13]

Developing countries, which pursued economic autonomy and self-sufficiency, found themselves confronting technology-intensive growth trends in the developed world and a globalizing market place. The long shadow of the multinational corporation was falling over more and more lands.[14] Advanced technologies were moving the world closer to a stage of "near workerless production" with fewer job opportunities while the populations of developing countries continued to rise.[15]

Growth, Infrastructure, Jobs and Services

By the 1970s the World Bank was pushing its loan portfolio beyond large infrastructure projects to include the human aspects of development, such as education, health and sanitation. This departed from the Bank's prior focus on strictly defined economic activity with a higher probability of return on investment than the riskier realm of social lending.

Social lending was justified on grounds that it would accelerate the development process. To maximize growth and employment required a new element to the set of antipoverty strategies. To deal with the world of work in a capital intensive, technologically grounded global economy, the poor needed a network of supportive social, educational and health services to meet their basic needs.

The basic needs approach adopted in the late 1960s and early 1970s included basic education, health care, food and housing subsidies augmented by skill training, childcare, and transportation. As part of labor-intensive growth strategies, newer aid projects highlighted food security, adult literacy, public health (for example, inoculations), credit for small farmers and technical assistance.

The arsenal of global antipoverty strategies now included Growth, Infrastructure, Jobs, and Services. But simply adding services on a project-by-project basis was insufficient and not infrequently counterproductive.

Social assistance programs like subsidized health care disproportionately benefited middle and upper income groups. In some countries, food subsidies went to the more well-off residents of urban areas rather than the destitute rural poor. Housing projects tended to serve as political showcases for governments while barely making a dent in national housing crises.[16]

Devils lurked in the details of implementation. Social service organizations tripped over one another. International donors overwhelmed national governments and local communities alike with burdensome grant conditions and excessive reporting requirements. Determining who should be counted as "poor" proved controversial.

Developing countries were induced to undertake reforms in "sectors" like health care, education and housing. Reforms foundered due to inadequate coordination across sectors, insufficient funding and political realities.

Education, for instance, was characterized by a tug of war over whether to invest more in universal primary schooling or post-secondary and university-level graduate programs. With decisive political support from wealthier classes, the latter tended to win out. Basic education for the poor took a back seat.

Subsidized housing benefited urban workers and civil servants while either ignoring the poor or harming them through the clearance of shantytowns without adequate relocation plans. Food subsidies were allocated mainly to civil servants, police, families of members of the armed services and factory workers. Health care programs, being concentrated in urban areas, tended to benefit middle and upper income groups far more than the poor.[17]

Many local projects proved innovative and effective. The dedication of aid workers, both domestic and international, was inspiring. Individuals and communities benefited. Yet, in general innovative local projects were not widely replicated even when recognized as models. Donors tended to fund innovation, not replication. And host governments lacked the resources to rigorously evaluate local projects and replicate those deemed successful.

One notable exception was the expansion of microfinance to support budding entrepreneurs in poor communities. But even here the aggregate impact on global poverty reduction has remained depressingly small.

Microcredit programs like the pioneering Grameen Bank in Bangdalesh typically make loans to groups of poor people operating a small business. These programs have had demonstrable success. They have been touted as a means of empowering women. However, for all the good they do, they are not the complete answer to extreme poverty.

First, in rural areas where they predominate, it would require restructuring of the economy to raise productivity and boost wages generally. The microcredit programs are not large or extensive enough to have such an impact. Most microcredit programs are not self-sustaining but depend on outside subsidies.

Second, in the "mini-economy" where the extremely poor live, transactions are small, informal and irregular. This makes it harder for microcredit programs to monitor activities or charge standard administrative costs. The more entrepreneurial members of a community tend to self-select into the programs. And there is the natural tendency for such programs to seek out those whose creditworthiness is higher.

To have a large effect on extreme poverty, microcredit schemes need to function as part of more integrated approaches involving literacy, health care, housing and other support systems. In some cases this occurs (for example in rural Bangladesh), in others not.[18]

With advances in mechanization, information and communications technologies, and biotechnology, both developing and developed countries will witness productivity gains in the future. In the former, the declining demand for unskilled labor accompanied by high population growth rates means that creative new solutions are required to avert economically bifurcated societies and a worsening poverty situation for those left out of the economic mainstream.

Growth, Infrastructure, Jobs, Services and Transfers

At the outset of this new century, there were welcome signs that the number of people in extreme poverty was dropping. However, the vast number of those still stuck in extreme poverty—minimally in the hundreds of millions—tempers the cause for celebration.

It is axiomatic in social welfare systems that the hardest cases remain until the last. The blend of growth, infrastructure, jobs and services has proven insufficient. Rural to urban migration has not always alleviated poverty. "The option of migrating is not available to all poor people, least of all the chronically (long-term) and severely (poorest) poor."[19] This is due to the cost of moving and the risks of losing whatever small assets they possess.

For those who do migrate, urban jobs often proved scarcer than expected and migrants lost touch with community-based kinship networks that provided them with an informal social and economic safety net. The beneficial effects of remittances notwithstanding, poverty and income inequality in sending rural areas can be exacerbated insofar as communities lose their most productive members to migration.[20]

The role of transfers in alleviating poverty has begun to attract more attention. The poor are most affected by shocks to the economic and social systems of their countries. Such shocks include crop failures, high inflation rates, natural disasters, civil conflict, crime, illness and disability, unemployment and the adversities of aging. Transfers are a means of reducing the risk of such shocks or at least softening their impact.

Social protection schemes take many forms including food subsidies, means-tested welfare payments, unemployment insurance, subsidized housing, universal health care and social security benefits. Such schemes are commonplace in rich countries but are often unaffordable in the poorest countries. "Less than ten percent of the population in the poorest countries have adequate social protection."[21]

Hence a pilot project by the International Labour Organization to establish a Global Social Trust. Rich countries would voluntarily contribute about five dollars per person per month to the Trust, which would be used to "jump start" social protection systems in the least developed countries.[22]

The World Bank has increased its involvement in the social protection sector. "Lending [in the sector] has increased more than six-fold since 1994."[23] In fiscal year 1999, lending reached $3.76 billion or thirteen percent of the World Bank's total.[24] The World Bank has concluded that, while individual social protection programs serve a useful purpose, a "more holistic approach" is needed to achieve significant poverty reduction in the developing world.

Under an approach dubbed "social risk management," it advocates a flexible approach to the design and implementation of social risk management strategies, depending on the nature of the particular risk (natural disaster versus economic downturn, for example) and the characteristics of the affected populations.[25]

Despite such conceptual frameworks, however, social protection systems tend to be categorical, that is, targeted not on the population in poverty as a whole but on selected subsets. Thus there are separate systems for the unemployed, seniors, and persons with disabilities. Different types of benefits and services are administered differently. Each demands the specification of its particular eligibility criteria, certification and periodic recertification of an applicant's entitlement to benefits, determination of benefit levels, and in some cases monitoring of how benefits are used (e.g. food stamps).

Social protection systems require the establishment of large and often intrusive bureaucratic structures. Expenditures must be audited to make sure that only eligible persons receive benefits and that benefits are pegged to the appropriate level and duration. The systems lose popularity in periods of economic downturn and rising government deficits. Complaints of waste, fraud and abuse grow louder. More basically, conservative critics contend that social protection fosters widespread dependency on government largesse and impedes prospects for economic growth. Beneficiaries tend to be stigmatized as unproductive drones.

Despite the criticism, social protection systems are more likely to expand than contract. The displacements created by the global economy will fuel such expansion. More and more international attention is being directed not only to growth strategies but also to the scope and financing of social protection in developing countries.

According to the World Commission on the Social Dimension of Globalization, "[a] minimum level of social protection for individuals and families needs to be accepted and undisputed as part of the socio-economic 'floor' of the global economy....Donors and financial institutions should contribute to the strengthening of social protection systems in developing countries."[26]

At the same time, the downsides of social protection persist, including such factors as administrative complexity, rising costs, stigmatization of recipients, perpetuation of dependency and potential work disincentives. The search to minimize these downsides and reduce reliance on social protection goes on.

Globalization, Equity and Social Protection

Unsurprisingly, globalization has provoked a rise in global tensions. Too few people influence its shape, affect its course, or share in its benefits. The relationships among economics, social structures and political power affect the ways policy is developed and implemented in poor countries. Yet these relationships are not well understood. History remains the best available guide to what does and does not work to foster growth and alleviate poverty and what role a global guaranteed income scheme might play in the process.[27]

Recent history reveals a pattern of unregulated capital flows and unfettered market access by global economic powers that have generated unbalanced outcomes within and among societies. While poverty reduction has become a central development theme, old ideologies and inflexible nostrums have proven inadequate. Around the world people seek decent jobs and promising futures for their children. Despite the growth in global wealth, hundreds of millions of people remain in the shadows of the informal economy without rights or benefits. They are unable or unwilling to function as part of an open private economy. They tend to live in "a swathe of poor countries that subsist precariously on the margins of the global economy."[28]

The phrase "social protection" covers a wide array of public programs aimed at overcoming the risk or consequences of economic insecurity and related adversities. Social protection schemes are designed to provide citizens with a minimum level of resources for living. They may be augmented by measures geared to personal growth and skill development through education, training, and supportive services. The most familiar types of schemes are social insurance, family allowances and means-tested welfare payments.

Social insurance refers to contributory systems with defined benefits that protect individuals and their families from economic insecurity due to job loss, retirement or health care expenditures. The financing of these systems is shared among participants, employers and governments.[29]

Family allowances are periodic cash payments made by governments to ensure the security of children and the economic stability of their families. Family allowance programs must cope with changing structures and patterns in contemporary family life. While means-testing may play a part, some minimum benefit is commonly provided to families regardless of their socio-economic status.

In welfare, means-tested cash assistance is provided from general revenues to eligible beneficiaries in designated population subgroups such as the poor, persons with disabilities, expectant mothers, and elderly persons.

Other forms of social protection include vouchers (e.g., for food, housing, schooling), in-kind benefits (such as the distribution of clothing or food), tax breaks, social services and job-related "activation" measures. Despite the individual and cumulative importance of these schemes, a significant proportion of low-income people continues to fall through society's safety nets.

In the developed world, and most notably in North America and Western Europe, a variety of social protection schemes has evolved incrementally from country to country. New schemes emerged to promote social objectives (e.g.

family formation) or in response to adverse conditions (poverty, unemployment, disability, etc.) affecting particular categories of people (women, children, single parents, seniors, racial and ethnic minorities).

Collectively the schemes comprise a crazy quilt of protection, with gaps in some areas, overlaps in others, unwelcome disincentives, and administrative complexity. In developing countries, where extreme poverty is concentrated, social protection schemes are generally less extensive, less generous, and more vulnerable to mistargeting and outright corruption.

As their economies grow and the disparities between rich and poor widen, these countries will face a choice. Their social protection schemes can follow the haphazard evolutionary path of the developed countries. Alternatively, they can skip past piecemeal solutions and respond to extreme poverty in a more integrated and technologically advanced manner.

To borrow an analogy from telecommunications, they can install telephones in homes and string the landscape with copper wires. Or they can skip immediately to cell phones and other wireless communications devices.

In social protection, with financial and technical assistance from the international community, they could opt for a simplified but comprehensive remedy for anyone in extreme poverty—a guaranteed minimum income. There are signs that the social welfare systems of so-called developed countries are themselves evolving in that direction.

A floor under the incomes of the world's poorest people is a logical first step for alleviating global social tensions and tapping into latent human capabilities. One approach is simply to provide a guaranteed basic income for all people regardless of their circumstances.

For the most part, proposals for a guaranteed income are limited to individual nations. International forums advocate the concept, track progress in implementing it, and compare various approaches. Here and there, calls are heard for a global guaranteed income. Too often the proposals are so utopian that even their advocates despair of full implementation. Whatever the fate of these proposals, on a global scale, something more concrete is called for.

A more affordable and potentially more politically palatable alternative is a negative income tax that takes the form of a refundable tax credit. This approach would entail a partnership among developing countries, donors and international organizations. The philosophy and history of social welfare systems, taken in conjunction with recent trends, provide the grounding for this approach. The philosophy indicates public sensitivity to the need for income security. The history reveals the inadequacy of current systems for achieving the goal.

END NOTES

1. United Nations (2000a).
2. This chapter is more of an essay than history. For the latter you may wish to go to my *Victory Deferred: The War on Global Poverty (1945-2003)*.
3. United Nations Economic and Social Council (1995) 4.

4. Nobel prize winning economist Simon Kuznets (1901-85) hypothesized that, in a traditionally agricultural economy with a low level of income inequality, the shift toward industrialization would lead to an increase in income inequality for a period of time. At some critical point, income inequality would start to decrease. This was represented by the famous U-shaped Kuznets curve. Despite much research, scant empirical evidence has been uncovered to fully substantiate the hypothesis.

5. Bhalla, Surjit S. (2002) 206.

6. Ayres, Robert L. (1983) 2.

7. United Nations Economic and Social Council (1995) 4.

8. Australian Reproductive Health Alliance and Family Planning Association International Development New Zealand (1998) 2.

9. International Labour Organization, Regional Office for Asia and the Pacific, "Roadways to Employment: Linking Infrastructure to Jobs," press release, 10/26/99. www.ilo.org/public/english/region/asro/bangkok/newsroom.

10. International Labour Organization, Regional Office for Asia and the Pacific, "Indigenous People Still the Poorest of the Poor," press release, 8/8/01. www.ilo.org/public/english/region/asro/bangkok/newsroom.

11. One example. In the wake of the Asian financial crisis of the late 1990s, Indonesia expanded its public works program. In the ILO's People's Security Survey, 2.4% of households with incomes *sufficient* for their food needs were engaged in public works schemes. One would expect the percentage to be higher for households with incomes that were not sufficient for food needs; in fact, the percentage was 2.6%. See International Labour Organization (2004) 371-372.

12. International Labour Organization (2004) 371-372.

13. Rifkin, Jeremy (1995) 204.

14. In 1999, of the world's one hundred largest economies, only forty-nine were countries; the rest were corporations. The top five corporations, General Motors, Wal-Mart, Exxon Mobil, Ford Motor and Daimler Chrysler, ranked number 23 (just ahead of Denmark), 25, 26, 27, and 28 respectively. (The study directly compares the sales of corporations with the Gross Domestic Product of countries.) See Anderson, Sarah and John Cavanagh (2000) 9.

15. Rifkin, Jeremy (1995) 207.

16. Bird, Richard M. and Susan Horton (1989) 11-16.

17. United Nations Economic and Social Council (1995) 5.

18. The preceding discussion on microfinance draws on International Labour Organization (2004) 373-376.

19. Waddington, Hugh and Rachel Sabates-Wheeler (2003) 18.

20. Op. cit.: 9-10.

21. International Labour Organization (2003) 11.

22. Ibid. For the United States, for example, the contribution would be $5 times 12 months times 280 million people or $16.8 billion a year.

23. World Bank (2001e) vii.

24. Ibid.

25. Ibid.

26. International Labour Organization (2004) xiii.

27. Bird, Richard M. and Susan Horton, editors (1989) 15-22.

28. International Labour Organization (2004) x.

29. The term "insurance" is a bit misleading since such systems are financed on a pay-as-you-go basis. There is no necessary relationship between participants' contributions and their subsequent benefits. The systems disburse benefits from current tax receipts and tend to accumulate large unfunded liabilities.

8

Rationale

While trends in economic growth worldwide are positive, there is disturbing evidence of gross inequality within and among countries and regions. The ratio in per capita gross domestic product between the more developed and less developed regions of the world stood at 3:1 in the early nineteenth century. The ratio had reached approximately 20:1 by the end of the twentieth century.[1]

For several decades, Latin America and the Caribbean have suffered from one of the most unequal income distributions in the world, particularly Haiti, Central America, the Andean region and Northeastern Brazil.[2] The demand for unskilled labor has not kept pace with growth and the wage gap between skilled and unskilled workers has increased.

Lacking opportunities in the formal employment sector, unskilled workers must resort to an informal cash economy characterized by very low wages, lack of benefits and job transience. Under annual per capita growth rates of three percent, it would take decades and, for some countries, literally a couple of centuries, to eliminate poverty in Latin America and the Caribbean.[3] It could take longer if national poverty lines were used (rather than the PPP$1 a day standard), if growth rates declined or if inequality accelerated.

The situation in some other regions, for example, Sub-Saharan Africa and parts of Asia, is if anything worse. In short, economic growth is an insufficient condition for the elimination of poverty. Developing countries are particularly vulnerable to falling prices in the commodities they export (e.g. coffee, cotton), rising prices in those they import (e.g. oil) and generalized slowdowns in the global economy. Market economies need a formal publicly-financed system for protecting the poor against such economic shocks.

Conversely, "reducing the risk of people falling below minimum subsistence could have a positive growth effect."[4]

Some Structural Employment Dynamics[5]

Investment in technology to augment or in some areas replace human labor can generate higher productivity. With the goal of maximizing productivity, employers in developed and some developing nations are rushing to adopt information and communications technologies, automate production processes, require technologically literate labor forces and implement cost-cutting measures.

Such measures are designed to enable countries with high labor costs to stay competitive globally. One adverse consequence is the reduction of job opportunities for less skilled workers. The growth of productive capacity creates some new jobs but the number remains insufficient to absorb the hard-core unemployed. Such structural unemployment dynamics, which in earlier times were localized and intermittent, are gradually becoming global and permanent.

Oddly, many governments react by promoting "work first" policies over welfare. The unemployed are discouraged from relying on social assistance through negative incentives like intrusive means tests, extensive recordkeeping and reporting requirements, and social stigmatization.

On the "positive" side, many governments subsidize employment through public sector employment, wage subsidies or job creation schemes. In the short term these policies do indeed generate more paid work for low-income people. Over the longer haul they may however prove counterproductive. By perpetuating low wage, low skilled jobs rather than promoting technology-based initiatives, these policies retard a country's drive toward global competitiveness.

An alternative is to subsidize income, not employment.

Work Ethic Obsession

Consider the following propositions. Minimum wage legislation is designed to alleviate poverty and raise workers' living standards. However, the relationship between minimum wage guarantees for workers and household poverty reduction is tenuous. To cope with higher labor costs, employers will seek to increase productivity by replacing some workers with new technologies and by inducing the retained labor force to become ever more efficient.

With a premium on a technologically attuned work force and with the increased automation of repetitive tasks, the poor will face major obstacles to finding and keeping jobs in low wage labor markets. Workers whose marginal work product is worth less than the legal minimum wage will be let go.

These latter will be forced into unemployment or into occupations not covered by minimum wage provisions. Even for retained workers, poverty can persist since the minimum wage is not adjusted for household size and needs. Opportunities for upward mobility will be extremely limited.

Inherently, a minimum wage bifurcates the labor force into those whose work product is worth at least the minimum wage and those whose work product is not. Some of the former and most of the latter are put at risk of extreme poverty. Then there are those persons who have no ties to the labor force. They remain at risk as well.

This is not a reason to eliminate the minimum wage. It is a reason to consider means of alleviating poverty among those who do not benefit from it. One sure means of alleviating poverty is to predicate income on household need, not employment. To be sure, providing income support directly to households in poverty will impair work incentives.

For this reason, there is much to commend in a mechanism like the negative income tax. It can be implemented with a minimum of new administrative machinery. And it can be structured such that households have some incentive to increase their incomes beyond the level provided through negative tax rates.[6]

At present social policy in both developed and developing countries dictates that the poor must at all costs be kept busy. The goal is focused less on eliminating poverty than on eliminating unemployment. Work equates to worth. Developing countries in particular are encouraged to embrace pro-poor growth by providing job opportunities for as many poor people as possible without unduly sacrificing points in overall growth rates.

As a general proposition, individuals can have an overdeveloped or underdeveloped work ethic. So too for society. Since there is more to life than paid work, a balance is needed. Beyond that self-evident proposition, there is the societal question as to how much human labor is actually required for economic productivity and real growth. Conversely, how much if anything would a society lose by assuring that its poorest members did not have to live on less than PPP\$1 a day?

For people in poverty, income is disproportionately dependent on their labor compared to the non-poor who are more likely to receive a portion of their income from sources like investments, savings and inheritances. They are also less likely to own assets like real property that can be converted into cash.

As the twenty-first century unfolds, productivity gains will depend less on human labor and more on technological innovation and diffusion. There will be advances in renewable energy, information and communications technologies, transportation, commercialization of outer space, biotechnology, and medicine.

Furthermore, labor-intensive growth strategies do not necessarily make the most sense over the long term for developing countries. That could leave them forever unable to achieve parity with more developed countries whose productivity gains are due more to advances in technology and the migration of capital than reliance on human labor.

Growth and productivity gains do not occur linearly, of course. Nor are their consequences uniformly benign. Within any given country and, for that matter, across regions of the globe, the pattern is more erratic. For short-term and transitional purposes, governments can and arguably should cushion the adverse impacts of growth on vulnerable groups. This includes strategies to provide training and foster job creation, both public and private, for displaced workers. Social protection schemes can help people absorb some of the shock.

The issue is the extent to which such interventions should comprise the core of a nation's antipoverty strategy. Can the extremely poor afford (literally) to wait patiently until a sufficient number of jobs become available that will require their labor? Will existing social protection schemes fully take up the slack for those unable to function in a modernizing economy?

Success in these endeavors has so far eluded societies everywhere, especially given the endless search for cheaper production costs. Existing social policy provides bandaids to hemorrhages. So-called pro-poor growth strategies for developing countries as advocated by international aid agencies risk being oxymoronic unless they are situated within a larger antipoverty context.

Reduced work incentives may be unwelcome in moral terms to some societies but they need not be so in economic terms. For a guaranteed income plan, the question is not simply whether human work effort is reduced but whether it is reduced to the point of being detrimental to society. A more interesting question is whether it might not in fact serve as a long-term spur to growth.

Robotics as Synecdoche.[7]

Robotics is maturing as an industry. "We are standing right now on the threshold of the robotic era. [R]obots [will soon] have the potential to dramatically change the world economy."[8] The relative importance of human labor in the global economy will decline.

Robots have become smarter, smaller and less power hungry. According to the United Nations Commission for Europe, the installed base of industrial robots in 2004 is estimated minimally at 800,000 and possibly over one million. The market appears to be growing at about 5.7 percent a year.[9] The prices of robots relative to labor costs have been falling.

Industrial robots are found overwhelmingly in developed economies. In 2002, Japan accounted for over half the world's industrial robots, followed by the United States and Germany. Other countries making more and more use of industrial robots include France, Italy, Republic of Korea, Russian Federation, Spain, and United Kingdom. Countries in the developing world will soon face the choice of adapting to the robotic era or losing ground in the industrial workplace. In transitional economies like Brazil, Mexico and China, investments in robotics are accelerating.[10]

In absolute terms, the number of industrial robots is small relative to the global labor force. However, mirroring predecessors like television sets, personal computers, and wireless phones, their presence is likely to become ubiquitous in the coming decades. Robots are showing up in non-industrial areas like construction, building cleaning and maintenance, security, firefighting, courier delivery, agriculture, hotel management, lawn care and housekeeping. Robots can also be used for surgery, undersea exploration, surveillance and demolition.

During the 1990s, robotics improved due to advances in computing, telecommunications, software, electronic devices and lightweight materials. Advances in robotics already have led to the replacement of humans by robots on many industrial assembly lines. In Japan, Italy and Germany, for every ten automobile production workers, there is at least one robot.[11] As companies acquire greater familiarity with the technology and with their own production processes, investment in robotics will grow apace.

Over the next decade or two, robots will continue to replace human beings in many types of employment, especially those involving repetitive tasks, heavy lifting and hazardous conditions involving smoke, chemicals, intense heat and the like. Increasingly they will either supplement or even replace those with more specialized skills as well.

In the automotive industry, for instance, robots are being used not only in basic assembly operations but also in areas with a higher risk of injury like welding and painting. Robots have the potential of lowering the risks associated with dangerous tasks, reducing industrial accidents and minimizing the incidence of labor disputes. National defense agencies are turning to robotic applications for unmanned surveillance aircraft and even for weapons systems.

The ceaseless quest for higher productivity virtually assures the emergence of a sizable robotic work force in developed and eventually developing nations. Employed human beings will perform less physical labor but will take on more mentally-oriented tasks and functions, including greater responsibility for quality control, maintenance and productivity targets.

Employees will undergo continuous training, geared not only to the use of new technologies but also adaptation to changed work environments. Education and evidence of "trainability" will be prerequisites for the jobs of the future.

Robots are finding their way into the home. For the 2004-2007 period, the UNECE/IFR study projects that an estimated 6.6 million domestic robots will be sold for services like lawn mowing and vacuuming and an additional 2.5 million units for leisure and entertainment (e.g. toy robots).[12]

All this is hardly news. Over forty years ago, economist Robert Theobald, an early advocate of a guaranteed income, predicted that employment in a technologically advanced economy will depend largely on "the level and skill of the job applicant...[T]he decline in job opportunities will be most severe for those who perform repetitive tasks and whose work can most easily be done by machines."[13]

Robotics is but one manifestation of technology-based, capital intensive growth that relies less and less on the prime asset of the poor, their labor. Other advanced technologies are eliminating traditional jobs such as supermarket cashiers, airline ticket agents and bank tellers. Developments in fields like biotechnology, nanotechnology, commercialization of space and a variety of information and communications technologies will exert powerful influences on the world's economy. They offer exciting opportunities for the world's labor force.

Labor Market Dynamics in the Developing World

To take advantage of emerging opportunities, members of the global labor force will require the requisite levels of education and technical skills. For many of the jobs being created in these specialized fields, the extremely poor need not bother to apply.

In industry, technological innovation occurs most commonly in large enterprises and multinational corporations. New work arrangements and production methods usually make job tasks more complex and require the hiring of people with the requisite skills and the retraining of existing workers.

In rural areas, large agribusinesses have impoverished small farmers, who cannot afford the cost of new technologies. Hand in hand with the modernization and commercialization of agriculture has been the increased consolidation of landholdings. Often denied access to land they once farmed, sharecroppers and tenant farmers join the migration to cities.[14] Those who cannot adapt to ever changing work settings, whether urban or rural, risk becoming redundant in the formal economy.

They then face the prospect of being unemployed or finding work in the informal economy that is "characterized by a lack of social protection, lack of regulatory safeguards and general precariousness."[15] While some informality is inevitable, and perhaps even indispensable, a large informal economy distorts the overall economic picture and reduces tax revenues that are the lifeblood of public social protection systems.

With the accelerating pace of globalization, developing countries that have not felt the impact of robotization and other advanced technologies soon will. In the production of both goods and services, the supply of labor will outpace the demand. The capacity of the economy to absorb minimally skilled workers will diminish. Developing countries in Asia, notably India, are witnessing the phenomenon of jobless growth propelled by technology-intensive industries and services.[16]

The process of deindustrialization has been occurring in the member countries of the Organization for Economic Cooperation and Development for several decades. The loss of manufacturing jobs is not limited to these affluent nations. Transitional and emerging economies like those of China, Republic of Korea, Russian Federation, Ukraine and Mexico experienced significant declines in manufacturing jobs during the 1990s.[17]

The demand for labor is subject to an ongoing international redistribution. In a global economy, jobs more readily migrate to countries where wages and benefits are lower. It is more difficult for workers themselves to migrate. The global economy fosters the free flow of goods, services and capital but is less tolerant of unrestricted labor flows.

The nations losing industrial jobs can remain competitive only through technologically driven gains in productivity. In the case of manufacturing, when labor-intensive assembly-line jobs go abroad, automation tends to take their place at home. The developing countries that gain these labor-intensive jobs obviously benefit for a time. Eventually, as real wages rise, they affect production costs. If a country's internal market for goods is large enough, the domestic economy may be able to fully absorb the associated increase in consumer prices.

However, even in China, the country with the world's largest population and fastest growing economy, "labor market insecurity...is very widespread."[18] In part, this is due to labor market dislocations caused by a restructuring of the Chinese economy. Despite its rapid growth, China's economy is burdened by structural imbalances that include a banking system laden with nonperforming loans, inefficient state-owned enterprises, widening regional disparities and substantial fiscal deficits.[19]

Using specially constructed poverty lines, the World Bank's Martin Ravallion and Shaohua Chen have identified a dramatic decline in extreme poverty in China from 53 percent to eight percent in the 1980-2001 period.[20] Macroeconomic stability contributed to overall economic growth and poverty reduction. Agricultural restructuring (such as decollectivization) pursuant to Deng Xiaoping's 1978 market reforms played a large—but mainly one-time—role in China's success.

However, "progress was uneven over time and across provinces."[21] Unless addressed, the rising levels of income inequality in many provinces will slow future rates of poverty reduction.[22] On the industrial front, the sale of some state-owned enterprises in China, with their costly cradle-to-grave welfare orientation, has led to a shedding of surplus labor costs by the acquiring private interests.

If growth is export-dependent, manufacturing jobs will tend to migrate again to even lower wage nations. The developing or transitional country losing those jobs will be forced to regain its competitiveness through technology and automation. Such trends may suggest why in China it appears that "aggregate growth is increasingly coming from sources that bring limited gains to the poor."[23] The Chinese government is aware of this problem.

With greater revenue from industrial and urban taxes, China like other industrializing countries has begun to reduce age-old taxes on agriculture and to provide farmers with subsidies.[24] The goal is to cope with growing rural-urban income inequality, maintain food production capacities and preserve the rural way of life. The economic impact of the new measures so far has been small but the direction of government policy is significant.

In China and elsewhere, as the standard of living improves and real wages rise, economic restructuring will entail increasing reliance on advanced technologies in production processes. The trend toward global labor redistribution and technological substitution shows no sign of ending ever, let alone soon.

Employment Security and a Minimum Income

In developing countries, the rate of population growth and the attendant increase in labor force supply are outpacing their ability to create jobs.[25] In sectors like manufacturing that traditionally provided job opportunities, automation and related technologies have taken over. The poor in particular will experience the shrinkage of labor market demand as advanced technologies inexorably substitute for the world's unskilled or at least irrelevantly skilled labor.

With the delivery of products and services becoming dependent more on technology than labor, the long-cherished goal of full employment through free market mechanisms will fall by the wayside. Two possibilities will remain. There will not be full employment. Or, there will be full employment but it will not result from free market mechanisms.

In the latter case, unskilled workers will become increasingly dependent on their governments, which will be endlessly pressured to institute retraining schemes, create labor-intensive public service jobs and expand welfare or social protection benefits.

Although never strong, employment security has been weakened by global and internal competitive pressures.[26] Workers have lost protections against unfair and arbitrary dismissal and avenues of redress. Surveys by the International Labour Organization found that in no country did a majority of the respondents expect their income to be higher in a year's time.[27]

The International Social Justice Project fielded large-scale surveys of popular opinion in thirteen countries in 1991 and six countries in 1996.[28] In all the participating countries, these surveys found support for some kind of minimum income to cover basic needs. Similar findings emerged from the People's Security Surveys, conducted by the International Labour Organization between 2000 and 2003. The levels of support by groups that were differentiated by age, gender and education did not vary significantly.[29]

A guaranteed minimum income would provide workers with a degree of economic security plus the freedom to pursue a wider range of career options. For qualifying low-income jobholders, it would reward work, reinforce their sense of responsibility and fight poverty at the same time. As an underpinning of society, it will enable the private sector to invest more readily in advanced technologies as a source of economic growth. Advances in technologies like robotics and other labor-saving (or rather labor-replacing) technologies will offset to some degree the potential decline in work effort among the poor (or others) resulting from a guaranteed income.

The diffusion of advanced technology plus a guaranteed income for all could lead to overall improvement in the global quality of life. With a guaranteed income system in place, governments could direct their attention to supporting high tech, capital-intensive production. Emphasis would shift from creating jobs for the unskilled to building a skilled labor force capable of incorporating new technologies.

These processes are already underway in developed countries. By contrast, developing countries are encouraged to engage in labor-intensive growth strategies. While well-intentioned (one assumes), these strategies may undermine the long-term growth prospects of the developing world. It will simply fall further and further behind the developed world.

There is an alternative. A global guaranteed income system could serve as a vital precondition for technologically driven growth in the developing as well as the developed world. With the rapid emergence of a post-industrial world, a refundable tax credit to alleviate extreme global poverty would represent a modest but meaningful step in that direction.

Guaranteeing Income

In a recent book, Peter Townsend and David Gordon include an antipoverty Manifesto. Among its eighteen items for international action, the second calls for legally enforcing the right to an adequate standard of living. This right would be recognized through "state-defined minimum earnings [plus] state-defined minimum cash benefits for those not in paid work."[30]

The Basic Income Earth Network (BIEN) advocates a basic income that is granted unconditionally to every individual without a means test or work requirement. In the fall of 1983, Paul-Marie Boulanger, Philippe Defeyt and Philippe Van Parijs at the Catholic University of Louvain in Belgium jointly elaborated this idea, which one of them had proposed with the name "allocation universelle."

In April 1985, the group, then known as the *Collectif Charles Fourier*, spelled out the idea in a special issue of the Brussels monthly *La Revue Nouvelle*. They summarized their idea and its potential consequences in a prize-winning essay for a competition on the future of work sponsored by the King Baudouin Foundation.[31]

With the prize money gained from the competition, the *Collectif Charles Fourier* organized the first international conference on basic income, held in Louvain-la-Neuve, Belgium in September 1986, with sixty invited participants. This event brought together many hitherto isolated but kindred spirits.[32]

The conference led to the creation of a more permanent association, called the Basic Income European Network. Since 1986, BIEN has organized a major international congress every other year. From 1988 through 1999 BIEN published a newsletter, which more recently has been superseded by a regular NewsFlash.

The group maintains a website with among other items an extensive bibliography on the basic income concept.[33] Reflecting the global character of its membership, the group voted in September 2004 to change its name to the Basic Income *Earth* Network.

In the United States, the concept has gained footing through an informal network of advocates called the U.S. Basic Income Guarantee Network (US-BIG).[34] Other similar networks recognized by BIEN exist in Argentina, Austria, Brazil, Denmark, Germany, Ireland, Netherlands, Spain, Switzerland and United Kingdom. Additionally basic income advocacy groups are active in other countries, notably Australia, Canada, France, New Zealand, South Africa and Sweden.

In Europe, support for guaranteed income schemes has arisen from diverse parts of the political spectrum. In 2003, a particularly conservative component of President Jacques Chirac's right-wing coalition in France advocated a universal dividend. Under this plan, everyone would be guaranteed a monthly income of 300 euros without regard for a means test or work requirement. In Germany, the Party of Democratic Socialism, heir to the East German communist party, has fostered public debate over an unconditional basic income.

Despite the diversity and occasional intensity of advocacy efforts in particular countries, one must not make too much of them. They can give a false sense of inexorable progress. For the foreseeable future in most countries, the prospects of implementing a guaranteed income scheme are dim, given existing political realities.

Conceivably basic income advocacy groups in various nations could choose to coalesce around the issue of extreme global poverty. Along with focusing on discrete national reforms, they could endorse a global guaranteed income system, subsidized in part by transfers from wealthier countries to the least developed. Thus far, however, their attention has centered mainly on reforms in their individual countries.

Features

A guaranteed income does away with employment status as a condition of eligibility and with the application of marginal tax rates. The Earned Income Tax Credit in the U.S. requires that at least one member of the household be an earner. A global tax credit by contrast would be predicated on income regardless of source.

Under even the most generous social welfare schemes, poor people who are capable of working are expected to seek work as a condition of assistance. As a route to increasing self-sufficiency for individuals and overall economic growth for developing countries, a work requirement approach is questionable at best.

The mandatory search for work as a condition for receiving benefits all too often leads to former welfare recipients being trapped in low-wage jobs and encumbered by heavy transportation and childcare expenses. The loss of benefits when people find work acts as a disincentive to seek work. If they find and subsequently lose a job, they begin again the lengthy and degrading process of applying for welfare.

A guaranteed income as a form of poverty alleviation would do away with the stigma of means-tested and work-conditioned social welfare programs. It would thus help eliminate poverty and unemployment traps within the social welfare system. The additional income would expand the range of choices for recipients.

Hardly anyone disagrees that existing social welfare systems are complex, cumbersome and stigmatizing. By doing away with categorization of beneficiaries (by age, health status and disability, for example) and conditions of assistance, a guaranteed income scheme would simplify the administration of benefits. Overlaps among a government's tax, welfare and social security systems would be addressed. Information about beneficiaries would be kept private and confidential.

Arguably, the reduced work effort under a guaranteed income could be positive. Firms would rely for productivity gains on technology and higher capital investment. They may have to raise wages and improve training to retain qualified workers. The national labor pool would make up in quality what it lacks in quantity.

By giving recipients more flexibility in the labor market, the tax credit would function as an instrument against inhumane working conditions such as exploitation of child labor, pitifully low wages, excessively long hours and unsafe work environments.

It would also lower the incentive for extremely poor people to engage in survival-oriented work that harms the environment. This includes abusive land use practices like deforestation, overgrazing, soil erosion and desertification; overfishing; and destruction of wildlife populations (such as elephant, hippopotamus, giraffe, and lion) because of poaching and habitat destruction

A guaranteed income would free individuals from the trap of dead-end jobs and give them an expanded opportunity to upgrade their skills and pursue more remunerative work. Or it could enable one or both parents to spend more time with their children. Or it could enable young people to study rather than be forced to seek work, often by terminating their education prematurely.

The potential for a regularized income level can reduce stress among the extremely poor. More than likely it would open their eyes to other sources of support and increase take-up rates in educational and social service programs for which they are eligible. The credit could indirectly foster innovation in the delivery of social services, as public agencies shift somewhat from a basic needs approach to emphasis on educational and economic opportunities for their clients.

Based on the evidence from a series of negative income experiments in the United States and Canada during the 1970s, complete withdrawal from the labor force is unlikely. The pattern observed in the earlier experiments was not complete withdrawal but rather longer periods of unemployment between jobs and fewer hours worked per week.[35]

Under a guaranteed income scheme, any foregone labor will be disproportionately unskilled, precisely where demand is diminishing proportionate to total labor demand. Unskilled guaranteed income beneficiaries will have the option to reduce their participation in the labor force or use part of their income to acquire skills demanded by a globalizing economy.[36]

Finally, a nondiscriminatory refundable tax credit would move the world closer to the goals of fairness and social inclusion. It acknowledges the dignity and autonomy of each individual. It embodies the concept that the earth and its products are not the exclusive property of a few but the common patrimony of all.

END NOTES

1. Economic Commission for Latin America and the Caribbean (2002) 76.
2. Canadian Foundation for the Americas (FOCAL) (2001) 3.
3. Lustig, Nora and Ruthanne Deutsch (1998) i., 3-5.
4. U.S. Agency for International Development (2004) 53. On the same page, the report goes on to say that "poor families...will have less need to pull their children out of school during a macroeconomic crisis or plant low-return but stable crops rather than riskier crops with higher profits."
5. The writing of this section benefited greatly from the line of argument advanced in Mitschke, Joachim (2000) 107-120.
6. This and the preceding paragraphs of this section are my summary of Stigler, George J. (1946) 358-65, which, despite not having a single equation, remains a classic argument

on behalf of the negative income tax. Perhaps there is something to be said for plain speaking, after all...

7. This section draws on Clark, Robert F. (2005)

8. See http://marshallbrain.com/robotic-freedom.htm. Marshall Brain is a writer and consultant who has written extensively on the impact of robotics on the U.S. and world economy. He advocates giving every U.S. citizen a stipend of $25,000 to distribute the benefits of the robotic revolution equitably and guarantee economic freedom for all.

9. United Nations Economic Commission for Europe, "UNECE Issues Its 2004 World Robotics Survey", October 20, 2004. Press release ECE/STAT/04/P01, Geneva. The survey is conducted in cooperation with the International Federation of Robotics.

10. Ibid.

11. Ibid.

12. Ibid.

13. Theobald, Robert (1965) 8.

14. International Labour Organization (2004b) 114-115.

15. International Labour Organization (2004b) 115.

16. "Out of a total [Asian] labor force of around 1.7 billion, at least 500 million are conservatively estimated to be unemployed or underemployed." Asian Development Bank (2005) iii.

17. International Labour Organization (2004b) 116-117.

18. International Labour Organization (2004b) 120.

19. Shane, Matthew and Fred Gale. 2004.

20. Ravallion, Martin and Shaohua Chen (2004).

21. Ravallion, Martin and Shaohua Chen (2004) Abstract.

22. Ravallion, Martin and Shaohua Chen (2004). The poverty lines they used, which were derived from the prices of regional food bundles, were 850 yuan for rural areas, 1200 yuan for urban.

23. Ravallion, Martin and Shaohua Chen (2004) 31.

24. Gale, Fred; Bryan Lohmar; and Francis Tuan (2004) 14.

25. Within ten years, an estimated one billion jobs would need to be created to absorb the growth in the global labor force. International Labour Organization (2004b) 135.

26. International Labour Organization (2004b) 13.

27. International Labour Organization (2004b) 94. The ILO's Socio-Economic Security Programme examines patterns of economic security around the world. There are three macro-level databases (SES Primary Database, SES Secondary Database, SES Social Security Database) and one meso-level database (Enterprise Labour Flexibility and Security Survey). Its micro-level data come largely from a series of household-based People's Security Surveys. Between 2000 and 2003, fifteen surveys were conducted in eleven countries, covering forty-eight thousand respondents. The countries were Azerbaijan, Brazil, Chile, China, Indonesia, Moldova, Pakistan, Philippines, Russia, Tanzania and Ukraine. The survey addresses various forms of work-related security as well as respondents' aspirations and sense of social justice. See International Labour Organization (2004b) xvii, 48-49.

28. The survey questionnaire included some one hundred standardized questions administered in hour-long face-to-face interviews. For each country there were nationally representative samples of about 1,500 respondents. The countries for the 1991 survey were Russia, Estonia, Poland, Hungary, Czechoslovakia, Bulgaria, Slovenia, East Germany, West Germany, United States, United Kingdom, Netherlands, and Japan. Those for the 1996 survey, which replicated most of the 1991 survey questions but also added new ones, were Russia, Estonia, Hungary, the Czech Republic, Bulgaria and Germany. See www.butler.edu/isjp/intro.html.

29. International Labour Organization (2004b) 307-311. Also, see End Note 12 above.

30. Townsend, Peter and David Gordon, editors (2002) 433 (Appendix A).

31. The King Baudouin Foundation was established in 1974-1976 by the Belgian government as part of a celebration of the twenty-fifth anniversary of the King's coronation. The Foundation supports activities dealing with social exclusion, employment, sustainable development, local administration, citizen involvement, media, sports and culture, among others. After King Baudouin died in 1993, Queen Fabiola assumed the Foundation's Honorary Presidency. Since 1999, the Foundation's main emphases have been on poverty and justice. Among other activities, it manages a Poverty Fund that supports microcredit loans. The Foundation receives an annual grant from Belgium's National Lottery. For more information, see www.kbs-frb.be.

32. They included, among others, Gunnar Adler-Karlsson, Jan-Otto Andersson, Peter Ashby, Yoland Bresson, Paul de Beer, Alexander de Roo, Nic Douben, Ian Gough, Pierre Jonckheere, Bill Jordan, Greetje Lubbi, Edwin Morley-Fletcher, Claus Offe, Riccardo Petrella, David Purdy, Guy Standing, Robert van der Veen and Georg Vobruba.

33. See www.etes.ucl.ac.be/bien/Index.html. The website is the source of this brief overview of BIEN.

34. www.widerquist.com/usbig/home.html. The group was founded in the Fall 1999 by Fred Block, University of California-Davis; Charles M. A. Clark, St. John's University; Pamela Donovan, City University of New York; Michael Lewis, State University of New York-Stony Brook; and Karl Widerquist then of the Levy Institute, now of Oxford University. The most recent USBIG conference as of this writing was held in New York City, February 21-23, 2003.

35. Widerquist, Karl (2002) 10.

36. For more, see Murray, Michael L. (1997)

9

Program

The Plan Spelled Out

A refundable tax credit would entitle individuals with incomes below a designated threshold to receive a payment from the government that brings them to the threshold. It is as simple as that. As an antipoverty measure, it would mean that individuals living on less than a dollar a day would receive the difference between their annual income and PPP$365 dollars. Households of one or more persons would file an annual tax return. For those whose annual income exceeded an average of PPP$365 per person, the household's tax liability would range from zero to some positive number.

For those whose annual income fell below PPP$365 per household member, the government would transfer an amount that made up the difference. This would apply to persons regardless of age or any other circumstance. As an antipoverty measure, this would guarantee an annual income per person of $365 in purchasing power parity or PPP$1460 for a four-person household.[1]

In the world's poorest countries the income differential between people living on less than PPP$1 a day and those at the median income will not be great. Without external assistance, the richer half of the population would entirely subsidize the poorer half. That is patently infeasible. The rest of the world community will be asked to take up most of the slack.

In most poor countries, this amount in the aggregate would strain the national budget. Hence, the international community, as represented by the United Nations, would subsidize a portion of the total in accordance with an agreed-on formula. The United Nations would establish a global tax credit fund, which would rely on periodic replenishments from its members. Participation in the tax credit scheme would be entirely voluntary on the part of developing countries.

Less Attractive Options

Why a refundable tax credit and not another option? Because it potentially is more feasible to implement on a global scale.

Under a universal demogrant, every citizen receives a basic income but then, except for the very poorest, part of the total household income is taxed away. A universal demogrant is often touted as preferable to a negative income tax or tax credit scheme in part because of its conceptual simplicity, in part for its universality. A universal basic income eliminates the need for costly, complex, and error-prone means testing. The targeting of benefits to designated groups brings in its wake a host of administrative and social costs.

These are powerful theoretical arguments that regrettably bump up against hard practical considerations, particularly for a global poverty reduction program that is implemented mainly in developing countries.

Within budget constraints, governments would have to lower the average benefit in order to provide universal coverage. A universal demogrant program that succeeded in providing PPP$1 a day to every citizen would be far more costly than a refundable tax credit limited to those below that income threshold.

International participation would require massive transfers from rich countries that would face political resistance domestically. Under the goal of reducing extreme poverty, a more targeted and less costly approach appears more feasible.[2]

For middle and upper income households, the universal demogrant scheme becomes partially redundant, and hence inefficient, as they receive back in the form of a demogrant a portion of the taxes they paid as tax filers. It adds a step to the administration of the tax system in countries where administrative capacities are limited. It opens up a potential new avenue for waste, fraud and mismanagement. Under a global tax credit, only a subset of tax filers stands to benefit. This simplifies the process, lowers transaction costs and reduces the chance for error.

Wealthier households that are subject to higher and higher marginal tax rates to finance a universal demogrant will work harder than at present to evade or avoid taxes. Indeed at the extreme some will manipulate the tax system so as to receive the demogrant without paying any taxes. Similarly, for our purposes, and notwithstanding its attractiveness for developed countries, a stakeholder grant system in developing countries with partial international subsidization seems most unlikely and maybe even undesirable. Again, rich international donor participants are likely to demur.

No, the preferable option for reducing poverty on a global scale is a refundable tax credit.[3] It is not as simple and straightforward as a universal demogrant or a stakeholder grant but it is more likely to succeed as a politically and administratively viable option.

An income guarantee at the extreme poverty threshold hardly qualifies as a state of economic well-being. A large proportion of other needed social services and benefits would remain unaffected. Certain nonmonetary aspects of poverty such as political freedom would remain unaddressed. Overly complex, incompetent or corrupt tax administration is an ever-present danger. Most importantly, declines in mean work effort have been well-documented among the beneficiaries of past and present income transfer schemes and related subsidies.

For some, such problems are overriding obstacles. For others (like myself), they are significant but not overriding, along the lines of "the perfect is the enemy of the good." In this latter view, a negative income tax, for all its drawbacks, is worthwhile so long as it reduces extreme global poverty.

Income Taxation in Developing Countries

The tax systems of individual countries are a function of a country's economy, policy framework and institutional structures. In these respects each country stands alone and no one size fits all. Effective systems of taxation depend on public confidence that the administration is honest and competent, revenues are spent wisely and penalties for cheating are enforced.

In all countries, achieving social and economic objectives requires tax revenues. Globalization poses a challenge to the tax systems of one and all. Despite advances in research, modeling and data collection in the past two decades, development economists' understanding of how tax systems of developing countries actually work is sadly deficient.[4]

The prevailing view is that tax administration in developing countries is inefficient, non-transparent and riddled with corruption. The tax system, particularly with respect to income taxation, is regarded as an inappropriate vehicle for achieving distributional objectives.

As things stand, it is hard to dispute these propositions. But times change and so do tax systems. Under the impact of globalization, developing countries will feel increasing pressure to modernize their methods of revenue collection. Developed countries will seek to counter the loss of revenue from corporate entities that seek tax shelters outside their borders. They will press for greater openness, accountability and administrative capability in the tax systems of developing countries.

The latter will need dependable revenue sources to finance the social services and infrastructure development required to reduce poverty. The extremely poor, who exist largely outside the tax system, would have an incentive to file tax returns if, instead of making a payment, they receive one.

Normatively, tax systems tend to rest on two principles. First, those who benefit from public goods should share in their cost. Second, as a matter of fairness, the level of taxation should depend on one's ability to pay. A consequence of these principles is that taxes should not make the poor poorer but they should make the rich less rich.

Theoretically, the personal income tax is the type of tax most congruent with the principle of fairness. It can treat earned and unearned income the same and through progressivity it can gear the level of taxation to the ability to pay. Ideally, all income would be treated alike, regardless of its source.[5]

In developing countries, there is a tendency to impose high marginal tax rates on the groups where income is concentrated. While arguably equitable, the strategy often proves counterproductive in political and administrative terms. For, in reality tax systems are often designed by wealthy elites whose goal is to minimize the impact of these principles. Tax evasion and the proliferation of legal exclusions, deductions and exemptions are commonplace.

In many developing countries, governments set revenue targets without caring much how they are met. Absent detailed revenue statutes and regulations, tax officials, themselves living on low salaries, negotiate payment levels with taxpayers. Wealthier taxpayers pay less than their fair share and tax officials supplement their incomes from payments on the side. Tax laws are not rigorously enforced and transparency is lacking.[6]

Small wonder that redistributing income through progressive tax systems "has fallen very much into disfavor in the past two decades."[7] The ease with which individuals can escape domestic taxation by investing abroad has contributed to the declining share of total tax revenue attributable to the personal income tax.[8]

Personal income tax systems rely on a base of corporations and wage and salary earners in government. The size of this base and the share of the economy it covers vary considerably among developing countries. In practice in most developing countries, personal income taxes constitute "little more than a tax on wages and salaries in the organized sector of the economy."[9]

Taxes are schedular, that is, with differential treatment of income from earnings, interest, capital gains and dividends. Opportunities for the exploitation of loopholes and outright fraud abound.[10] So long as people outside the base can avoid income taxes and people inside strive to evade them, fair and honest administration of the tax system is rendered very difficult.

Income tax systems are thwarted by economic underdevelopment, unrealistically high marginal tax rates, large agricultural sectors outside the formal economy, inadequate accounting standards, low literacy levels, barriers to market entry, and the concentration of economic activity in small establishments.

Residents often are liable for higher marginal rates than non-residents. In Guatemala, despite recent reforms, non-residents pay a lower tax rate on interest owed to foreign creditors and no tax at all on interest owed to domestic institutions. Distortions are created by tax exemptions for public enterprises, non-profit organizations and cooperatives, as well as for sectors like tourism and forestry.[11]

The costs of compliance by taxpayers, agents and third parties (e.g. firms that withhold taxes) are extremely high. In India, with only twenty million income taxpayers (in a workforce of over 450 million), compliance costs in 2001 were estimated at 60 percent of income tax revenue, compared to 3.9 percent in the United Kingdom (1986-87) and between 7.9 and 10.8 percent in Australia (1990s).[12]

The costs of compliance for non-salaried taxpayers were seven to ten times higher than for salaried earners. Even with bribes excluded, individual low and middle-income non-salaried taxpayers can pay more than double their income tax in compliance costs.[13]

Participants in the informal economy seek avenues of escape from the system. Because of red tape, high fees, fear of high taxes, or simple ignorance of the law, they do not register their enterprises with government entities. The rich, including professionals like doctors and lawyers, small entrepreneurs and well-off farmers, resist efforts by tax authorities to obtain information about their operations.

Scraping along day-to-day, the working poor may simply not know their total income. They bake bread, sell fruits and vegetables, work as mechanics and hairdressers, and clean houses and office buildings. The money they earn is not recorded as income but quickly goes to purchase necessities or pay off debts.

This informal or shadow economy predominates in developing countries. Not surprisingly, income taxation under such conditions has not performed well in most developing countries. The income tax burden falls disproportionately on the recipients of wages and salaries in the formal economy, which is the smaller share of the total economy.[14]

As a proportion of the total population, individual income tax payers in developing countries range between 0.14 percent and 12.0 percent, with a mean less than 5.0 percent.[15] One study of eighty-six countries found that in the aggregate individual income taxes accounted for only 1.9 percent of Gross Domestic Product and just 10.3 percent of total tax revenues.[16]

A Simple Fantasy?

As mechanisms for income redistribution, developing countries' tax systems face major constraints. The very countries where income redistribution is most warranted lack fully functioning income tax systems. They find it extremely difficult if not impossible to maintain a complete and current roster of tax filing units, administer income reporting and withholding schemes, or enforce compliance.

Those that would meet the minimum standards for such systems would still fall short of their poverty reduction goals because most extremely poor people simply do not file tax forms. Dependent on farming, barter and other informal transactions, they function outside the formal economy and hence outside the income tax system.

Once in place, income tax laws and regulations invariably become ever more complex, even to the point of impenetrability. They tend to generate too many exemptions and excessively differentiated rate structures. High marginal tax rates in the upper ranges foster tax avoidance through preferential income shelters or outright evasion.

Thus, income tax systems grow incrementally and illogically, favoring some, penalizing others and breeding popular distrust. Even with simplification of the tax system, noncompliance would remain an issue in countries where local cultures endorse tax evasion.[17]

In developing countries with significant income inequality, low-income households make up a very large fraction of all tax filers but contribute only a small fraction of total tax revenues.[18] For enforcement purposes, they consume huge chunks of administrative time and effort with relatively little payoff. This reduces the government's incentive to enforce compliance across the board.

There appears to be a trend to greater reliance on indirect taxes (for example, taxes on consumption) and immobile factors like domestic physical investment. There is correspondingly less reliance on taxes on income, profits and assets, which are more progressive.[19]

Aversion to taxation is widespread. Mexico's tax revenue to GDP is 13 percent, about the same as Uganda's and less than Senegal's. India's is 10 percent.[20] Low tax revenue to GDP ratios hamper the ability of developing and transitional countries to redistribute the benefits of higher growth through their fiscal systems. However, such low ratios are not inevitable. For example, "Ethiopia has increased its national tax to GDP ratio from 11% to 15% since 1998. . . ."[21]

In many developing countries, the state of tax collection is not good. Along with other aspects of public administration, taxes are collected by low-paid, inadequately trained and insufficiently motivated staffs. There is widespread tax evasion and cheating. Governments are not well positioned to adapt their tax systems to the forces of global economic integration.

The real time goals of tax policy often conflict with one another. One goal is to stimulate growth, savings and investment: hence, lower taxes on the rich. Another is to reduce income inequality and assure a fairer distribution of society's resources: hence, increase taxes on the rich.

To the extent that the first goal predominates, inequality persists. To the extent that the second does, the rich have an incentive to evade their fair share— and inequality persists. Political predictability and the protection of private wealth as defined by a country's governing elites tend to trump normative considerations around development, redistribution, equity and sound tax administration.

A badly designed and badly run personal income tax system is "not costless".[22] Those costs arise from a host of political, economic, regulatory and compliance issues. Thus, in one view, "the personal income tax is not a useful tool for protecting the poorest . . . and devices such as the negative income tax are not relevant for them."[23] The idea of a centrally managed, smoothly administered tax-transfer system in most developing countries has with some justification been derided as "simple fantasy."[24]

Individual Disincentives

Such doses of reality appear to doom the prospects for a global tax credit. And that is not all. The sort of credit advocated in this book requires a declaration by the tax filing household that total money income comes out to less than $365 per year per person. Such a declaration depends on household literacy, adequate financial records and willingness to file. These elements are more often absent than present in the poorest households.

Fraud, abuse and error are inevitable, most especially in the start-up phases. The system would be vulnerable to dishonest reporting and corrupt administration, though perhaps decreasingly over time. Simple mistakes could be made in eligibility determination, benefit calculations and payment transfers.

Individuals would have an incentive to hide income in order to qualify for the benefit. This would appeal to some persons with intermittent or unstable employment histories. Others would resist converting non-liquid assets into cash in order to remain eligible for the guaranteed income. Administrators might set up sham accounts and pay themselves.

The poorer people who receive a tax credit payment will be inclined more toward consumption than saving. Their spending will increase demand in certain areas but could adversely affect aggregate capital investment.

Some beneficiaries would inevitably waste their new resources on drugs, alcohol, gambling, speculative investments or other counterproductive purposes. In this they would be not unlike some of their wealthier fellow citizens. A guaranteed income does not guarantee a secure future, only its possibility.

Those from whom income has been taken will be understandably resentful toward the program's abusers. Society may decide either that the scale of waste, fraud and abuse is so large that the program should be terminated. Or it may decide that the number of abusers is small and that beneficiaries have for the most part made choices that enhance the future for themselves and society as a whole.

New Factors in Play

So why proceed? Because important new factors have come into play. They include the impact of globalization, the spread of information and communications technologies, the availability of international expertise and the inadequacy (or at least the insufficiency) of traditional antipoverty policies. The path of development will increasingly require a more effective use of human capabilities through education and training and "the redistribution of income and wealth on a more equitable basis through taxation."[25]

A world without borders can foster trade and development. It can also provide havens for dishonest taxpayers. Multinational firms connive with developing country elites to create tax havens. Revenue losses to such havens in developing countries amount to as much as $50 billion a year.[26] Since the sources and amounts of money are often hidden, corruption flourishes.

The governments in both developing and developed nations have an incentive to ensure that tax systems everywhere are managed with clarity, consistency, openness and accountability. "Nations have been and will continue to experience far-reaching but gradual changes in the level of tax revenue, tax mix and systems of tax administration and tax compliance."[27] The more open and market-based economic environment of recent years has spurred a broadening of national tax bases and a reduction of their tax rates.

Clearly, for purposes of raising the revenue needed to finance physical infrastructure and social service delivery, governments of developing and developed countries alike will continue to depend on taxation. *How* to tax multinational corporations, electronic commerce, and migratory workers are among the issues that bedevil the world community. Whether the adverse impacts of globalization on the poor will be ameliorated through changes in tax systems remains to be seen.

In any event, tax reform will be needed in the global economy. Harmonizing national tax systems as a response to global economic integration seems rational on one level but "dead on arrival" in the political realm, where the notion of national fiscal sovereignty reigns.

At present, international bodies like the United Nations and the Organization for Economic Cooperation and Development have chosen to emphasize tax cooperation among countries through greater transparency and sharing of information. For example, knowing how multinational corporations and others in one country are exploiting tax havens elsewhere can help with the appropriate enforcement of national tax laws.

This could lead to the relatively rapid modernization of tax systems in developing countries. And such modernization need not follow the same long tortuous path of the developed world. Among its principles for mobilizing tax revenues in developing countries, the World Bank includes the raising of personal income tax collections through low top marginal rates, closing of loopholes and enforcement of compliance.[28]

A reformed tax system requires political commitment, well-trained and dedicated tax administrators and incentives for voluntary compliance. Additionally, "a simple tax structure induces better tax administration."[29]

Developing countries have an opportunity to design systems that minimize complexity (fewer rates, lower rates, broad base) and incorporate cutting edge technologies to foster taxpayer compliance. They can reduce compliance costs and the potential for error by harmonizing or even merging income taxation with contributions to national social security schemes.

Advanced technologies can facilitate tax withholding and electronic filing of returns. The electronic assessment, collection and refunding of taxes in all national tax systems become increasingly attractive as a response to globalization. Among other factors, the growth of electronic commerce within and across national borders has generated pressure for modernizing and coordinating consumption tax administration.

To prevent the outflow of owed revenue, developed countries have an incentive to assist in transferring new communication technologies and providing other technical assistance to the developing world. It is clear that new international tax standards will be required as the twenty-first century unfolds.

OECD's Center for Tax Policy and Administration is designed precisely to address such issues. The taxation of foreign capital, tax subsidies for multinational corporations and the tax implications of Internet-based transactions are but three issues on the front burner of national (and, implicitly, international) tax policy development. Many changes will occur under the radar screen of public scrutiny.

In the twenty-first century, e-commerce will play a transforming role in global economic development. It can also play havoc with national tax collection systems. Reform of revenue policy and administration is being seen as essential for development and for countering sophisticated tax evasion and tax avoidance schemes. Tax officials around the globe will be forced to modernize and coordinate their revenue collections systems. Richer nations will be motivated to assist poorer nations to upgrade their tax policies and procedures.

Setting standards for multinational corporations and correcting tax abuses in individual countries are gaining stature as an international priority. The current international tax regime is based on a consensus among nations, which has evolved since the 1920s. It has metamorphosed into an elaborate system of compromises embodied in tax treaties that are based largely on OECD's Model Tax Convention on Income and on Capital.

Whereas OECD's Model is best suited to negotiations between developed nations, the United Nations Model Double Taxation Convention emphasizes tax issues between developed and developing countries, with more taxation rights being granted to the latter than in the OECD Model.[30]

Systems of finance are coming in for greater scrutiny from citizens' organizations. ATTAC (Association for the Taxation of Financial Transactions for the Aid of Citizens) is a decentralized network of local and national groups that seeks "democratic control of financial markets and their institutions."[31] While not opposing globalization, ATTAC serves as a counterweight to the prevailing neoliberal orthodoxy. Among other things, it advocates measures like Tobin taxes, "fair" rather than "free" trade, publicly supported social security and health care systems, cancellation of developing countries' debt and elimination of international tax havens. Created in France on June 3, 1998, ATTAC has affiliates in forty countries.[32]

Taxation: Higher on the Radar Screen

The proximate incentive for international tax reform is the impact of corruption, money laundering and evasion on the global economy. Attention to the more basic questions of fairness, inequality and redistribution is gaining ground.

The United Nations, World Bank and Organization for Economic Cooperation and Development have all raised the issue of taxation to a higher point on their policy radar. The 2002 Monterrey Consensus on financing for development encouraged countries to "strengthen international tax cooperation...giving special attention to the needs of developing countries and countries with economies in transition."[33]

The United Nations addresses taxation through its Committee of Experts in International Cooperation in Tax Matters.[34] The Committee examines and advises on a variety of tax-related matters such as: tax treaties between developed and developing countries; debt collection issues; the interactions of taxation, trade, investment and equity market development; tax treatment of cross border interest income and capital flight; and taxation of electronic commerce.

The World Bank promotes dialogue on cooperation on tax policy and tax administration among its member countries. In January 2004, the OECD launched its Forum on Tax Administration, an initiative that promotes exchanges on tax administration issues and dissemination of best practices among members and selected non-members alike.

For four decades, the International Monetary Fund has provided technical assistance to developing countries on fiscal and monetary matters, including tax policy and administration. It has aided countries like Indonesia to include more individuals and businesses on the tax rolls, improve auditing systems and collect taxes in arrears.[35]

Since 1993, to aid groups of small island countries with similar problems, the IMF has worked through the Pacific Financial Technical Assistance Center and the Caribbean Regional Technical Assistance Center. In 2002 and 2003, it established African Regional Technical Assistance Centers in Dar es Salaam, Tanzania and Bamako, Mali. These centers work closely with the African Development Bank and various donor partners. By providing training and expert assistance, the centers help countries in East and West Africa build up their institutional and human resource capacities in tax policy and revenue administration.[36]

Technology is beginning to play a role in revenue collection. The pioneering online tax system of Chile's Servicio de Impuestos Internos (Internal Taxation Service) saves money on printing, distribution and processing time. The system has proven to be fast and accurate for taxpayers while reducing the government's tax collection costs. In 2000, some 734,000 of the country's roughly two million individual and corporate taxpayers used the service.[37] Under a government agreement, a private company, CTC-Internet, offers very low cost Internet access. This service, called "Republic 2000", is intended for people with little Internet experience.[38]

In August 2001, Guatemala initiated BancaSAT, an online tax filing and payment system supported by the World Bank and managed by the Guatemalan tax agency, Superintendencia de Administración Tributaria. Some sixteen months later, the new system accounted for 84 per cent of the country's tax revenues.[39]

The income tax is a relatively minor source of revenue in developing countries. This is due more to its political and administrative cost than its theoretical desirability. There is evidence that income taxes grow more important as per capita income rises.[40] Hence, it is reasonable to infer that "as the economy grows, the population becomes better educated and, accounting more widespread ... the income tax will play an increasing role."[41]

Even critics of progressive personal income tax regimes as a device for redistribution in developing countries hesitate to recommend scrapping them. After all, ". . . such taxes can contribute by generating revenues and by building a more politically cohesive and stable state."[42] They can serve as a visible counterweight to inequality and a symbol of government's "concern with the distributive outcomes of the market system."[43]

Beyond Social Protection Patchwork

As the economies of developing countries improve, their governments will be compelled to modernize their tax systems. Could the opposite be true? By preemptively modernizing their tax systems, might they not spur development?

Some developing countries are embracing e-government approaches that speed the two-way flow of information and resources between people and public agencies. This in turn is leading to greater consistency, openness and accountability

It is not inconceivable that the early introduction of a global tax credit could jump-start the process. The program would underscore the need for advanced information and communications technologies, adequate recordkeeping systems and the imposition of severe penalties for cases of fraud and abuse. With appropriate international support, equitable and efficient administration of a negative income tax system is within reach.

Even with high participation rates, a refundable tax credit would shift the state of global poverty only from "extreme" to "severe." Most likely, it would not lead to the elimination of social services, noncash benefits (like food subsidies) or other cash benefits like Social Security. However, reductions in one or more of these areas could potentially be made to offset the additional budgetary impact.

Within the member states of the Organization for Economic Cooperation and Development, social protection is provided through an eccentric patchwork of categorical supports, services and income transfers. Since each has its political constituency, governments have little incentive, let alone ability, to bring about system-wide reform.

Consequently, developed countries are endlessly forced to address the inequities and excessive complexities of their social insurance schemes, including the overlaps with the broader tax system. By contrast, developing nations need not repeat this history. Instead, they have an opportunity to design from scratch an integrated income support system that minimizes "targeting," provides basic security to the poor, and fosters economic growth.

A global tax credit could serve as the driver for such a system.

With some outside help.

END NOTES

1. For tax filing purposes we use the household rather than family, since the latter term can be more ambiguous. A household is one or more persons who may be but need not be related but who collectively comprise an economic unit. The phrase "economic unit" needs more precise operationalization but in general refers to one or more persons residing in the same premises and sharing the same pool of resources to support day-to-day living. This is not to minimize the difficulty in determining who actually should be in or out of a household for tax purposes. As underscored by experience in Hindu and Islamic countries, it is often difficult to determine the appropriate tax unit, which is a "culturally relativistic concept." See Bird, Richard M. and Oliver Oldman, editors (1990) 213. For tax credit purposes, countries can define "household" in any way that suits them.

2. "In practice, tagging [targeting] obviously cannot be perfect.... [N]evertheless...even with exogenous classification errors...it remains optimal to pay a larger basic income to the tagged population." Salanié, Bernard (20030 176. For his more formal treatment of this question, see Salanié, Bernard (2002) 319-324.

3. Please keep in mind that we are referring to a global poverty reduction initiative. Individual countries, particularly wealthier ones, might well opt internally for a universal

demogrant in order to achieve certain related policy purposes, such as assured participation or reductions in income equality.

4. Many aspects of the general discussion on taxes owe a considerable debt to Bird, Richard M. (1992), especially ix, 3, and 49-60.

5. Bird, Richard M. (1992) 11. Income taxes have the additional advantage of giving citizens the "most proof that they are contributing to the public purse", and thereby strengthening public pressure for governmental accountability. See United Nations Development Program, Arab Fund for Social and Economic Development and Arab Gulf Program for United Nations Development Organizations (2005) 152.

6. Jenkins, Glenn and Rup Khadka (2000) 1-2.

7. Zee, Howell H. (1999) 3.

8. Tanzi, Vito and Howell H. Zee (2000) 30. In Arab countries, for example, taxes account for a very small proportion of public revenue — 17 percent in Arab non-oil countries and 5 percent in Arab oil countries. The share of total tax revenues accounted for by income taxes dropped from about 34 percent in 1992 to about 28 percent in 2002. See United Nations Development Program, Arab Fund for Social and Economic Development and Arab Gulf Program for United Nations Development Organizations (2005) 152, 153 (Figure 6-1).

9. Bird, Richard M. (1992) 15.

10. This may be contrasted with a global income tax that combines income from all sources for tax purposes. While thought to be the most equitable in terms of the ability-to-pay principle, some observers conclude that global income taxation systems are more difficult for developing countries to administer than schedular taxation system, since the former is accompanied by a greater incidence of non-filing and under-reporting. Schedular income taxation can foster greater compliance through methods like withholding at the source. See Alm, James and Sally Wallace (2004).

11. Cavallo, Sonia (2000) 14.

12. Chattopadhyay, Saumen and Arindam Das-Gupta (2002) v-vi.

13. Chattopadhyay, Saumen and Arindam Das-Gupta (2002) 64.

14. Bird, Richard M. and Oliver Oldman, editors (1990) 297.

15. Bird, Richard M. and Eric M. Zolt (2005) 26.

16. Tanzi, Vito, "Quantitative Characteristics of the Tax Systems of Developing Countries", Chapter 8 in Newberry, David and Nicholas Stern, editors (1987) 205-241, esp. 224.

17. One approach to reaching hard-to-tax groups like self-employed professionals, farmers and small businesses is to impute income to them based on some criteria (like the group average) and tax members of a group on that basis. This estimated income approach covers those who cannot or will not keep books or who have a record of low compliance. Two examples are Israel's *tachshiv* system and France's forfait system. See Musgrave, Richard A. "Income Taxation of Hard-to-Tax Groups" 299-309 and Goode, Richard, "Some Economic Aspects of Tax Administration" 482-83 in Bird, Richard M. and Oliver Oldman (1990).

18. The Gini coefficient, named for Corrado Gini (1884-1965), an Italian statistician, is used to measure income (and, for that matter, asset) inequality in a society. The coefficient ranges between 0 and 1, where 0 means that everyone has an equal income and 1 means that one person has all the income. Thus, the higher the coefficient, the greater the income inequality. The coefficient is computed using the Lorenz curve (for its creator, Max Lorenz). It is twice the area between the 45-degree line of perfect equality and the curve.

19. Ibid.: 29.

20. United Nations Development Program (2005a) 71, 122.

21. United Nations Development Program (2005a) 97.
22. Bird, Richard M. and Eric M. Zolt (2005) 2.
23. Ahmad, Ehtisham and Nicholas Stern (1991) 86.
24. Bird, Richard M. (1992) 53.
25. United Nations Development Program, Arab Fund for Social and Economic Development and Arab Gulf Program for United Nations Development Organizations (2005) 173.
26. Oxfam International (2005) 69.
27. Asher, Mukul G. and Ramkishen S. Rajan (1999) 28.
28. World Bank (2005b) 177.
29. United Nations Department of Economic and Social Affairs, Development Policy and Planning Office (2004) 11.
30. The most recent version of the UN Model was issued in 2001, while the 2000 OECD Model was most recently updated in 2003. For this and more on the historical development of international model tax conventions, see Kosters, Bart (2004) and United Nations Secretariat (2003).
31. www.attac.org.
32. ATTAC grew out of a December 1997 editorial in *Le Monde Diplomatique* in which its author Ignacio Ramonet advocated creating an organization to pressure governments to adopt the Tobin tax. This would be a tax on international currency transactions to counter rampant speculation, an idea first proposed by economist and Nobel Prize winner James Tobin. The organization subsequently expanded its scope to address other aspects of globalization. For more information, see www.attac.org and its affiliate websites as well as the online encyclopedia, Wikipedia (en.wikipedia.org/wiki/ATTAC).
33. United Nations (2002a) 15.
34. A precedent of sorts was set by the 1928 League of Nations' Fiscal Committee. At the United Nations, an Ad Hoc Group on Tax Treaties between Developed and Developing Countries was established in 1968. In 1980 the UN's Economic and Social Council renamed it the Ad Hoc Group on International Cooperation in Tax Matters, whose members included ten tax administrators from developed countries and fifteen from developing and transitional countries. In November 2004, pursuant to Resolution 2004/69, the ECOSOC redesignated this group as the Committee on International Cooperation in Tax Matters, thereby converting it into a permanent body of the UN. See www.un.org/esa/ffd/ffdtaxationoverview.htm.
35. International Monetary Fund (2004) 18.
36. International Monetary Fund (2004).
37. See www.oecdobserver.org/news/fullstory.php/aid/424/Taxing_time_for_e-government.html.
38. See http://www1.worldbank.org/publicsector/egov/taxadmin.htm.
39. See www1.worldbank.org/publicsector/egov/taxadmin.htm.
40. Tanzi, Vito, "Quantitative Characteristics of the Tax Systems of Developing Countries", Chapter 8 in Newberry, David and Nicholas Stern, editors (1987) 205-241, esp. 226.
41. Ibid.: 87-88.
42. Bird, Richard M. and Eric M. Zolt (2005) 45.
43. Ibid.: 46.

10

Administration

The United Nations

The United Nations came into existence on October 25, 1945. Today it plays an indispensable role in global affairs. Unless superseded by another entity, its role will only grow for the rest of this century and beyond, as the pace of global integration accelerates.

Disparities between rich and poor nations and rich and poor people wherever they live will stand out in bolder relief. On behalf of international security if nothing else, a supranational mechanism will be needed that confronts these disparities. In particular, the persistence of extreme poverty in a prospering world will demand international action.

In the current geopolitical environment, the United Nations is the best available vehicle for administering a coordinated global initiative aimed at assaulting extreme poverty. In the scheme I elaborate here, the United Nations would serve as the overall international administrative agency for a global tax credit program in collaboration with cooperating national governments.

There is an institutional basis. The number of experts worldwide in international taxation is very limited. However, the UN's Committee (previously designated as the Ad Hoc Group) of Experts on International Cooperation in Tax Matters has been in existence since 1968. Its twenty-five members, who represent fifteen developing and ten developed countries, explore ways to help conclude tax treaties between developed and developing countries and improve international income allocation.[1]

The United Nations is a uniquely relevant forum for forging stronger linkage between taxation and development. It can help restrain the kind of tax competition used by developing countries to attract foreign direct investment. It can also foster initiatives aimed at curbing tax avoidance, tax evasion and capital flight.

Given its governance structure, it is in the best position to oversee design and implementation of a global tax credit program. To finance the program, the United Nations will establish a global tax credit fund. It will accept contributions from individuals, private organizations and governments. These funds will serve as a supplementary resource to national governments that make negative tax payments to their citizens in extreme poverty.

For countries choosing to participate in the program and qualifying under the UN's criteria there will be a match rate derived from a standardized formula. The formula could include variables like total population, gross domestic product, per capita income, income inequality, and the population in extreme poverty. A country with negative tax payments totaling PPP$1 billion and a forty percent match rate would receive PPP$400 million from the global tax credit fund to support those payments.

The United Nations will also set forth the requirements for participation in the program. Each country's refundable tax credit program will have to be certified as complying with United Nations standards for simplicity, transparency and accountability.

Individual countries will incorporate the global tax into their internal revenue systems. International organizations like the United Nations, World Bank, its counterpart regional banks and the International Monetary Fund will provide countries with technical assistance and, if necessary, resources to upgrade their internal revenue systems.

Such an arrangement would permit participation by the poorest countries that lacked the financial and administrative capability to implement the program on their own. Some of the financing could come from new sources of revenue like the proposed Tobin Taxes.[2]

Because of its more democratic governance structure, the United Nations is better suited to oversee the global tax credit than other international bodies. At the same time, the United Nations could delegate (though contractual arrangements) responsibility for some aspects of program implementation. For example, the World Bank alone or along with regional development banks (such as the Asian Development Bank) could function as fiscal intermediaries for the program for specific sets of participating countries.

In this capacity, these bodies would handle ongoing administrative tasks like formula-based reimbursements to the governments of participating countries. This could include a review of the validity of reimbursement claims submitted by these governments.

Essentially fiscal intermediaries would function as conduits between the United Nations and developing countries offering the tax credit. General program supervision and policy development would remain within the United Nations. For example, the United Nations would monitor the system to assure consistency in the interpretation and application of tax credit provisions across fiscal intermediaries.

The global tax credit will not be easy to administer, particularly at the outset. Its success will depend on realistic planning and implementation. Efforts to establish a large international bureaucracy will doom its prospects.

A Hypothetical Scenario

Here is one way events leading to the program could unfold. After vigorous debate, the General Assembly votes in favor of the credit. Recognizing that extreme poverty bears on global security issues, the Security Council endorses the program. The Economic and Social Council assumes overall responsibility for program implementation.

Under the direction of the Economic and Social Council, one of its subsidiary bodies, the United Nations Development Program, establishes a global tax credit trust fund. A number of donor countries contribute to the fund, which achieves an initial capitalization of $50 billion.

The Economic and Social Council organizes a tax credit task force. Its membership includes representatives from UN functional commissions, regional commissions, standing committees, expert groups, subsidiary bodies and specialized agencies. Task force membership is also extended to other international organizations like the Organization for Economic Cooperation and Development, as well as non-governmental organizations.

The task force is responsible for developing the policies, procedures and administrative mechanisms for implementing the tax credit program. The work is highly technical, requiring the involvement of development economists, tax specialists and public administration experts. The Department of Economic and Social Affairs provides staff support.

When the task force's work is done, the United Nations announces the availability of the global tax credit program. Interested developing countries submit applications to the Economic and Social Council. These applications provide evidence of the country's governance capacity as well as its plan for implementing the tax credit internally.

Although participation is voluntary, countries must implement the tax credit program in accordance with the United Nations policies and procedures. The United Nations develops a model global tax credit program with prototype tax forms and filing procedures for use by participating countries. It also provides technical support and guidance to countries seeking to comply with the program's requirements.

In its application, a country must designate a single agency as the one responsible for program administration. Ordinarily this will be the country's revenue ministry. For oversight purposes, a country must also establish a tax credit advisory committee consisting of public officials, representatives from the private sector (both profit and non-profit) and tax credit beneficiaries.

The program can be implemented in a participating country once the United Nations formally approves the plan in the country's application. The approved plan is a living document that is subject to modifications and amendments as circumstances warrant in the participating countries. Periodically, for example, every third year, a country must submit a comprehensive new application for the UN's review and approval.

The global tax credit program is financed through a combination of country expenditures and disbursements from the United Nations global tax credit trust fund. The United Nations matches a country's expenditures on tax credit reimbursements at a rate that is established by formula and that varies from one country to another.

Thus, the United Nations, donor countries and developing countries all share a stake in the program's management and effectiveness. Because of the match rate provisions, developing countries have an incentive to participate in the program. At the same time they are accountable for the way funds are managed and spent.

Administrative Criteria

As money moves from rich to poor countries, donors will want to be assured that it ends up in the hands of the extremely poor. They will demand that administrative costs are minimized, targeting is precise and implementation timely. These considerations suggest three criteria: (a) simplicity, (b) transparency, and (c) accountability.

First, simplicity. The global tax credit will operate in any country that chooses to participate. The beneficiaries will be located primarily in the least developed countries. These countries will not have fully developed internal revenue systems.

In any country, rich or poor, tax codes tend to become more complex and arcane over time. The tax systems of developed countries are too complex to be transferred to developing countries. In developing countries tax revenues tend to be small and unstable. Tax collection is irregular and enforcement of the law spotty. Tax evasion and corruption are not uncommon.

Any of these characteristics will undermine the global tax credit program. Ambiguity about any aspect of the design and implementation of the global tax credit will open the door to misjudgments, errors and corruption. To be implemented in these settings, the global tax credit program will have to be easily understood and administratively straightforward.

Second, transparency. The policies, laws, regulations and operating procedures governing the global tax credit program will be open and available to anyone in the world. So too will any reports about the system's operations and effectiveness. In other words everything about the program will be available for public scrutiny, short of individual tax returns. Though not the principal objective, this could have salutary effects on the personal income tax systems of participating countries.

The system's openness has a downside. It increases the risk that despite precautions unscrupulous entrepreneurs will be able to identify and prey on legitimate recipients of negative tax payments. They will devise schemes to siphon off the new money flowing to extremely poor households. Some of these abuses are unavoidable; but new laws and strict law enforcement in participating countries will be needed to mitigate the adverse consequences.

Third, accountability. Almost everything done under global tax credit will be fully documented and subject to inspection by anyone in the world. This will be true at the level of the United Nations and individual national governments. The tax returns of individuals and households will remain confidential but still subject to audit by appropriate United Nations' representatives.

A question arises over whether the tax credit scheme should be administered solely by the public sector or whether some or all aspects should be contracted out to the private sector. Arguably, the latter approach could assure more rapid implementation, insulate the system from political interference, and improve the efficiency and quality of service. In fact, in a number of developing countries, responsibility for the delivery of social services has been privatized or at least contracted out to private firms. Private sector management, however, would raise issues of taxpayer privacy and confidentiality. The degree of regulatory oversight by public sector agencies would need to increase proportionately.

Price Tag

What would it cost? The data on extreme global poverty are at best provisional. We work instead with hypothetical conditions that roughly approximate global realities as presently understood. Our cost estimates intentionally err on the high side.

Assume that on average, each of the world's 1.1 billion poorest persons had incomes averaging PPP$.50 a day. They need an equal amount to reach PPP$1 a day. This works out to PPP$.50 a day times 365 days times 1.1 billion people or PPP$200 billion a year. To simplify the calculations, arbitrarily add PPP$25 billion for administrative and transaction costs. This gives a total program cost of about PPP$226 billion.

In 2002, the gross world product stood at an estimated PPP$49 trillion. Dividing PPP$226 billion by PPP$49 trillion yields .0046. Hence a global tax credit that guaranteed an income of PPP$1 a day and that reached every extremely poor person (something that will not happen . . .) would absorb at most about half of one percent of the gross world product.

We will assume that no one living on an income of PPP$2 a day should be required to finance the global tax credit for persons living on less than PPP$1 a day. Of the world's 2002 population of about 6.3 billion persons, about 3.6 billion people have incomes above PPP$2 a day. The cost of financing a PPP$226 billion credit by this group works out to PPP$62.78 per person per year.

There is some evidence that the extreme poverty gap—the difference between the income of the average extremely poor person and the PPP$1 a day threshold—is shallower than PPP$.50.[3] Many of the world's one billion extremely poor people have incomes that are clustered just below the poverty threshold.

If instead of PPP$.50 a day, the extremely poor had incomes on average of PPP$.75 a day, the poverty gap per person per day would decline to PPP$.25. That would cut the cost of a global tax credit in half, assuming (unrealistically) one hundred percent coverage. Based on our example above, the cost would drop from PPP$226 billion a year to PPP$113 billion or PPP$31.39 per person above the PPP$2 a day threshold.

If only half the extremely poor were covered, the cost would drop by half again. Financing by the non-poor in this latter scenario would come out to $15.69 per person above the PPP$2 a day threshold. If official estimates of the number of people in extreme poverty prove to be too high, the cost would go down further for that reason. Table 2 illustrates several hypothetical cost scenarios.

Table 2. Global Tax Credit Cost Scenarios

	- Five Hypothetical Scenarios -				
Variables	A	B	C	D	E
NEP	1.1B	1.1B	1.1B	1.1B	1.1B
MIN	.50	.50	.50	.75	.75
PGP	.50	.50	.50	.25	.25
DYR	365	365	365	365	365
PRT	100%	50%	25%	50%	25%
PCOST	200.8B	100.4B	50.2B	50.2B	25.1B
ADM	25.1B	12.5B	6.3B	6.3B	3.1B
TCOST	**225.9B**	**112.9B**	**56.5B**	**56.5B**	**28.2B**

Definition of Variables:
NEP = No. of people in extreme poverty (income <PPP$1 a day) in billions.
MIN = Mean income per day of NEP.
PGP = Poverty gap per person per day = (1 minus MIN).
DYR = Days per year.
PRT = Participation rate of NEP in tax credit program per year.
PCOST = Direct program cost (in PPP$) = NEP x PGP x DYR x PRT.
ADM = Administrative cost (in PPP$) @ 12.5% of PCOST.
TCOST = PCOST + ADM (in PPP$).

Formula: (NEP x PGP x DYR x PRT) + ADM = TCOST.

Total annual costs range from a high of PPP$226 billion under scenario A to a lower and more plausible PPP$28 billion under scenario E. Under scenario E, the financing cost per person above the PPP$2 a day threshold comes out to PPP$7.83 a year.

If the World Bank's estimates of the current number of extremely poor persons is too high and/or the poverty rate continues to fall for reasons not associated with the credit, then the cost of the credit will drop further. If global wealth continues to rise, the share of gross world product required to finance the credit will drop.

The numbers I have used are of course largely hypothetical. Cost projections for an actual global tax credit program will include many more "realistic" factors. Actual costs will inevitably surprise the most expert prognosticators. However, the essential point from this highly speculative exercise is that, based on what we think we know now, significantly reducing extreme global poverty through a tax credit mechanism is both feasible and affordable.

To achieve consensus on detailed program design and implementation will demand the best talents of the international community. The final shape of any real program will incorporate a high degree of progressivity in its financing, given the disparity of wealth within and among nations.

The plan will gain acceptance once the members of the United Nations are persuaded that a refundable tax credit effectively reduces global poverty while fostering global growth. After introduction of the global tax credit, participation rates by developing countries and household take-up rates within those countries are likely to be low. On both scores, they will rise gradually over time. Initial costs will therefore also be low as the global community gains experience from administering the program and evaluating its impact.

END NOTES

1. The Secretary-General of the United Nations proposed that the ad hoc group be upgraded to the status of an intergovernmental commission or committee. See press release GA 10197 from the 58th Plenary of the UN General Assembly. www.un.org/News/Press/docs/2003/ga10197/doc.htm. Under resolution 2004/69, November 11, 2004 (doc. E/2004/L.60), the UN's Economic and Social Council renamed the Ad Hoc Group of Experts on International Cooperation in Tax Matters as the Committee of Experts on International Cooperation in Tax Matters.
2. Tobin Taxes, first proposed by Nobel laureate economist James Tobin, is a sales tax on international currency transactions. Currency speculators trade over $1.0 *trillion* a day across borders. These transactions would be taxed at a rate in the 0.10 to 0.25 percent range. The tax could dampen currency speculation and help head off financial crises. Of equal or greater importance, it could generate an estimated $100-300 billion a year for urgent international priorities like environmental protection, disease prevention and poverty eradication. Global citizen action is needed since national legislatures would have to pass Tobin Taxes and international cooperation would be required for enforcement. For more information, see www.ceedweb.org/iirp.
3. Nathan Associates, Inc. (2002) 13. The poverty gap can be calculated as follows. Let PG be the Poverty Gap, PP the proportion of people living below the poverty line (in this case, PPP$1 a day), PA the average income of the poor, and PL the poverty line. Then PG=PP*(1-PA/PL). Thus if 40 of 100 people are extremely poor and their average income is PPP$.60 a day, PG=.40*(1-.60)=.16.

11

Effects

Among the problems with many antipoverty programs in developing countries are imprecise definitions of poverty and failure to apply eligibility standards consistently. Consequently, the benefits from programs like food subsidies, microcredit assistance and infrastructure development are all too often siphoned off by the more well-to-do.

Because of funding constraints, many programs that are successful locally are not replicated or expanded to a level where they significantly affect the incidence and prevalence of poverty. The global tax credit will be target inefficient as well, particularly during the startup period and for an indeterminate period thereafter. This will include errors of exclusion or undercoverage of eligible persons, and errors of inclusion or "leakage" of benefits to ineligible persons.[1]

However, with the data collected, it will be easier to quantify the extent of the inefficiency, conduct audits and other related investigations and improve targeting through remedial and enforcement measures. Compared to many other types of intervention, a nationwide program grounded in a country's tax system can more easily be modified in response to new needs or persistent problems.

In contrast to certain types of welfare programs that foster dependency, the global tax credit would function as a temporary palliative. It would bring its recipients up to a minimum subsistence level. The regularity of annual income provided under the credit would establish an economic floor for each participating household.

Few recipients will remain content with a standard of living based on an income of PPP$1 a day. The benefit level is not so high as to discourage individual efforts to gain greater self-sufficiency, yet high enough to underwrite such efforts, at least at the margins.

A precarious job situation may induce a person to cling to a job, no matter how hard, how dangerous, or how low paying. With additional income support from the credit, the same person will be better able to seek out higher paying and more stable work or to upgrade his skills through education and training.

The notion of subsidizing an individual's income so that he or she is free to take advantage (or not take advantage) of education or training opportunities is hardly novel. Parents—usually with government assistance—do just that with their children. The subsidy may take the form of tuition payments, living allowances and purchases of goods and services (books, clothing, rent, vehicles, health insurance).

Whether the subsidy is direct or indirect, it enables the recipient to concentrate on self-improvement with less fear of economic insecurity. On balance every society feels compelled to invest in the education and training of children, even though some waste their opportunities. The basic proposition is simple enough: economic security for children now in return for an enhanced contribution from them later. There is no reason to limit the proposition to children alone.

In addition to preventing ineligible persons from claiming the benefit, the government will have an incentive to reach out to those who are potentially eligible but fail through ignorance or by choice to apply. This includes small farmers, unemployed industrial workers and other persons outside the formal economy. Parenthetically, it would also provide an impetus for more comprehensive reform of developing countries' tax systems, including greater emphasis on the personal income tax.

Straightforwardness of Administration

In principle, a refundable tax credit minimizes transaction costs for the government and minimizes the stigma of means-tested benefits for recipients. The burden on applicants is reduced since they fill out one form, not many. If eligibility for certain other programs and benefits services is tied to receipt of the credit, social service agencies will spend less time on eligibility determination and more time on service delivery. There is potential for eliminating redundant data in government information systems.

For developing countries with functional and corruption-free income tax systems, the refundable tax credit could be administered with comparative ease. For those lacking these characteristics, it could be riddled with inefficiency, high costs and mistargeting. The same is true for other approaches to social protection.

As countries develop, some may find an expanded tax credit approach preferable to establishing separate schemes for child benefits, parental allowances, housing subsidies, unemployment assistance, means-tested welfare payments, et al. All too often such systems grow administratively piece by piece until eventually they become large, fragmented and badly coordinated.[2]

Whether the tax credit is central to the country's social protection strategy or simply another instrument in the orchestra will vary from one country to another. The system *in toto* could be highly centralized at the national level or extremely decentralized under national standards.

Under one model, the national government would administer the tax credit while sub-national governments (states, provinces, *départements*, counties, municipalities, other public authorities) would provide direct services, perhaps based on shared responsibility contracts with recipients. Under these contracts, recipients would agree to participate in work and training programs offered by governmental authorities either directly or through community-based non-governmental organizations. Income supplements beyond the tax credit could be part of the package.

The legal status of such contracts, including their enforceability, and the array of benefits made available, would vary from country to country and even from one sub-national government to another within a country.[3] Whatever the specific form of the contract, the goal is not only to alleviate poverty but also to foster economic opportunity and social solidarity.

Recipients' Incentives

The tax credit like any public subsidy has its downsides, most prominently moral hazard and induced demand. Some persons barely above the line of extreme poverty level will be tempted to slacken their efforts in order to qualify for the credit. The long-term poor who have adjusted to living just below the line will have less incentive to climb above it. This form of moral hazard essentially exploits the tax credit to sustain one's condition rather than to improve it.

Its complement is induced demand. In large numbers, people who otherwise would remain outside the system of social protection are motivated to apply for the credit and perhaps other benefits as well. If not anticipated, this could put a strain on the government's resources.[4]

Without denying the impact of moral hazard and induced demand, one can still question what proportion of recipients will be content to continue living in or just above extreme poverty indefinitely.

The tax credit will create some drones in society. It will also give others a needed boost toward permanent self-sufficiency. Which group will predominate is an empirical question. I suspect the latter. The credit enables people to survive but falls quite short of assuring a decent standard of living. With a survival income assured, most would apply themselves to bettering their circumstances.

If eligibility for services such as food subsidies or housing vouchers is made automatic by virtue of receipt of the credit, the issue becomes more complex. In this case, the net value of the credit rises above PPP$1 a day. That would constitute an added incentive for recipients of the credit to maintain their status "by hook or crook." For cost-conscious policymakers, that would argue for decoupling the tax credit from eligibility for other benefits.

Not so for social service administrators, particularly social workers, who are invariably burdened (sometimes to the point of burnout) by complex eligibility determination rules, changes in benefit levels and endless paperwork.

If qualifying for the credit automatically made individuals eligible for other benefits, the administrative burden of eligibility determination would be lightened. Receipt of the tax credit reimbursement would constitute proof of eligibility. Hence, for these administrators, the notion of categorical eligibility for services based on receipt of the tax credit is attractive. They could concentrate more on individual and family needs assessment, planning, case management and service delivery.

As a matter of efficiency, linking recipients of the credit to the larger social service and benefits system makes administrative sense. Leaving very poor people unaware of their right to antipoverty resources as a cost-cutting tactic seems unfair and perhaps unjust. To reduce the moral hazard incentive, the system could be structured so that benefits and services continue based on other criteria even after individuals increase their income over the PPP$1 a day level and they no longer qualify for the tax credit reimbursement.

Financing Employment, Not Unemployment

By lifting recipients to a subsistence level, the global tax credit would affect government, employers and low-skilled workers. The pressure on governments to introduce or increase minimum wages would diminish (but not disappear). So too would the pressure to expand public employment or provide wage subsidies. At the same time, there would be an incentive for governments in developing countries to finance education and training programs.

Workers would demand wages that raise them sufficiently above the subsistence level to make paid work attractive. Employers in turn would demand higher skill levels since they resist paying wages above the productivity level of underskilled workers. Some workers would be motivated to upgrade their skills, while others would exit the labor force and remain content with a subsistence-level income.

"Widespread unemployment and underemployment remains a global challenge" despite global growth in Gross Domestic Product.[5] Poverty contributes to the phenomenon of jobless growth, since the poor lack access to the education and training that enhance economic opportunity.

In all regions of the world, youth unemployment rates in 2003 were at least twice as high as overall unemployment rates.[6] In the developing world, particularly in the Middle East and Sub-Saharan Africa, young people between ages 15 and 24 comprise 40 percent or more of the population. The unemployed among this "youth bulge" constitute an attractive recruiting pool for organized crime and violence-prone rebel groups.[7] A refundable tax credit would give the extremely poor among unemployed younger people some welcome relief and help reduce political tensions.

Industries with high minimum wages are threatening to the jobs of their least skilled workers. These workers would not feel quite so compelled to cling to these jobs. With an income subsidy as grounding, workers could shift more readily to jobs not covered by statutory or negotiated minimum wages. Some workers would choose to reduce their work hours, thereby opening up job opportunities for others.

With more discretionary time, a portion of these workers would seek to upgrade their skills and therefore their job prospects through education and training. Some would opt to start their own small or micro-businesses. The tax credit would serve as a safety net for those individuals plunged into poverty through job loss. Women in poverty would face pregnancy and childbirth with greater equanimity, while both men and women would cope better with career changes, illness and child rearing.

Employers would feel less pressure to keep their industries labor-intensive. Instead they would have more discretion to invest in labor-saving technologies. Or, conversely, they could create more jobs at lower wages. In these circumstances, the credit would function like a partial labor subsidy. It would be a refundable tax credit that "finances employment instead of unemployment."[8] For developing countries, and with such a small tax credit, such a reorientation would be measured more in baby steps than large strides. But the possibilities are there.

The impact of the credit on migratory patterns is hard to gauge. By assuring every eligible tax filer at least a minimal income, a properly administered tax credit would reduce the incentive of some extremely poor people to migrate either within their country or from it to others where job prospects are greater. Others previously unable to afford the expense of migrating would use their new resources to do so. The net effects are likely to be small and to depend not only on the credit but also on the extent to which overall economic opportunity expands at home.

In its 2005 World Development Report, the World Bank maintains that, for developing countries, well designed social and tax policies can "be consistent with strong growth" provided they pay "careful attention to productivity impacts."[9] Furthermore, by compensating those adversely affected by broader governmental reforms (for example, liberalized trade, greater fiscal restraint, new revenue-enhancing measures), they can help make such reforms more politically feasible.[10] A refundable tax credit could contribute to accomplishing these ends.

Target Efficiency, Growth and Social Protection

Individual social assistance schemes like unemployment assistance are portrayed as target-efficient. Resources go only to those in specific categories of need. The refundable tax credit addresses a more basic need.

Take, for example, people who lose their jobs and qualify for unemployment assistance. Some of them will have income from investments, inheritances or savings. The unemployment assistance system will not take other sources of income into account, whereas a global tax credit would. In a developing country this form of targeting is especially critical, since the overall economy of a developing country is not robust enough to support those who can manage without an income subsidy.

Refundable tax credit schemes are sometimes advocated as a means of folding income taxation and social assistance into one system. The particular global tax credit advanced here does not make this claim since the benefit is designed solely to eradicate extreme poverty.

Extremely poor people have basic needs in education, health care, housing and employment that cannot be met with incomes of PPP$1 a day alone. The tax credit could possibly substitute for some parts of a country's social assistance system but certainly not all.[11] At the same time, it could foster a fundamental reappraisal of a developing country's strategy for long-term economic growth coupled with social protection for its most vulnerable residents.

A large complex program like a global tax credit must contend with a number of statutory and administrative considerations. If each country's tax laws apply, tax filers will want to apply for the credit based on net taxable income rather than gross income. This would increase the number of qualifying households. Developing countries may choose this route on their own but, in my opinion, it should not be part of a UN-sponsored program.

The internal flaws of the Purchasing Power Parity measure would only be exacerbated by a net income standard. Given different rules in each country regarding deductions, exemptions and the like, a net income of PPP$1 a day in one country will be even less equivalent to a net income of PPP$1 in another country. Applying a gross income standard preserves a greater degree of tax filer equivalency across countries.

Since tax filers will come from the informal economy, their income is subject to fluctuation over the course of a year. They literally may not know their annual income. This raises the issue of the appropriate recall period. Tax filers could submit estimates of their income weekly, monthly, quarterly, semi-annually or annually. Each participating country will have to make its own determination subject to international guidelines.

A similar issue arises around the schedule of payments. They could be made monthly, quarterly or annually. Despite the nice symmetry, the schedule of payments need not coincide with the recall period. For example, the tax filer's recall period could be quarterly while the government reimbursement is made annually. Finally, no less than for the tax filing public overall, the privacy and confidentiality of information submitted by households applying for the credit will need to be protected.

In view of inevitable implementation problems, the program could provide an impetus for the direct administration of a country's tax credit program by the international community. Very poor countries in Sub-Saharan Africa are potential candidates, for example. This impetus could come from the country itself or international bodies.

Such a step is risky for both parties. An alternative is technical support to these countries as they bring their tax systems into compliance with international standards. In an extreme case, the United Nations or another entity to which it delegates the responsibility could administer the tax credit on an interim basis with a date certain set for the country to reassume this role.

Second Fictional Interlude: Political Debt

"Perhaps I should resign before I am fired," thought Karim Amadou, Regin's minister of finance, as her driver pulled onto the grounds of the presidential palace. Five years ago, she had pressed forcefully for her country's participation in the United Nations' Global Tax Credit Program. Now, because of the program's problems, her party could lose the upcoming national elections.

Her Sub-Saharan West African nation, twice the size of Texas and land-locked, had a population of twenty-four million and a Gross Domestic Product per capita equivalent to US$175. In Regin, this equated to a purchasing power of PPP$890. In other words, what would cost about five dollars to buy in the United States would cost only one dollar in Regin.

The Global Tax Credit Program seemed a godsend. When the program began, the country ranked close to the bottom in the United Nations Development Program's Human Development Index. Half the population was under age 15 and only two percent 65 or over. The mean number of children born per woman was an astonishing eight. Life expectancy at birth was 45 years. Three-quarters of the population was functionally illiterate.

The tax credit program, she was convinced, would pull the country's poorest people above the international threshold for extreme poverty. With the aid of a United Nations team of technical experts, she had led the modernization of Regin's tax system.

After years of bone wearying work, she had brought the country's tax system into compliance with international standards. Regin had now competed its third year of participation in the program. It remained highly controversial.

The economy of Regin was based on subsistence agriculture, animal husbandry and re-export trade. Exports consisted largely of livestock, cowpeas, onions, and cotton products. World demand for the country's uranium stores had declined.

Future growth prospects depended on the exploitation of gold, oil, coal and other mineral resources. Apart from those employed by a few large transnational mining corporations, most people in the labor force operated in the informal economy of seasonal farm work, day jobs and home-based small businesses.

Under its decade-old Constitution, Regin had adopted a semi-presidential form of government. The president, elected for a five-year term, was head of state. The president appointed a prime minister to serve as head of government. The prime minister, with the president's concurrence, appointed ministers for each of the government's cabinet-level departments.

Rumor had it that the president was not happy with his current prime minister. "And I am largely to blame," Karim Amadou thought miserably as she passed through security. A guard accompanied her to the president's office. There she waited.

The government's success at attracting foreign private capital had been less than stellar. The entire continent of Africa attracted less than one percent of international capital flows and accounted for less than one percent of global trade. Regin's share of Africa's share was depressingly small. The country continued to lose ground to the forces of global economic integration. The people of Regin worked hard but could not compete with more technologically advanced societies.

Instead, Regin was more dependent than ever on bilateral and multilateral aid. Recently the World Bank had approved a structural adjustment loan of $100 million and the International Monetary Fund had approved a $75 million poverty reduction and growth facility. The country had been promised $125 million in debt relief under the Heavily Indebted Poor Countries (HIPC) initiative.

All this assistance served to stave off disaster but had little positive effect on the country's subsistence economy or future growth prospects. Twelve million people (half the total population) lived in extreme poverty, with incomes that averaged the equivalent of PPP$183 a year (or PPP$.50 a day). To boost each of them to the PPP$1 a day threshold would require an additional PPP$183 a year per person, or approximately PPP$2.2 billion a year total. The Global Tax Credit program, she insisted, would enable the country to raise this money and eliminate extreme poverty.

In speech after speech, the finance minister had hammered home the need for the program. Foreign direct investment was small and declining. Regin needed an infusion of external capital. The refundable tax credit would guarantee an income for the country's poorest people, bring in new money that would be spent for essential goods and services and stimulate the economy. Civil rights groups and other non-governmental organizations enthusiastically backed the plan.

Karim Amadou personally lobbied (some say badgered) the president until he finally voiced his support for the program. By sheer persistence, she won over skeptical members of the national assembly.

Based on a United Nations formula, the government of Regin was responsible for ten percent of the total cost of the credit. The United Nations would make up the remaining amount. The infusion of this funding was the one element that preserved the program. On other grounds, it had become extremely unpopular among the country's small but influential upper income groups.

The new program had thrown the fledgling income tax system into administrative chaos. The taxes on upper income groups rose to pay for Regin's share of the credit. This stimulated increased tax evasion among taxpayers through dubious income shelters and outright false reporting. Program participation rates were far lower that one hundred percent.

In the previous year, refundable tax credit payments were made to one million households, consisting of 5.33 million individuals. Each household received an average of PPP$975.40 for a total cost of PPP$975.4 million. Regin's ten percent share was PPP$97.5 million, with the United Nations providing the remaining PPP$877.9 million.

A preliminary United Nations audit estimated that two-thirds of those eligible for the credit either did not apply for it or were wrongfully denied. Conversely, about a quarter of those who did receive the credit were not eligible. In other words, about $243.4 million in tax payment credits had gone to persons who should not have received them.

Investigation continued into what shares of this total were due to fraudulent tax filing, official corruption or bureaucratic incompetence. In one sensational case, a millionaire had managed not only to evade paying any taxes but also had claimed—and received!—the refundable tax credit. Television news programs outdid each other uncovering similar instances of waste, fraud and abuse in the program.

An interim report by the economics department at the University of Regin on the first year of the program indicated that the effects of the credit could be deleterious. In some households, members—parents, working-age children—cut back on their hours of work or in rare instances withdrew from the labor force altogether.

The credit was blamed for marital instability and household breakup. Although typically households filed as a unit, in theory each eligible individual, regardless of age, gender or other circumstance, could claim the credit separately. In this traditionally male-dominated culture, poor women suddenly found themselves less dependent on their husbands. Their assertiveness began to be felt even in traditionally staid upper-income groups.

The opposition decried the fact that the government's own expenditures on the credit, as well as the money from the global tax credit fund, were being "frittered away" on the poor. Far better, they contended, would be the concentration of this wealth in the hands of venture capitalists and entrepreneurs who would invest in new and expanding industries.

The poor, they said, would spend rather than save, thereby drying up the pool of investment capital. Furthermore, the tax credit was but the camel's nose under the tent. Already non-governmental organizations were advocating an expansion of the credit to persons whose income fell below PPP$2 a day. The country risked becoming a permanent ward of the international welfare system. The global tax credit was the old colonialism in thin disguise.

"Without our participation in the program," Amadou insisted, "there would be no reimbursement from the United Nations at all, let alone any to invest." So far this argument had carried the day, but future support in the national assembly was precarious.

Newspaper editorials lamented the loss of traditional values and the threat to social cohesion posed by the influx of unearned income. Television news programs gleefully ran exposés of "tax credit junkies" who spent their windfall on new cars and expensive clothes. Many ran up unpayable debts. "We have sold our souls for a mess of pottage," cried the pastor of one congregation.

In vain did the finance minister and her allies point out that such behavior had long been a staple of wealthier groups in society. It would take time for the country's poorest to learn how to use a minimum income to their best advantage.

Now the national election was looming. Polls showed the country evenly divided at present over the tax credit but reflected a downward trend over time. It was the single biggest issue affecting the outcome of the election. If the trend continued, her party's fate was sealed.

Engrossed in such gloomy reflections, the finance minister was startled to see that the president himself had appeared in the waiting room. A short, rotund, beaming man, he exuded energy and drive. A former economics professor, he had commissioned the study being conducted by the University of Regin.

"How are you, my dear?" he asked solicitously. "I am so sorry to have kept you waiting but the quarterly conference call with other African leaders ran on and on. I am always amazed at the amount of small talk that occupies us heads of state." He rattled on until he had escorted her into his private office and they had settled themselves in plush armchairs.

Karim wondered if she should anticipate the president by offering her resignation. As she hesitated, the president explained the purpose of their meeting.

"I have some information to share with you," he said. "As you know, I was quite skeptical when you first approached me about Regin's participation in the Global Tax Credit program. And, indeed, there have been setbacks over the past four years."

"I understand, Mr. President," Karim said, took a deep breath and added, "I accept full responsibility for the program's failures and—"

"Failures? No, my dear, setbacks that were fully to be expected. Any large new program will experience growing pains. Since you are eager to accept responsibility, you must also be willing to take credit for the program's success."

"Success?" Karim was astonished.

"Indeed. I have recently been briefed on the final report issued by the University of Regin. It covers the first three years of the program. The researchers conducted extensive interviews with people living below the $1 a day poverty line."

Despite her overwhelming curiosity, Karim struggled to appear impassive as the president continued.

"On almost all of the survey's measures," he said, "people who had received tax credit payments showed significant improvement in their quality of life compared to people who did not file for the credit or who were wrongly denied.

"What measures?" Karim broke in before stifling a gasp at her impertinence.

The president proceeded benignly. "A number of generally accepted quality of life measures. Adult recipients were more likely to have attended adult education classes, started small businesses, and become more involved in community activities. Compared to families without the credit, a higher proportion of their children attend school regularly. Their use of local medical clinics has declined, indicating an improvement in health status. Their expenditures on consumer goods like food and clothing and medicine have boosted the economy."

"But those findings are quite different from their interim report," said an astonished Karim.

"Yes, but those earlier findings were very preliminary, covering only the first year, well before the full effect of the credit took hold. There is some reduction of work effort and there are cases of marital breakup attributable to the credit but overall the longer-term results are much more positive."

"In what way?" Karim broke in again, despite herself.

The president by now was in his full professorial mode. "While some people leaving the workforce have become slackers, most have attempted to upgrade their skills through education and training. The family issues are partly due to the autonomy and expanded opportunities enjoyed by women, which in my view is a healthy development. Foreign investors have lately been showing interest in our small nation."

"In my position, Mr. President," Karim ventured, "I have little time to keep abreast of the latest research. I seem to hear nothing but complaints and problems relating to the tax credit program. It will boost the morale of my staff when they hear of these new findings."

"There is more, Karim," the president smiled. He had never before called her by her first name. "The data show that a significant proportion of tax credit recipients have registered to vote, they plan to vote in the upcoming election and—" here he paused for effect— "they plan to vote for our party. According to the latest polls, my reelection is virtually assured."

The dark cloud over Karim Amadou's head seemed to dissipate, allowing in the political sunshine. The Global Tax Credit had paid off in the most unexpected ways.

When the president again paused, she decided the session was over and began gathering up her papers.

"There is one last matter," the president said, holding up his hand. "You may have heard that I am not entirely satisfied with the prime minister. There is evidence that he has been receiving kickbacks from foreign corporations seeking official favors. Our country suffers from too much corruption but I will not tolerate it in my administration."

Karim was puzzled. Why was she the recipient of such political intelligence? Perhaps it was to signal that everyone under the prime minister would be asked to resign as well. It was understandable that the president would want to launch his second term with a fresh new team.

Well, she mused, at least the tax credit program stood a better chance of surviving her tenure in office.

The president had dropped his academic persona and resumed his role as politician-in-chief. He looked at Karim with well-practiced earnestness as though the fate of Regin depended on her answer.

"Madame Amadou, will you do me the honor of serving as prime minister in my next term?"

END NOTES

1. Grosh, Margaret E. (1994) 16-17.
2. Germany, the nation that gave the world its first government-sponsored social insurance system and which has an elaborate system of social protection, is a case in point. In that country 155 different social assistance policies financed by taxes and contributions are administered by "38 different authorities and semi-authorities". See Mitschke, Joachim (2000) 113.
3. This model with attendant national and sub-national variations is standard for European countries that use minimum income schemes to promote the inclusion (or, as it is also called, the "insertion") of individuals into the wider society. See Standing, Guy, editor (2003).
4. This is sometimes referred to as the "woodwork effect", a phrase I and others find demeaning.
5. International Labour Organization (2004a) 4.

6. International Labour Organization (2004a) 5.

7. United Nations (2005) 95.

8. Mitschke, Joachim (2000) 117.

9. World Bank (2005b) 149. The experience of Europe in the last half of the last century is cited as evidence.

10. Ibid.

11. An unconditional citizens income would achieve many of these results, but less efficiently and at a cost that developing countries would find prohibitive. It is less efficient in that some income taxed from the non-poor is recycled back to them. Why not leave it there in the first place? The sheer volume of increased taxes and benefits expenditures would create insurmountable political resistance. The impetus toward tax avoidance and tax evasion among upper-income tax payers would accelerate.

12

Objections

A proposal for a global tax credit must confront a number of objections from the left and the right. On the far right, it flies in the face of those whose *summum bonum* is the creation of wealth with little regard for those excluded from its benefits. This leaves no room for any scheme involving income redistribution, let alone a refundable tax credit. On the extreme left, it runs up against those who espouse antipoverty strategies based on training, jobs and supportive services. They see risk in letting people make the "wrong" choices with unearned income.[1]

With respect to the poor, the former attitude reflects conservative dismissiveness, the latter liberal condescension.

Both sides share certain aims. They want the economies of their countries, developed or developing, to stay competitive in an ever-changing global environment. They see growth as the key to social and economic prosperity. They concur on the desirability of higher living standards and a better quality of life for all their fellow citizens. They aspire to a fairer and more inclusive world.

The more moderate members of both camps seek consensus around effective and politically palatable means of attacking poverty. Moderate conservatives favor providing poor people with a minimum income as an alternative to perpetual dependence on state-sponsored social services. Moderate liberals like the idea of folding the benefit into the larger tax system where it operates more unobtrusively and with less stigmatization than direct service provision.

For many in this middle band, an income guarantee such as a refundable tax credit offers a certain appeal. A tax credit is less visible on the political radar and hence less controversial. Take a small example. In the United States, some food stamp recipients abuse the program. They buy luxury food items rather than necessities. They sell or trade food stamps illegally. While such abuses are a small part of the total program, they receive a lot of publicity and energize critics.

A refundable tax credit eliminates the illegality of such abuses since the additional income could be spent as beneficiaries choose. They may not choose wisely or well but their choices are legal. With fewer highly publicized cases of cheating, public disdain for social welfare programs would diminish. The political temperature around the programs would be lowered. For recipients, tax-based income would eliminate the stigma and embarrassment that comes from paying with food stamps in the grocery store.

This seems to be the experience with the U.S. Earned Income Tax Credit. Tax credit schemes are far from perfect but with all their flaws they do have a measurable effect on poverty. Needless to say, they have not so far attained universal acceptance.

The following objections to the approach rest on many grounds—philosophical and moral, historical, economic, administrative and strategic. So do the ripostes. Let us review the bidding.

1. *Global poverty is decreasing without such schemes.*

Yes, but progress is unacceptably slow and the future holds no guarantees. Despite several decades of global growth, hundreds of millions of people at a given point in time survive on incomes of less than $1 a day. There is no assurance that global growth will continue at its previous pace. In addition, growth is uneven within and among countries. Growth creates economic dislocations, providing upward mobility for some people but plunging others into extreme poverty. War, civil conflict, natural disasters and macro-economic shocks (e.g. sudden currency depreciation) take their toll. A global tax credit will cushion people at risk against such adversities.

2. *No country, developed or developing, has such a program.*

Developed countries do not have people living on less than $1 a day. Developing countries that do will not risk such a program on their own. However, there are enough harbingers at the national level in both developing and developed countries to indicate the administrative feasibility of the program on a global scale.

Though in the aggregate their social protection schemes are overly complex and bureaucratized, a number of western European nations in the end provide that individual and family incomes do not fall below a set level. The tax system typically forms part of the total structure of social welfare benefits. Their experience in administering such schemes is relevant.

The lack of an explicit precedent in individual nations is not an overriding obstacle. With the dissemination of information and communications technologies buttressed by technical and administrative support and partial subsidy from international organizations, even the least developed countries can mount the program.

3. *A global tax credit will discourage work effort.*

Social justice requires a degree of reciprocity between donor and donee. By breaking (or rather loosening) the link between work and income, say the critics, the tax credit represents a moral hazard. It would rob people of the dignity that comes from paid labor. It will retard career advancement and development prospects. In this view, income support should go only to the "deserving" poor: children, seniors, persons with disabilities or other special needs, and temporarily unemployed persons. Able-bodied persons are not entitled to a free ride. The tax credit would reward laziness.

This perspective assumes that recipients of the credit would choose not to work. While this may be true for some, as a blanket assumption it is contestable. The low level of the credit will not lift people out of poverty, only diminish its intensity and severity. At the extreme poverty level, work will still be sought if only to enhance one's capacity to consume.

The self-respect that comes from paid work and the social stigma attached to slackers cannot be discounted. Nor can the contributions made by parents, caregivers, and community service volunteers. The demands of reciprocity can be satisfied by more than paid labor alone.

A more serious problem is that the economies of developing countries cannot manage full employment. Jobs in market economies in particular are simply not available to everyone who wants one. Job guarantee schemes provided through public sector employment perpetuate the bias toward labor-intensive job growth.

The informal sector is not an adequate fail-safe mechanism. Jobs there are in inadequate supply, less secure and cut off from social insurance. Unemployment in both the formal and informal sectors is structural. The question is how to cope with these conditions in the context of global growth.

Critics fear that beneficiaries of income support schemes will squander their money on alcohol, drugs, cigarettes and gambling; women will have unwanted children in order to collect more money. While one should not expect the extremely poor to be more saintly than their non-poor counterparts, it is more likely that money from the tax credit will go to necessities like food, education and transportation.

Antipoverty policies have traditionally been tied to the outmoded goal of minimizing the loss of work effort among beneficiaries. Designing social welfare systems around the idea that every able-bodied adult can find work is disingenuous at best. Global growth depends more on technology and innovation than human labor, especially unskilled labor. A global tax credit scheme would provide a push toward more capital-intensive development strategies.

Yes, a refundable tax credit will diminish the intensity of job searches and lead to a reduction in work effort. However, since the size of the credit is so small, the amount of any foregone work will be minimal. Furthermore, it will be concentrated in the unskilled and underskilled sector of the labor force.

Foregone work will be more in the form of reduced hours rather than total withdrawal from the labor force. A severely deleterious impact on any country's economy is unlikely. With reduced availability of unskilled or semi-skilled la-bor, countries will be motivated to invest in labor-saving and labor-substitution technologies.

For a significant proportion of beneficiaries the credit will open up new ave-nues for training and education. People will be able to pursue opportunities that are now denied them due to poverty and discrimination. This scenario will fail if the majority of recipients simply bless their good fortune, reduce their hours of work, and do little to improve their circumstances.

Given the extreme nature of their poverty, such individuals are more likely to be in the minority (though they will feature prominently in news coverage of the credit...). In short, it is reasonable to hypothesize that a refundable tax credit for the extremely poor would over time improve labor productivity, raise living standards, accelerate technological progress, and buttress prospects for long-term economic growth.

4. *It will have adverse effects on family structure.*

There is some evidence from extant (though dated) negative income tax studies in the United States that a guaranteed income could foster a breakdown in kin-ship networks and higher divorce rates. Other studies find no negative effects on marital stability and family structure. As noted in chapter five, these studies taken all together leave the issue unsettled.

To the extent that traditional families exist by virtue of economic necessity, marital instability arising from a guaranteed income is a potential consequence. To the extent that other factors like love and mutual respect govern, the impact could be just the opposite. Since the size of the proposed tax credit is small, any effect it has on family structure should likewise be small.[2] The direction of the effects will vary from one society to another. At the margin, women will be more empowered, more able to control their own destinies, better able to free themselves from abusive relationships.

The credit could lead to larger families since it tends to reduce the level of work effort and the amount of the credit per individual (child or adult) is not cut back to adjust for economies of scale. Both men and women will be marginally better positioned to devote more time to parenting. Conversely, a modicum of economic security could foster less childbearing and smaller families. Children would not be seen as the sole source of support in one's later years. Women might limit childbearing in order to pursue skill training and job opportunities.

Alternatively, the impetus could lie in the direction of shared living arrange-ments that may or may not involve traditional marriage or family growth. These are empirical questions, where the findings are likely to vary from country to country and culture to culture.

5. *It will foster antisocial behavior.*

With its reduced work incentive, the credit could conceivably foster antisocial behavior among nonworking recipients, with special reference to bored and bitter young people in countries where their share of the population they represent is growing and unemployment rates are dauntingly high. Two points can be made in response.

First, the credit does little more than lift one from extreme poverty to a state of still severe poverty. The size of the credit is small enough that behavioral effects in any direction are not likely to be pronounced. Second, any incentives triggered by the credit cut two ways—toward antisocial behavior among some and toward self-improvement and upward mobility in others. Essentially, the credit releases human capabilities that are suppressed due to extreme poverty. How those capabilities are used then becomes a function of human freedom.

6. *Poor people will hide income to qualify for the credit.*

Even with precautions, waste, fraud and abuse can be expected. The tax credit could induce people to shift from the formal, wage-paying economy to the informal economy where documentation of income is scarcer and less reliable. The unverifiability of many tax filings will make false reporting more tempting.

Some people who would qualify for the credit will not file for it out of ignorance or fear. Eligible people who apply will be denied through administrative error. Some who do not qualify will receive it fraudulently or simply erroneously.

No tax system can eliminate fraud, waste and abuse but their incidence can be managed. Judging from examples like the U.S. Earned Income Tax Credit and Ecuador's Bono Solidario, a significant degree of mistargeting is foreseeable, especially in the early years of implementation. With tax systems, however, such problems are (in principle at least) identifiable and fixable.

The program would be designed to be as easy to understand and administratively simple as possible. Tax filers will have to swear to the accuracy and completeness of their declarations and submit supporting documentation. Their returns will be subject to cross-checking within government databases. They will be subject to audit.

Improving the target efficiency of the credit will require governments to upgrade their information and communications systems. For example, as proposed in South Africa, smart cards with electronic data chips could be issued to beneficiaries and used to store data regarding their eligibility for the credit. Biometric data (via, for example, thumbprints or eye scans) would be stored as well to confirm the cardholder's identity. Beneficiaries could present their cards at local banks to receive payments at scheduled intervals. For beneficiaries with bank accounts, the refundable portion of the credit could be transferred electronically. The card could also be used for expenditures.

Critics of the credit will seize on instances of fraud to press their case. Hence, strictly enforced anti-fraud measures will be required to overcome negative public stereotypes of the credit. Penalties for proven fraud will be severe and widely publicized. The role of institutions like the United Nations as monitors and evaluators and developed nations as contributors will spur movement in these directions.

Interestingly, with its reliance on advanced technologies for eligibility determination, administration and monitoring, a global tax credit program could move the world community, including the poorest nations, closer to becoming a network of cashless economies.

7. Poor people outside the tax system will not benefit.

Many if not most poor people in developing countries operate in the informal economy as farmers, small entrepreneurs, and self-employed day laborers. They survive outside the formal economy and do not pay taxes. There are in addition semi-nomadic indigenous peoples living in remote areas of Africa, Latin America and Asia.

For some critics, a refundable tax credit is undesirable due to the lack of financial literacy and paperwork sophistication among these poor. Compared to a universal demogrant, the takeup rate will be low since the extremely poor must file a tax return to qualify for the credit. This is true, though outreach efforts and tax-preparation assistance by governments and non-governmental organizations can partially overcome these hurdles.

The global tax credit will attract some of these marginalized persons into the formal economy since they would expect not to pay taxes but rather to receive a payment. Tax filers who claim the credit will swear to the accuracy of their assertions. With the aid of new communications and information technologies, the documentation and data they provide can be more easily verified.

There are advantages to an initially low takeup rate since it will permit the administrative system to gain its sea legs. Once in the tax system, people will find it harder to avoid paying positive taxes as they move out of poverty and up the income scale.

8. Many poor people may have no income but they have assets.

True. And the assets are not subject to the terms and conditions of the tax credit. Hence there will be real differences in total wealth between persons with incomes below $1 a day. The treatment of assets like a house, land, and other personal property, real or intangible, for purposes of establishing eligibility for a public benefit is complex. Factoring in the value of assets would complicate the tax credit program immensely. For purposes of simplicity and transparency, it makes the most sense to begin with income only. A mature program may be able to address the question of how to factor in assets in determining who qualifies for the credit.

9. The scheme in toto is too costly.

The size of the credit is small. It brings the income of an extremely poor individual from where it is up to $1 a day. The international community will assist in financing the credit. The amount of the assistance will depend on a formula that takes into account factors like the country's GDP and poverty rate.

Globally, it will be affordable, with a maximum annual cost of PPP$200 billion under the highly unrealistic assumption of one hundred percent participation by the governments and eligible citizens of developing countries. Actual annual expenditures could be much less than half that amount. Cost-sharing by participating countries will reduce the drain on the global tax credit fund.

Despite precautions, some costs would be incurred due to payments being made improperly to ineligible households. This error-driven upward bias in costs will be more than offset by initially low overall take-up rates by individuals, due to factors like illiteracy, distrust of government (especially tax collection agencies), and lack of recordkeeping. The country will also have to demonstrate compliance with UN standards for tax collection systems.

Over time some waste, fraud and abuse will be weeded out while the proportion of eligible households actually receiving the credit will rise. The process will be politically and administratively painful, but sustainable so long as the benefits to society are seen as outweighing the costs, financial and otherwise.

Tax avoidance and tax evasion can be countered with modernization of the country's revenue system and greater enforcement. International assistance with tax credit financing will be governed by a formula that takes each participating country's social and economic conditions into account. The reduction in extreme poverty generated by the credit will have a payoff in terms of long-term growth and higher and more sustainable tax revenues.

10. *It will depress national savings rates and discourage investment.*

Since they struggle to meet their basic needs, the poor will tend to spend rather than save their additional income. This might change somewhat over time as some poor people see the value of setting aside some income for future contingencies. However, meeting immediate needs through spending will predominate.

This could stimulate economic activity, as demand for consumer goods rises. Poor households tend to buy goods produced by more labor-intensive industries. That will stimulate local economic activity and job creation.

Large capital investment may decline, to the extent it is financed from domestic savings. However, with the lessening of extreme poverty, the country may be more inclined to open its markets and be better able to attract international investors. A country where everyone is entitled to a minimum income guarantee through the tax system is at lower risk of social and political instability. In short, the credit could have a substantial and positive developmental impact.

11. *It will be undermined by inefficient, even corrupt, tax administration.*

The UN would set standards for participation in the global tax credit program. It would provide advice and assistance to those countries that seek to comply with the standards. This would involve assisting with recruitment, training and compensation of tax collection staffs, as well as incorporation of more up-to-date information technologies.

In some cases, developing countries may decide to delegate aspects of their tax systems to the United Nations or contract them out to private firms. The penalties for systemic corruption at the country level would be severe, up to removal from the program and even economic sanctions against the most serious offenders.

The initially low take-up rates by countries and by the extremely poor within those countries will permit the United Nations to more easily eliminate "bugs" from the system. The smaller the number of program participants initially, the easier it will be to ferret out cases of waste, fraud and abuse. It will enable the United Nations, its donors and the participating countries to improve program administration before the program operates fully on the international scale.

12. *The tax credit provisions will grow more complex over time.*

Income tax systems as a whole invariably grow more complex as patent inequities, administrative problems and political pressures trigger new legislation and regulations. This certainly could happen with the refundable tax credit but is not inevitable. As a global system operating in many developing countries, the United Nations will be under pressure to administer the program openly and transparently. This can be accomplished most easily by keeping the structure of the program as simple as possible.

The more complex the rules governing the credit, the greater the risk of maladministration, either from unintentional error or outright fraud. Maladministration in turn adversely affects the program's credibility with the public and induces tax evasion measures. At the cost of a degree of equity, there are advantages, especially at the outset, in operating a system that emphasizes transparency, accountability and comprehensibility.

13. *The 100 percent marginal tax rate on the benefit is too high.*

Once income from all sources, earned and unearned, rises to PPP$1 a day, a tax filer receives no payment under the scheme. Under more complex schemes, like the U.S. Earned Income Tax Credit, the benefit is phased out gradually rather than being terminated abruptly at a specified income level.

In other words, the EITC benefit is subject to a declining marginal tax rate as opposed to a 100 percent marginal tax rate for the global tax credit. While hardly flawless, the U.S. has a technologically advanced tax collection system with a high degree of taxpayer compliance. It can handle administrative complexities like declining marginal tax rates on benefits with relative ease.

This is not true for many of the least developed countries with relatively unsophisticated tax collection systems and histories of widespread tax avoidance and evasion. In these circumstances, simplicity of design and ease of administration are preferable to more equitable approaches, especially in the early years of implementation.

There are adverse consequences to this point of view. Absent a more graduated benefit reduction rate, someone accepting a job paying PPP$1 a day would have his credit "taxed" at 100 percent since by working the person gains no net income. A job that pays PPP$2 a day entails a tax of 50 percent and so forth.[3]

At some minimum level of compensation (which may include other elements besides pay, such as health care coverage and even intangibles like training and opportunities for advancement), any incentive inherent in the credit to reduce work effort is completely offset. Clearly the lower that minimum, the better. However, such concerns can only be resolved through political bargaining and administrative rulemaking.

14. *It is the camel's nose under the tent for other political agendas.*

Would the United Nations or any participating country rest content with the $1 a day threshold? Surely there would be pressures to raise it to $2 or beyond. No doubt. However, the minimal credit in order to overcome extreme poverty will have to demonstrate its feasibility first. When it is seen as operating efficiently and honestly, there will indeed be pressure to increase the size of the credit. Although "extreme" poverty will decline, there will still be "severe" poverty around the globe.

Any increase in the benefit will be up to the international community as represented by the United Nations and its member states. There will be countervailing pressures to keep the credit small. Some people, such as advocates of unfettered capitalism, will never endorse the idea of the credit, let alone its expansion.

Additionally, the larger the credit, the greater the temptation for countries and their citizenries to "game" the system, that is, to manipulate it on their behalf. To the degree that this occurs, it will provide ammunition to opponents. At some political libration point, any increase will be seen as unaffordable or otherwise counterproductive. Just because there will be pressure to increase the size of the credit does not mean it will be applied successfully.

Advocates of the credit might indeed move from seeking income support for basic needs to income support for a decent and dignified standard of living. The political pressure to increase the size of the credit would be unremitting. It could, horror of horrors, lead to calls for income redistribution on a larger scale.

Such scenarios have stiffened opposition to negative income tax approaches in wealthy countries like the United States. And true, lots of things *could* happen. For our purposes it is useful to re-set the context. The global tax credit would aim at alleviating extreme poverty in the world's poorest countries.

It would be implemented in developing countries whose main goal is sustainable economic growth. These countries will be wary of any scheme that diverts the focus from that goal. Countries contributing to the global tax credit fund would seek assurance that the funds were used for the intended purpose. Otherwise contributions would dry up.

Each case of proven fraud would generate an outcry against the very concept of the credit. The pressure to expand the program would be counterbalanced by calls for its elimination. To change the metaphor, some will see a global tax credit as a stalking horse for world government, global socialism and other perceived evils. Actually, it could just as well give a push to global capitalism and freer markets. With a guaranteed income for the world's poorest people, developing countries could devote a greater share of resources, both public and private, to capital-intensive development. This in turn would aid in leveling the playing field between developed and developing economies.

15. *Vital social services will be cut to finance the credit.*

It is a mistake to expect too much of an impact, either positive or negative, from a tax credit that merely provides an income floor of PPP$1 a day. While the credit will diminish the poverty gap ratio, most beneficiaries will be left with incomes below national poverty line levels. Hence the national poverty head count will be relatively unaffected. The demand for services will persist. Each country will have to make its own decisions with respect to public social service provision.

The existence of a refundable tax credit could aid in rationalizing the crazy quilt of social services found in many countries. There may be resistance from service providers who fear that resources will be siphoned off from their favored programs. But that need not be the case. And social services will still be needed. The guarantee of at least a dollar a day in income hardly lifts one to a state of affluence. People in poverty will still need jobs, education, health care, housing, transportation, and other forms of support in order to better their lives.

The tax credit is not a cure-all. It is not flexible enough to meet the entire range of human needs. But it does improve the prospects. With a refundable tax credit in place, social service systems will not be eliminated but rather transformed. For example, rather than providing services gratis, governments may require more cost-sharing by recipients. In place of complex eligibility requirements, for instance, receipt of the tax credit could automatically qualify one for services. With marginally more discretionary time, recipients may be in a better position to participate in the governance of these systems. The services themselves will be driven more by demand than supply.

A variant of this objection is that social services are geared to support people who engage in small farming, fishing, crafts and similar occupations. A tax credit approach could undermine these traditional livelihoods which have cultural as well as economic meaning. The response to this objection is brief. Whatever course people take as a result of the credit is up to them, romantic notions to the contrary notwithstanding.

16. *Participating countries will become dependent on subsidies.*

A formula will determine the extent of the subsidy from the global tax credit fund for each participating country. The formula will take into account variables like population, gross domestic product, per capita income, poverty headcount and poverty gap. The actual formula will depend in large part on the availability of valid and reliability data. Some variables may be weighted more heavily than others. As a country's gross domestic product grows and poverty declines, the amount of the subsidy will decrease. Governments will have to choose between maximizing the subsidy or fostering growth.

17. *The $1 a day standard is inherently arbitrary.*

That does not make it irrelevant. The PPP$1 a day standard emerged from a careful analysis of survey data from developing countries by World Bank economists. While its scientific grounding may be open to debate, it can safely be said that a person living on less than $1 a day is extremely poor. Others may qualify for this undesirable status on other grounds, but at least there are no false positives, only false negatives.

With all its admitted defects, the standard makes global comparability possible and provides a basis for global action against poverty. Political leaders have with good reason coalesced around it. It serves as the benchmark for the Millennium Development Goal on poverty reduction. Any other standard that meets these criteria is welcome.

18. *The credit will have a negative macroeconomic impact.*

The argument rests on the unassailable fact that a dollar transferred to a non-earning poor person is a dollar diverted from wealth-creating purposes like capital investment, technological enhancements or workforce skills development. This could adversely affect a country's international competitiveness, push up wage rates and cause unacceptably high inflation. In the short run these risks are real, though to an uncertain degree.

Over the longer run, the picture is blurrier but arguably brighter. The poor will spend the credit primarily on basic necessities like food, clothing and health care. Increased consumption will stimulate the production of local labor-intensive commodities. Sectors like agriculture, manufacturing and selected services will experience growth. Local markets, especially in depressed rural areas, stand to benefit.

With the additional income, some beneficiaries will seek more education, skill training or higher-paying jobs. Others will start their own businesses financed with microcredit loans. The wage-push effects of the tax credit will force larger firms to rely more on technology and automation for increases in output and productivity. Thus long-term growth will combine both bubble-up and trickle-down elements.

Since the mechanism is a refundable credit for qualified tax filers rather than a universal demogrant, the immediate impact on the economy, whether positive or negative, is not likely to be large. This is due to predictably low initial take-up rates and the exclusion of the non-poor from the benefit. Since change resulting from the tax credit will be incremental, countries and their international partner organizations will be able to anticipate and adjust for unforeseen disincentives and economic dislocations.

Essentially a global refundable tax credit that depends on voluntary participation by developing countries, their commitment to international standards for tax administration and low initial take-up rates would function as a natural experiment suited to research and evaluation on its macroeconomic impact, antipoverty effectiveness and a host of other policy relevant questions.

19. *The scheme will foster tax avoidance and tax evasion.*

According to this objection, a refundable tax credit will require higher government revenues, which will be obtained through higher average and marginal tax rates. Worse, the predicted decline in work effort will leave fewer people actually paying taxes. The refundable tax credit will only exacerbate the problem of tax avoidance and tax evasion, already widespread in developing countries. More and more pressure will fall on international donors to finance the credit.

With a refundable tax credit, overall expenditures for social protection will indeed rise. So will average and marginal tax rates on the taxpaying population. However, the increases will be less than they would be under a universal demogrant scheme. And there are offsetting considerations.

A country's participation in the scheme is voluntary and, with respect to international assistance, subject to United Nations approval. In practical terms, the scheme will not be implemented without a prior analysis of its likely impact on government revenues, employment and growth rates. Tax credit expenditures can be offset to some extent by savings elsewhere. At one extreme, the tax credit could be tied to wholesale reform of the social welfare system or, at the other, it could stand alone as an antipoverty measure. The former approach will stir opposition from groups vested in the social welfare system while the latter invites taxpayer antagonism.

Under domestic and international pressure to control public spending and open markets, governments will have to navigate between the two extremes. For example, there can be consolidation in the unruly thatch of income support programs in most countries. Consolidation will generate administrative efficiencies and cost-savings. Making the "sale" of the credit politically to taxpayers could depend on such reforms. There is risk in making the tax credit dependent on changes elsewhere in the social welfare system but for some developing countries it will be a risk worth taking.

END NOTES

1. Bergmann, Barbara R. (2002).
2. This seems to be the experience in France, which since 1988 has had a minimum income scheme called Revenu Minimum d'Insertion (RMI). The RMI has "brought relief to many low-income families...but...has not led to a complete breakdown in family solidarity." See Paugam, Serge, "The Revenue Minimum d'Insertion (RMI) in France" Chapter 3 in Standing, Guy, editor (2003) 45.
3. Most income support programs include a benefit reduction rate or BRR. If B is the basic benefit, T the benefit reduction rate, and I the income, the BRR formula for calcu-

lating the actual aid or A is A=B-TI. Thus, for B=100, T=.25, and I=50, A=100-[(.25)(50)]=87.50. Total income is I+A or 50+87.50=137.50. At I=400 (the break-even point), A drops to zero. Social welfare economists tinker endlessly with benefit reduction rates in an attempt to support income without decreasing work incentives. Over the range of PPP$0 to PPP$365, the refundable portion of the tax credit proposed here is reduced by PPP$1 for every PPP$1 of additional income and falls to zero once a person's income reaches PPP$365 a year (a 100 percent BRR). In time income will be subject to more sophisticated BRR tinkering. While more "equitable", the result will inevitably lead to overall cost increases and greater administrative complexity. On pragmatic political, economic and administrative grounds, I argue that such refinements are better added later rather than sooner.

13

Prospects

The refundable tax credit can be characterized as a bad idea; a good idea but politically infeasible; or an idea that is good, realistic and timely. I prefer to think of it as a good idea whose time is coming. It is not an immediately feasible solution to global poverty. Nor is it an idealistic scheme for the indeterminate future. It belongs among the mid-range list of possibilities. This concluding chapter is an examination of factors affecting the medium- to long-term prospects for the tax credit.

One authority on minimum income schemes has observed that "policies that have been regarded as unrealistic, unfeasible and out-of-the-question have a habit of suddenly becoming reality."[1] Sustained and measured advocacy enhances the possibility of "sudden" success. As political and economic conditions evolve, the gap between rich and poor countries will widen.

Religious bodies, labor unions, professional associations and various private multinational enterprises have all lent their voices to the cause of global poverty eradication. The Millennium Development Goals are shared by all 191 United Nations member states.[2] Even if there is no agreement about the remedy, the spectacle of hundreds of millions of people living on less than PPP$1 a day will continue to assault the world's conscience.

Little Cause for Cheer

On the surface, there is little cause for cheer. Dialogue about the effects of globalization appears frozen. People are locked into ideological mindsets and talk past each other. Neoliberal economic orthodoxy extends its sway, propelled by the United States, other industrialized nations and private sector enterprises. The governments of developing nations are urged and even coerced to open markets, cut spending, reduce budget deficits and step aside for private sector initiatives.

Antipoverty advocacy groups fight a rear-guard action, relying (incongruously) on an array of means-tested income support and social services to foster self-sufficiency among recipients. Some reflexively resist new social welfare paradigms, fearing to lose what few gains they have made. Under any circumstances, consensus is difficult to achieve in an untidy global "network" of local communities, sub-national governance units, nation-states, and regional organizations.

Global entities like the World Bank, International Monetary Fund and the United Nations Security Council are noteworthy for their lack of democratic underpinning. Might may not make right but it does make the rules. International capital markets effectively constrict national policy options. The unpredictability and the lack of regulation of these markets have undermined growth prospects and provoked crises in transitional and emerging economies.

Developing country governments, donor nations and international organizations have not faced up to their shared responsibility for failed poverty reduction policies and ineffective program interventions. The informal economic sectors of developing countries put the poor beyond the reach of labor laws and social insurance systems. Corruption is widespread in developing countries, at times abetted by foreign investors and governments.

A recitation of obstacles to the global tax credit can be off-putting. However, each of the obstacles must be evaluated in light of the pace and direction of global change. Disparities in the distribution of resources, opportunities and economic impacts are too great to be wished away.

If growth alone does not eliminate existing poverty (and contributes to creating new poverty) and if current targeted interventions fall short of filling global poverty gaps, then something else is needed. That something, I argue, is direct income support at least for people in extreme poverty. In weighing the costs and benefits of various alternatives, I end up in favor of accomplishing this through national tax systems with international cost-sharing. The approach may be controversial and lack political traction at present. But that need not always be so.

The right's misplaced confidence in growth alone and the left's myopic reliance on infrastructure-jobs-and-services strategies will each reveal their shortcomings and the debate will play out to a policy impasse. Both sides will agree on establishing an income floor for the world's poorest. Among competing alternatives, the tax credit will emerge as the most satisficing option.[3]

Just as the Earned Income Tax Credit acquired support in both liberal and conservative precincts in the United States, a global tax credit can bring together a disparate but nonetheless effective coalition of interests on behalf of the world's extremely poor. Proponents of the credit will have to be patient, respectful of opponents and smart about their advocacy.

Sense and Sensitivity

Donor countries and international organizations are trying harder to harmonize their aid initiatives with one another and with the domestic priorities of recipients. New civil society organizations within developing countries and on an international level have emerged, bringing moral force, fresh energy and stimulating ideas to the global marketplace.

In rich nations, greater domestic security and relief from terrorism are seen as flowing less from their own military prowess than from progress against poverty in developing nations. Below the political radar screen and invariably nuanced in concept or design, there are glimmerings of a coming system of global governance. Its underpinnings and contours cannot be fully foreseen. It will, however, reflect increasing concern over the effects of an economically integrated but politically fractionated world.

For the present, goal convergence and coordination of activities dominate the international policy paradigm. The United Nations as a voluntary compact among national governments plays an indispensable role in world affairs. Poverty reduction has risen to a high place on its agenda even if the means of achieving it are debated continually among its members.

The globalization of commerce and related capital flows has moved the coordination among tax systems to a higher place on the international agenda. Consensus is emerging among experts and within countries that "a comprehensive and accessible basis for international tax cooperation needs to be created," preferably under the aegis of the United Nations.[4]

Among most nations in the world, the principles of social insurance have been firmly grounded. Unemployment insurance and publicly financed pensions have become accepted as rights.

Social welfare systems for the poor are currently tilted toward "workfare"—time-limited benefits, work activation measures, job-related supports like transportation and child care. Even so, the obligation of society to provide support to its neediest and most vulnerable members through some form of public assistance is at least grudgingly acknowledged. Recipients may be seen as somehow less deserving than, say, social insurance beneficiaries but they should not be denied support altogether.

In part, public attitudes toward social welfare schemes may spring from feelings of altruism and social solidarity. In part they may reflect a defensive posture: providing for basic needs as a bulwark against crime, delinquency, social and political disruption.

Income distribution is embedded as an element of a decent fair-minded society. While resentful of waste and fraud, taxpaying publics generally endorse aid for those who cannot meet their basic needs through no fault of their own. The question in the early twenty-first century is whether the international community as a whole will deal systematically with the millions of "no-fault needy" created by global economic dislocations.

Framing the Credit

In several nations—France, Germany, New Zealand, South Africa, Brazil, for examples—the notion of a guaranteed basic income for all has entered mainstream political discourse. A world without poverty is being recognized as an achievable goal. Development and income security can go hand in hand.

Global poverty can be assaulted through growth alone, provision of jobs and related services, or income redistribution. The first two can be effective but, from a global perspective, the pace of poverty reduction under them is uneven and slow.

A redistribution system like a global tax credit cuts the Gordion Knot. It places a floor under the income of everyone in the world. The tax credit supersedes the essential conservative distrust of traditional welfare-based or services-based antipoverty programs—that they divert investment resources from capital markets and foster dependence on government bureaucracies.

Unlike welfare programs, the tax credit is not subject to complex eligibility rules. Unlike services-based programs, it sets no limits on how people use their additional resources. Even if other segments of society lament their choices, the money transferred to the poor is theirs to spend as they see fit. Thus, the program concept can be framed as a means of expanding personal freedom and unleashing human capacity. Slogans like "The Global Tax Credit: Making Freedom Real for Everyone" or "Tapping Human Capacity—The Promise of a Global Tax Credit" capture its essence.

One could do worse than amending the World Bank's slogan: "A World Free of Poverty" by adding "Support a Global Tax Credit". Making the credit a global reality will require sustained advocacy and technical expertise from a coalition of interested non-governmental organizations.

Coalition Building

Non-governmental organizations have gained an enviable degree of credibility in international settings. Compared to public officials and governmental institutions, they are seen as being in closer touch with people in poor communities and as being more sensitive to their needs. Non-governmental organizations are forming coalitions and acting in concert on broad policy issues like trade and debt relief that affect the poor. When non-governmental organizations coalesce around a shared objective, the results can be impressive.

Increasingly, the world's poor are making their voices heard through entities like ATD Fourth World. That movement, founded in 1957 by Father Joseph Wresinski (1917-1988), who was himself born in poverty, has a full-time volunteer corps with teams in twenty countries and correspondents in ninety. It engages some one hundred thousand people worldwide and enjoys consultative status with the United Nations. Its mission, quite simply, is to rid the world of extreme poverty, which is seen as a violation of basic human rights.

The Jubilee 2000 campaign on behalf of debt relief for the poorest countries is emblematic of the revival of public pressure on international organizations through grassroots mobilization, board room advocacy and street protest. In 1996, under pressure from a coalition of aid agencies, trade unions, churches and other groups, the World Bank announced its Heavily Indebted Poor Countries (HIPC) initiative, which was designed to address the debt of the poor countries in a comprehensive way.

In the United Kingdom, members of the coalition like the Catholic Agency for Overseas Development (CAFOD), Christian Aid, Tearfund and the World Development Movement lent their support to a new campaign launched by the New Economics Foundation, called Jubilee 2000. On May 16, 1998, the Group of Eight (G-8), representing the globe's richest economies, held their annual meeting in Birmingham, England. The Jubilee 2000 campaign organized a human chain of some seventy thousand people who ringed the conference center and called for cancellation of the debts of poor countries by 2000.

In the months and years following, the activities of the Jubilee 2000 campaign have kept the issue of debt relief on the international agenda. Jubilee 2000's global petition collected over twenty-four million signatures. In the United States, the campaign reached out to non-traditional allies. Impressively, it won over an influential conservative, Representative Spencer Bachus (Republican, Alabama), who helped raise the visibility of the issue in the U.S. Congress.[5] This paved the way for support from other conservative Republicans, including North Carolina Senator Jesse Helms.

In 1999, at the Cologne G-8 meeting, world leaders agreed to cancel $100 billion of debts owed by the poorest countries. Jubilee 2000 and its successor, Jubilee Research, have demonstrated the power of collective global action to remedy economic injustice. The campaign itself includes an extensive international coalition of faith-based and secular organizations. It operates with offices in sixty countries. The Jubilee 2000 Campaign has set a precedent for the type of joint action that could lead to a global tax credit initiative.[6]

A more recent example. In 2005, the United Kingdom held the presidency of the European Union and hosted the G-8 summit. The Make Poverty History campaign, based in the United Kingdom, took advantage of its government's higher international profile to mount a coordinated assault on global poverty. It advocates fairer trade, debt cancellation, and more and better-focused aid. The campaign brings together more than two hundred charities, campaign groups, trade unions, faith-based organizations and celebrities around these objectives.

The Global Tax Credit campaign could bring under one umbrella a number of traditional and non-traditional allies that, however much they may differ on other issues, could agree on the one ingredient that indisputably reduces poverty—more disposable income.

United Nations as a Target Audience

Let us assume that a tax credit coalition has come into being. To whom does it deliver its message? A tax credit campaign would need to focus on a variety of audiences that include national political leaders, international organizations, other advocacy groups, non-traditional allies and, needless to say, the publics of United Nations member countries.

The bull's-eye on the target of audiences is the United Nations itself. Familiarity with its structure and operation is therefore critical. The United Nations operates through six principal organs: Secretariat, General Assembly, Trusteeship Council, Security Council, International Court of Justice and Economic and Social Council.

The General Assembly, Secretariat and Economic and Social Council shape the organization's approach to poverty reduction. The General Assembly, the largest of the United Nations' subgroups, meets September to December. Much of the support for the General Assembly is generated in committees, especially the Economic and Social Committee, where decisions on poverty reduction policy are hammered out.

The United Nations Secretariat is responsible for much of the organization's ongoing activity. The Secretariat includes a number of departments and offices. Two that address global poverty most directly are the Office of the Secretary-General and the Department of Economic and Social Affairs.

Under the United Nations charter, the Economic and Social Council is responsible for promoting higher standards of living, full employment, and economic and social progress. The Economic and Social Council's purview extends to over seventy per cent of the human and financial resources of the entire United Nations system.

A campaign aimed at gaining the support of the United Nations system for a global tax credit program faces not a monolith but a welter of discrete entities with discrete institutional missions. Within this complex are entities whose support of the global tax credit would be invaluable. Chief among these is the United Nations Development Program, which devotes most of its $2.2 billion annual budget resources to the world's poorest countries. Published annually since 1990, the UNDP's *Human Development Report* exerts wide influence on issues of poverty and development.

Under the umbrella of the United Nations Development Program are lodged the Development Fund for Women and United Nations volunteers. Additional parts of the group consist of the United Nations Population Fund and the United Nations Children's Fund. Within the United Nations system, a number of individual entities in addition to the UNDP have taken up the banner of poverty reduction while espousing philosophies of growth and development that fit snugly with their institutional missions.

These include the United Nations Fund for Population Affairs, United Nations Conference on Trade and Development, World Food Program and Office of the High Representative for the Least Developed Countries, Landlocked Developing Countries and the Small Island Developing States.

A number of other specialized agencies use the machinery of the Economic and Social Council to coordinate with each other and the United Nations as a whole.

The global tax credit program would benefit from the support of specialized agencies like: (1) International Labour Organization (2) Food and Agriculture Organization (3) United Nations Educational, Scientific and Cultural Organization (4) World Health Organization (5) World Bank Group[7] (6) International Monetary Fund (7) International Fund for Agricultural Development and (8) United Nations Industrial Development Organization.

Forward progress can be slowed or stalled not only by outside opposition groups but also by internal debate among UN entities. While one entity, say, hypothetically, the United Nations Development Program, could sponsor the tax credit program, the success of a global campaign on its behalf will depend on support from multiple entities within the UN system.

Targeted Appeals

The chief appeal of the global tax credit is its potential for reducing extreme poverty in the developing world. However, there are carryover benefits of special interest to particular UN agencies. A global tax credit campaign would tailor its message to these agencies.

For the United Nations Children's Fund, the tax credit would mean a reduction in the intensity of child poverty.

For the United Nations Development Fund for Women, a step toward gender equity.

For the High Commissioner for Human Rights, assurance of a minimally acceptable standard of living for everyone.

For the World Bank Group and International Monetary Fund, a world freer of poverty and set more firmly on the path of development.

For the International Labour Organization, progress toward universal social protection.

For the World Health Organization, a break in the link between poverty and ill health.

For the International Fund for Agricultural Development, the alleviation of rural poverty.

And so on.

Research, Data and Monitoring

Changing international policies and practices is rarely simple and straightforward. Rough seas on the way to a global tax credit are unavoidable. In additional to persistent advocacy, staying on course requires high-level research and policy analysis. Part of the effort involves gathering, synthesizing, and demystifying economic information. (It is noteworthy that a successor to the effective Jubilee 2000 campaign is called Jubilee Research.)

Research support for the tax credit campaign will involve more than the preparation of bar charts. It will entail analyzing available data and marshaling arguments to counter opposition to the tax credit. It will mean critiquing the policies of international entities (prominently the World Bank and International Monetary Fund) and national governments that stand in the way of the credit. Conversely, it will highlight harbingers, such as Brazil's commitment to a guaranteed income or the OECD's emphasis on harmonizing the tax systems of developing and developed nations.

Models of such advocacy research are available. The Bretton Woods Project, which was created by British non-governmental organizations, serves effectively as an independent "networker, information-provider, media informant and watchdog" with respect to the World Bank and International Monetary Fund.[8]

Similarly, Social Watch, funded by the Netherlands Organization for International Development Cooperation and based at the Third World Institute in Montevideo, Uruguay, is an influential international network of national antipoverty advocates. Its genesis lay in the 1995 World Summit for Social Development in Copenhagen, where participating civil society organizations saw the need for an ongoing follow-up mechanism. As a global civil society alliance, the Social Watch network tracks the extent to which international commitments to poverty eradication and equality are fulfilled. Social Watch enables non-governmental organizations to influence the United Nations and other international bodies through its use of advanced communications technologies.

These and other similar initiatives serve as models for the development of a research-based and advocacy-oriented tax credit campaign. The tax credit campaign's research arm would also gain in credibility and legitimacy from ties to more academically oriented groups like the Comparative Research Programme on Poverty (CROP), an initiative of the International Social Science Council.

Public Education

With such models and resources at its disposal, a global tax credit campaign can begin its work not at the starting line but halfway down the course. Moving the global tax credit onto the international agenda requires making it a priority in developed and developing countries alike. To complement advocacy-based research there will be need for a program of public education.

This is because the campaign for a global tax credit will depend crucially on favorable public opinion, particularly among citizens of the member states of the Organization for Economic Cooperation and Development. After all, the taxpayers of these countries will be contributing the lion's share of the money to be transferred under this mechanism to the poorest people in the poorest countries.

Winning their support will require a public education strategy that communicates the nature of the global tax credit scheme through concise and consistent messages. These messages need to highlight the advantages of the scheme to themselves, their own country and the world community at large, not just the tax credit's recipients.

A public education campaign will stand a greater chance of success to the extent that the tax credit plan is designed and implemented in accordance with the following criteria.

First, it closes the poverty gap between the extremely poor and the $1 a day threshold.

Second, it minimizes the stigma attached to transfer payments.

Third, it is reasonably target-efficient, with administrative mechanisms for reducing access by the non-poor and for increasing the take-up rate by the poor.

Fourth, costs (including opportunity costs) are bearable.

And fifth, the impacts on the poor and on society as a whole with respect to factors like education, employment and economic growth are positive.

Many information channels exist for public education, such as newsletters, direct mail, speaker's bureaus, newspapers, radio, television, Internet websites, weblogs, and email communications. Advocates of the tax credit will seek out other more targeted venues like debates on university campuses, testimony before legislative bodies, and face-to-face meetings with public officials.

Other ways of getting out the message include print ads, billboards, public service announcements, press releases, brochures, videos, and Power Point presentations. These latter approaches can be used to convey the stark human cost of extreme global poverty and the loss to the world of people's latent capabilities.

Public education seeks more than diminished public opposition or even passive public support. It aims at motivating citizens who do support the tax credit to participate actively in open forums on the topic and to express their support forcefully to elected officials and other opinion leaders.

Responding to the Opposition

Opposition to a global tax credit will take predictable forms. One prominent advocate of minimum income schemes pithily sums up the most common criticisms to such schemes.

"Giving people money would encourage them to be idle...divert resources from other priorities...be unfair to those working hard...mean taxing those who have been working responsibly...and be administratively hard and costly."[9]

No, say these critics, social policy should instead be geared to increasing the capabilities of the poor and overcoming their social exclusion "by guidance, direction and coercion if necessary."[10] Additionally, critics descry the tax systems of developing countries as inappropriate vehicles for reform. A tax credit plan in these systems would be target-inefficient, unwieldy and subject to corruption.

In political discourse, there is a tendency to demonize the opposition. That would be a mistake in this case for at least three reasons. First, the criticisms need to be taken seriously. They are not totally invalid. At the heart of the debate is not whether they are valid or invalid, but whether or not their valid elements should be overriding.

Second, many of the critics themselves are humane and principled people. Few human beings enjoy the spectacle of their fellows living on less than $1 a day. They may disagree on what it takes to eliminate extreme poverty, but they need not deplore it less for all that.

Third, no one argues that the tax credit plan could be implemented universally and instantaneously. It will take time to get it up and running for every participating country. Under an incremental approach, both the United Nations and participating countries can learn from experience and adopt measures to meet the valid objections of critics.

A campaign respectful of opposing views can have a payoff—the recruitment of unlikely allies from among those who began as opponents. For example, there are those (mainly of a more conservative bent) who object to social services as an antipoverty strategy but who could come to endorse a non-categorical, non-welfare-based, income transfer scheme like a global tax credit. With commitment and energy behind the global tax credit, the prospects for implementation sooner rather than later would be enhanced.

Toward Global Poverty Intolerance

As an international initiative, a global tax credit would communicate the world's intolerance of extreme poverty. It would require coordination among donor and recipient countries. It would foster tax reform and literacy programs in developing countries. It would spur technology-based development by providing a safety net to many displaced workers.

It would give the world's poorest people not only essential income but hope for upward mobility. It would operate as a blow against terrorist networks that feed on the disparities between rich and poor nations.

The path to such accomplishments will hardly be rose-strewn. There are grounds for holding that a global tax credit is a good but politically immature idea. In the United States and Western Europe, whose support is essential, public sentiment on domestic social welfare programs is running against unconditional transfers and in favor of benefits that are tied to work effort. Pension reforms have tended to move in the direction of defined contributions in lieu of defined benefits.

There is no dearth of experts who insist that growth alone is the surest path to poverty reduction. Markets and free-floating capitalism trump global equity considerations. Support for antipoverty initiatives of any type is given grudgingly. In this context, a global tax credit scheme appears downright fanciful.

However, if one lengthens the lens, the picture brightens. Undeniably and irreversibly, the forces of globalization have led to the rapid diffusion of new technologies and the freer flow of people, goods, services and capital. The world as a whole has grown richer.

The spread of information and communications technologies has focused the spotlight of public scrutiny on some of the evils for which global economic integration is at least partly responsible. These include periodic crises in world financial markets, the wider reach of terror networks and the inexorable marginalization of extremely poor countries and their citizens.

The impacts, good and bad, of globalization on child labor, opportunities for women, democratic governance, labor standards and protection of the environment are staples of international discourse.

The United Nations as a multilateral institution with global legitimacy provides the framework for international action. Without raising the specter of world government, the United Nations, with the support of its member states and international partners, can build a consensus-driven system of rules and processes that steers global economic forces toward humanly desirable ends.

The United Nations can above all function as a forum for promoting shared human values that are reflected in its Charter, as well as the Universal Declaration of Human Rights and the Millennium Declaration. One of these shared human values is the right of everyone to a standard of living consistent with basic health and well-being. A global tax credit is a cost-effective means toward that end. The resources are available. The institutional structures and systems for tapping into those resources exist. The rest is up to us.

END NOTES

1. Standing, Guy, editor (2003) 9-10.
2. Unfortunately, that does not mean they all support the same thing. The eight Millennium Development Goals were enunciated in the Millennium Declaration adopted at the 2000 Millennium Summit. The United Nations Secretariat subsequently (in 2001) published a set of targets and indicators associated with the goals. These latter targets and indicators are routinely subsumed under the heading "Millennium Development Goals", although they were not part of the Millennium Declaration and were not formally adopted by the UN member states. And in fact, the United States, to cite one example, explicitly disagrees with one indicator associated with Goal 8, "Develop a Global Partnership for Development." The indicator assesses progress in achieving this goal by measuring official development assistance as a percentage of donor countries' gross national income (with 0.7 percent as the standard). The U.S. opposes numerical aid targets, regarding them as inputs, not outputs. See the "Dear Colleague" letter from Ambassador John R. Bolton, United States Mission to the United Nations, August 26, 2005 at www.globalpolicy.org/msummit/millenni/undocindex.htm#2005.
3. To "satisfice", a word coined by the late social scientist and economist Herbert Simon, contrasts with the conventional economic view that people act to maximize their utility based on a complete assessment of the costs and benefits. Instead, in the real world of constraints and bounded rationality, Simon argues, people settle for less than optimal but nonetheless satisfactory results. See his classic *Administrative Behavior* (4th edition, New York: Free Press: 1997). In this case, while more idealized schemes for establishing a floor under income will have their advocates, the refundable tax credit will be seen, despite its limitations, as the most feasible approach under real world political conditions.
4. International Labour Organization (2004) 104.
5. See Hoover, Dennis R. (2001). The article describes how Martin Dent, a retired British professor, conceived the campaign in an Oxford pub and, along with Bill Peters, a retired British ambassador, dubbed it Jubilee 2000 and went on to enlist the aid of Tearfund and other Christian aid agencies.
6. This is not to overdramatize the debt relief campaign's achievements. By the end of 2004, less than forty percent of the total debt of the forty-two HIPCs had been canceled. Debt servicing continues to absorb a large fraction of developing countries' budgets. In 2003, for example, Zambia spent more on debt payments than on education. "Low income countries are still paying out $100 million every day to their creditors." See Oxfam International (2005) 30, 38 and www.jubileeresearch.org.
7. For years, the "World Bank" was a shorthand reference to the International Bank for Reconstruction and Development. Over time, it added several quasi-independent and more specialized components. The World Bank Group is comprised of the International Bank for Reconstruction and Development; International Development Agency; International Finance Corporation; Multilateral Guarantee Agency; and International Centre for Settlement of Investment Disputes. The "World Bank" now refers to the first two of these.
8. www.brettonwoodsproject.org/project/index.shtml
9. Standing, Guy, editor (2003) 2.
10. Standing, Guy, editor (2003) 2.

Bibliography

Ackerman, Bruce and Anne Alstott. 1999. *The Stakeholder Society*. New Haven: Yale University Press.

Adams, Richard H. Jr., 2003. *The Effect of Economic Growth on Poverty and Income Distribution in Developing Countries: A Literature Review and Data Analysis*. Technical report prepared for U.S. Agency for International Development by Nathan Associates, Inc. (Contract No. PCE-1-00-00-0001). Washington, DC: USAID.

African Development Bank, Asian Development Bank, European Bank for Reconstruction and Development, International Monetary Fund, World Bank. 2000. *Global Poverty Report*. (May) Prepared for the G8 Okinawa Summit in Nago City, Okinawa, July 21-23, 2000.

Agence Française de Développement. 2001. *Rapport Financer 2000*. (May 28) www.afd.fr/english/activite/resultats_financiers_1.cfm

Aghion, Philippe and Peter Howitt. 1998. *Endogenous Growth Theory*. Cambridge, Massachusetts: MIT Press.

Adelman, Irma and Sherman Robinson. 1978. *Income Distribution Policy in Developing Countries: A Case Study of Korea*. Stanford, California: Stanford University Press.

Ahmad, Ehtisham and Nicholas Stern. 1991. *The Theory and Practice of Tax Reform in Developing Countries*. Cambridge: Cambridge University Press.

Allen, Jodie T. 2002. "Negative Income Tax." Entry in *The Concise Encyclopedia of Economics*. www.econlib.org.

Allen, Tim and Alan Thomas, editors. 2000. *Poverty and Development: Into the 21st Century*. New York: Oxford University Press in association with the Open University, United Kingdom.

Alm, James and Sally Wallace. 2004. *Can Developing Countries Impose an Individual Income Tax?* (August) Paper prepared for Conference on "The Challenges of Tax Reform in a Global Economy", Andrew Young School of Policy Studies, International Studies Program, Georgia State University, Stone Mountain Park, Georgia, May 24-25, 2004. Atlanta, Georgia: Georgia State University.

Anderson, Sarah and John Cavanagh. 2000. *Top 200—The Rise of Corporate Global Power*. (December) Washington, DC: Institute for Policy Studies. www.ips-dc.org/downloads/Top_200.pdf.

Aristotle. 1885. *Politics*. Translation of Benjamin Jowett. Web edition at www.mdx.ac.uk/www/study/xari.htm. Page references follow the numbering system of Immanuel Bekker (1785-1871).

Asher, Mukul G. and Ramkishen S. Rajan. 1999. *Globalization and Tax Systems: Implications for Developing Countries with Particular Reference to Southeast Asia*. Discussion Paper No. 99/23. (October) Adelaide 5005 Australia: Centre for International Economic Studies, Adelaide University.

Asian Development Bank. 2005. *Labor Markets in Asia: Promoting Full, Productive, and Decent Employment*. Manila: Asian Development Bank.

Asian Development Bank. 2002. *Asian Development Outlook 2002*. New York: Oxford University Press.

Asian Development Bank. 2002a. *Social Protection Strategy*. (August). www.adb.org/Publications.

Asian Development Bank. 2001. *Social Protection in Asia and the Pacific*. Isabel Ortiz, editor. Publication stock number 050301. Manila: Asian Development Bank.

Asian Development Bank. 1997. *Guidelines for the Economic Analysis of Projects*. www.adb.org.

Atkinson, Anthony B. 1995. *Public Economics in Action: The Basic Income/Flat Tax Proposal*. Oxford: Oxford University Press.

Australian Agency for International Development (AusAID). 1997. *One Clear Objective: Poverty Reduction through Sustainable Development*. Report of the Committee of Review, Commonwealth of Australia. This is often referred to as the Simons Report, after the Committee's chair, H. Paul Simons, AM. Canberra: AusAID. Available on the Internet at www.ausaid.gov.au.

Australian Reproductive Health Alliance and Family Planning Association International Development New Zealand. 1998. "Jobs, Income and Poverty," Chapter 16 in *Briefing Pack on Population and Development*. (January) Available at www.asiapacificalliance.org. Note: To access document, go to Sitemap and click on Examples of Good Advocacy Materials.

Ayala Consulting Company. 2003. *Workshop on Conditional Cash Transfer Programs: Operational Experiences - Final Report*. (March). Prepared for the World Bank following the Workshop, held at the Universidad de las Américas, Puebla, Mexico, April 29-May 1, 2002. Quito, Ecuador: Ayala Consulting Company.

Ayres, Robert L. 1983. *Banking on the Poor: The World Bank and World Poverty*. Cambridge, Massachusetts: MIT Press.

Baker, Judy L. 2000. *Evaluating the Impact of Development Projects on Poverty: A Handbook for Practitioners*. Washington, DC: World Bank.

Bardhan, Pranab. 2005. *Globalization and Rural Poverty*. WIDER research paper no. RP2005/30 (June). Helsinki: United Nations University/World Institute for Development Economics Research.

Basic Income European Network. 2004. *NewsFlash*. (January). Electronic newsletter for BIEN subscribers. www.basicincome.org.

Bell, Joseph G.; Philip K. Robins; Robert G. Spiegelman; and Samuel Wiener, editors. 1980. *A Guaranteed Annual Income: Evidence from a Social Experiment*. New York: Academic Press.

Bergmann, Barbara R. 2002. *A Swedish-Style Welfare State or Basic Income: Which Should Have Priority?* Paper prepared for Conference on Rethinking Redistribution, sponsored by the Real Utopias Project, University of Wisconsin, May 3-5, 2002. See www.ssc.wisc.edu/havenscenter.

Beveridge, Sir William. 1942. *Social Insurance and Allied Services: Presented to Parliament by Command of His Majesty*. CM 6404, HMSO (November). London. Note:

Since it was produced by the Beveridge Committee, the report is commonly cited as The Beveridge Report. For a summary, go to www.fordham.edu/halsall/mod/1942beveridge.html.

Bhagwati, Jagdish. 2004. *In Defense of Globalization*. New York: Oxford University Press.

Bhalla, Surgit S. 2003. *Not as Poor, Nor as Unequal, as You Think—Poverty, Inequality and Growth in India, 1950-2000*. Final report of research project for the Planning Commission, Government of India titled "The Myth and Reality of Poverty in India" (December 4). New Delhi: Oxus Research & Investments.

Bhalla, Surjit S. 2002. *Imagine There's No Country: Poverty, Inequality and Growth in the Era of Globalization*. Washington, DC: Institute for International Economics.

Bhalla, A. S. and Frédéric Lapeyre. 1999. *Poverty and Exclusion in a Global World*. New York: St. Martin's Press.

Bird, Richard M. and Eric M. Zolt. 2005. *The Limited Role of the Personal Income Tax in Developing Countries*. Working Paper 05-07 (March). International Studies Program, Andrew Young School of Policy Studies. Atlanta, Georgia: Georgia State University.

Bird, Richard M. 1992. *Tax Policy and Economic Development*. Baltimore, Maryland: The Johns Hopkins University Press.

Bird, Richard M. and Susan Horton, editors. 1989. *Government Policy and the Poor in Developing Countries*. Toronto: University of Toronto Press.

Bird, Richard and Oliver Oldman, editors. 1990. *Taxation in Developing Countries*. Baltimore, MD: The Johns Hopkins University Press.

Birdsall, Nancy, Allen C. Kelley, and Steven W. Sinding, editors. 2001. *Population Matters: Demographic Change, Economic Growth and Poverty in the Developing World*. Oxford: Oxford University Press.

Blank, Rebecca M., David Card, and Philip K. Robins. 1999. "Financial Incentives for Increasing Work and Income among Low-Income Families" (February). Revised version of paper presented at Joint Center for Poverty Research Conference on "Labor Markets and Less Skilled Workers." Washington, DC, November 5-6, 1998.

Blank, Rebecca M. 1997. *It Takes a Nation: A New Agenda for Fighting Poverty*. New York: Russell Sage Foundation and Princeton, New Jersey: Princeton University Press.

Blank, Rebecca M. 1996. "The Employment Strategy: Public Policies to Increase Work and Earnings", Chapter Seven in Danziger, Sheldon H., Gary D. Sandefur, and Daniel H. Weinberg, editors. *Confronting Poverty: Prescriptions for Change*. New York: Russell Sage Foundation and Cambridge, Massachusetts and London, England: Harvard University Press.

Blim, Michael. 2005. *Equality and Economy: The Global Challenge*. Walnut Creek, California: AltaMira Press.

Block, Fred and Margaret Somers. 2003. "In the Shadow of Speenhamland: Social Policy and the Old Poor Law", *Politics and Society* 31(2) (June): 283-323.

Block, Fred and Jeff Manza. 1997. "Could We End Poverty in a Post-Industrial Society? The Case for a Progressive Negative Income Tax," *Politics and Society* 25 (December): 473-511.

Boughton, James and K. Sarwar Lateef, editors. 1995. *Fifty Years after Bretton Woods: The Future of the IMF and the World Bank*. Washington, DC: IMF and World Bank Group.

Brainard, Lael; Carol Graham; Nigel Purvis; Steve Radelet; and Gayle Smith. 2003. *The Other War: Global Poverty and the Millennium Challenge Account*. Washington, DC: The Brookings Institution Press and Center for Global Development.

Brandt Commission. 1983. *Common Crisis North-South: Co-operation for World Recovery*. Second report of the Independent Commission for International Development. London: Pan World Affairs Books.

Brandt Commission. 1980. *North-South: A Program for Survival*. First report of the Independent Commission for International Development. Cambridge, Massachusetts: The MIT Press.

Brazil Ministry of Education. 2002. *Bolsa Escola Federal: The First Year*. (March) See www.mec.gov.br/bolsaescola.

British Chambers of Commerce. 2004. *A New Tax Horizon: How to Simplify Britain's Payroll Tax System*. (February). London: BCC.

Brodkin, Evelyn Z. and Alexander Kaufman. 1998. *Experimenting with Welfare Reform: The Boundaries of Policy Analysis* (September) JCPR Working Paper No. 1. Chicago: Joint Center for Poverty Research at Northwestern University and University of Chicago.

Bruton, Henry J. 1969. "The Two-Gap Approach to Aid and Development: Comment" in *American Economic Review* 59: 566-577.

Burman, Leonard E. and Deborah I. Kobes. 2003. *EITC Reaches More Eligible Families Than TANF, Food Stamps*. (March 17). Tax Facts (No. 1769) from the Tax Policy Center, a joint venture of the Urban Institute and the Brookings Institution. Washington, DC: Urban Institute and Brookings. Also see www.taxpolicycenter.org/taxfacts.

Burnside, Craig and David Dollar. 1997. *Aid, Policies and Growth*. Working paper 1777. Washington, DC: World Bank.

Cain, Glen G., and Douglas Wissoker. 1990. "A Reanalysis of Marital Stability in the Seattle-Denver Income Maintenance Experiment," *American Journal of Sociology* 95(5) (March): 1235-1269.

Campbell, David and Michael Parisi. 2002. *Individual Income Tax Returns, 2000*. www.irs.gov/pub/irs-soi/00indtr.pdf.

Canada, Government of. 1994. *Improving Social Security in Canada—Guaranteed Annual Income: A Supplementary Paper*. Catalog no. MP90-2/15-1995. Quebec: Ministry of Supply and Services. A copy of the paper is available at www.canadiansocialresearch.net/ssrgai.htm. Note: In 1994, the Canadian government launched a national Social Security Review, under which a discussion paper and a number of supplementary papers were released. This one on a guaranteed annual income provides excellent historical background and an analysis of the negative income tax and universal demogrant options.

Canadian Foundation for the Americas (FOCAL). 2001. *Addressing Poverty and Inequality in Latin America and the Caribbean*. Available at www.focal.ca.

Condorcet, Marie Jean Antoine Nicolas Caritat, Marquis de. 1988. *Esquisse D'un Tableau Historique des Progrès de L'Esprit Humain* (1st edition, 1795). Note: The book was originally published posthumously by his widow. Paris: GF-Flammarion.

Cassen, Robert. 1994. *Does Aid Work?* Oxford: Clarendon Press.

Caufield, Catherine. 1996. *Masters of Illusion: The World Bank and the Poverty of Nations*. New York: Henry Holt.

Cavallo, Sonia. 2000. *Tax Structure in Guatemala*. Discussion paper No. 645 (February) as part of the Central American Project of Harvard University's Center for International Development. Cambridge, Massachusetts: Harvard University.

Centre for International Economics. 2002. *Globalisation and Poverty:Turning the Corner*. (October) Canberra, Australia: Panther Publishing & Printing.

Chadwick, Laura and Jürgen Volkert. 2003. *Making Work Pay: U.S. American Models for a German Context?* IAW-Diskussionspapiere 8 (March). Tübingen, Germany: Institut für Angewandte Wirtschaftsforschung. www.iaw.edu.

Chattopadhyay, Saumen and Arindam Das-Gupta. 2002. *The Compliance Cost of the Personal Income Tax and Its Determinants.* Study prepared for the Planning Commission, Government of India, by the National Institute of Public Finance and Policy. (December). New Delhi: NIPFP.

Chen, Shaohua and Martin Ravillion. 2004. *How Have the World's Poorest Fared since the Early 1980s?* Policy Research Paper 3341 (June). Washington DC: World Bank.

Chen, Shaohua and Martin Ravillion. 2000. *How Did the World's Poorest Fare in the 1990s?* Policy Research Paper No. 2409 (August). Washington DC: World Bank.

Chenery, Hollis B. and T.N. Srinivasan, editors. *Handbook of Development Economics*, Volume I. 1988. Volume II. 1989. Volume IIIA. 1995. Volume IIIB. 1995, with Jere Behrman and T.N. Srinivasan as editors. Amsterdam: North Holland.

Chenery, Hollis B., Montek S. Ahluwalia, C.L.G. Bell, John H. Dulloy, and Richard Jolly. 1974. *Redistribution with Growth: Policies to Improve Income Distribution in Developing Countries in the Context of Economic Growth.* A Joint Study by the World Bank's Development Research Center and the Institute of Development Studies, University of Sussex. London: Oxford University Press.

Chu, Ke-young, Hamid Davoodi and Sanjeev Gupta. 2000. *Income Distribution and Tax and Government Spending Policies in Developing Countries.* IMF Working Paper WP/00/62. Washington, DC: International Monetary Fund.

Christiaensen, Luc; Lionel Demery; and Stefano Paternostro. 2002. *Growth, Distribution and Poverty in Africa: Messages from the 1990s.* Poverty Dynamics in Africa Series No 25244 (November). Washington, DC: World Bank.

Chronic Poverty Research Centre. 2004. *The Chronic Poverty Report 2004-05.* Manchester, United Kingdom: University of Manchester, Institute for Development Policy & Management. Note: The Centre is an independent body funded by the UK's Department for International Development (DFID). See www.chronicpoverty.org.

Citro, Constance F. and R.T. Michael. 1995. *Measuring Poverty: A New Approach.* Washington, DC: National Academy Press.

Clark, Charles M. A. 1997. "A Basic Income for the United States of America: Ensuring that the Benefits of Economic Progress Are Equitably Shared." *The Vincentian Chair of Social Justice: Volume 3.* New York: The Vincentian Center for Church and Society at St. John's University.

Clark, Charles M. A. and Catherine Kavanagh. 1996. Basic Income, Inequality and Unemployment: Rethinking the Linkages between Work and Welfare", *Journal of Economic Issues.* 30 (June): 399-406.

Clark, Colin. 1940. *The Conditions of Economic Progress.* London: Macmillan.

Clark, Robert F. 2005. *Victory Deferred: The War on Global Poverty (1945-2003).* Lanham, Maryland: University Press of America.

Clark, Robert F. 2002. *The War on Poverty: History, Selected Programs and Ongoing Impact.* Lanham, Maryland: University Press of America.

Cline, William R. 2004. *Trade Policy and Global Poverty.* (June) Washington, DC: Center for Global Development and Institute for International Economics.

Coady, David; Margaret Grosh; and John Hoddinott. 2003. *Targeted Anti-Poverty Interventions: A Select Annotated Bibliography.* (July) Washington, DC: World Bank.

Cole, G.D.H. 1935. *Principles of Economic Planning.* London: Macmillan & Company.

Collier, Paul and David Dollar. 1999. *Aid Allocation and Poverty Reduction.* Working paper 2041. Washington, DC: World Bank. (January 1) Note: The authors emphasize that the paper does not necessarily reflect the official views of the World Bank.

Collins, Mick. 2000. *Personality and Political Leadership Explored: Richard Nixon and the Family Assistance Plan.* Thesis submitted in partial fulfillment of requirements for M.S. degree in Political Science. Blacksburg, Virginia: Virginia Polytechnic Institute and State University.

Collinson, Patrick, "The Late Medieval Church and Its Reformation (1400-1600)", Chapter 6 (p. 233-266) in McManners, John, editor. 1992. *The Oxford Illustrated History of Christianity.* Oxford, New York: Oxford University Press.

Commission on Human Security. 2003. *Human Security Now.* New York: Commission on Human Security.

Committee for Economic Development. 2002. *A Shared Future: Reducing Global Poverty.* New York: CED.

Committee on International Relations, U.S. House of Representatives, and Committee on Foreign Relations, U.S. Senate. 2001. *Legislation on Foreign Relations Through 2000.* (June) Volume I-A: Current Legislation and Related Executive Orders. Washington, DC: U.S. Government Printing Office.

Congressional Research Service. 2003. *Cash and Non-Cash Benefits for Persons with Limited Income: Eligibility Rules, Recipient and Expenditure Data, FY 2000-FY 2003.* (November 25). Compiled by Vee Burke. Washington, DC: CRS.

Congressional Research Service. 2000. *The Earned Income Tax Credit: Current Issues and Benefit Amounts.* Order Code RS20470 (September 1). Report prepared by Melinda T. Gish. Washington, DC: CRS.

Consultative Group to Assist the Poorest. 2000. *Annual Report 2000.* Washington, DC: World Bank.

Cournot, Augustin. 1838. *Recherches sur les Principes Mathématiques de la Théorie des Richesses.* [*Researches into the Mathematical Principles of the Theory of Wealth*] Paris: L. Hachette. Translated into English by Nathaniel T. Bacon, 1897. English edition: New York: The Macmillan Company, 1927. Reprinted New York: Augustus M. Kelley, 1960, 1964, 1971 [Reprints of economic classics].

Cunliffe, John and Guido Erreygers, editors. 2004. *Origins of Universal Grants: An Anthology of Historical Writings on Basic Capital and Basic Income.* London: Palgrave Macmillan.

Cunliffe, John and Guido Erreygers. 2000. *Basic Income? Basic Capital! Origins and Issues of a Debate.* Paper prepared for the Eighth Congress of the Basic Income European Network, Berlin (October 6-7, 2000). (January; revised version of September, 2004 draft).

Dawood, N.J. (Translator). 1999. *The Koran.* London: Penguin Books.

Deaton, Angus and Valerie Kozel. 2005. *Data and Dogma: The Great India Poverty Debate.* (January; revision of September, 2004 draft). Working paper available at: www.wws.princeton.edu/deaton/papers.html. Note: The paper is an adaptation of the authors' introduction to Deaton, Angus and Valerie Kozel, editors; 2004; *Data and Dogma: The Great India Poverty Debate*; New Delhi, India: Macmillan.

Deaton, Angus. 2004. *Measuring Poverty in a Growing World (Or Measuring Growth in a Poor World).* (February) Review of economics and statistics lecture, presented at Harvard University, April 15, 2003. www.wws.princeton.edu/deaton.

Deaton, Angus. 2003. "How to Monitor Poverty for the Millennium Development Goals," *Journal of Human Development* 4 (3) 353-378. Also see www.wws.princeton.edu/~deaton/papers.html.

Deaton, Angus. 2001. "Counting the World's Poor: Problems and Possible Solutions." *World Bank Research Observer* 16:2 (Fall): 125-147.

Deaton, Angus and Margaret Grosh. 2000. "Consumption," Chapter 5 in Grosh, Margaret and Paul Glewwe, editors. *Designing Household Survey Questionnaires for Developing Countries: Lessons from Ten Years of LSMS Experience.* Washington, DC: World Bank.

Demery, Lionel and Michael Walton. 1998. *Are Poverty Reduction and Social Goals for the Twenty-First Century Attainable?* Washington, DC: World Bank.

De Ferranti, David, Guillermo E. Perry, Francisco Ferreira and Michael Walton. 2004. *Inequality in Latin America: Breaking with History?* (February) Washington, DC: World Bank. Note: See Chapter 9, "Taxation, Public Expenditures and Transfers".

De Janvry, Alain; Frederico Finan; Elisabeth Sadoulet; Donald Nelson; Kathy Lindert; Bénédicte de la Brière; and Peter Lanjouw. 2005. *Brazil's Bolsa Escola Program: The Role of Local Governance in Decentralized Implementation.* SP Discussion Paper No. 0542 (December). Social Safety Nets Primer Series. Washington, DC: World Bank Institute.

De Vries, Margaret Garritsen, editor. 1986. *The IMF in a Changing World.* (June 15) Washington, DC: International Monetary Fund.

Dikhanov, Yuri and Michael Ward. 2001. *Evolution of the Global Distribution of Income in 1970-1999.* (August). Paper (draft) prepared for the 53rd Session of the International Statistical Institute, Seoul, Korea, August 22-29, 2001.

Dollar, David. 2001. *Globalization, Inequality and Poverty since 1980.* (November) World Bank research paper. Washington, DC: World Bank.

Dollar, David and Aart Kray. 2000. *Growth is Good for the Poor.* Development Research Group Working Paper 2587.Washington, DC: World Bank.

Dollar, David and Lant Pritchett. 1998. *Assessing Aid: What Works, What Doesn't and Why.* Washington, DC: World Bank.

Domar, Evsey. 1946. "Capital Expansion, Rate of Growth and Employment." *Econometrika* 14 (April):137-147.

Domar, Evsey. 1957. *Essays in the Theory of Economic Growth.* New York: Oxford University Press.

Easterly, William. 2001. *The Elusive Quest for Growth: Economists' Adventures and Misadventures in the Tropics.* Cambridge, Massachusetts: MIT Press.

Easterly, William. 1997. *The Ghost of Financing Gap: How the Harrod-Domar Growth Model Still Haunts Development Economics.* (July) Draft working paper. Washington, DC: World Bank.

Economic Commission for Latin America and the Caribbean. 2002. *Globalization and Development.* (April) LC/G 2157(SES.29/3). New York: United Nations.

Emmerij, Louis, editor. 1997. *Economic and Social Development into the XXI Century.* Washington, DC: Inter-American Development Bank.

Emmerij, Louis; Richard Jolly; and Thomas G. Weiss. 2001. *Ahead of the Curve?: UN Ideas and Global Challenges.* First volume in the United Nations Intellectual History Project. Bloomington and Indianapolis: Indiana University Press.

Esping-Anderson, Gøsta. 1990. *The Three Worlds of Welfare Capitalism.* Princeton, New Jersey: Princeton University Press.

European Commission. 2002. *Annual Report 2001: On the EC Development Policy and the Implementation of the External Assistance.* Brussels: EuropeAid Cooperation Office.

European Commission. 2002a. *Social Protection in Europe 2001.* Report of the Directorate-General for Employment and Social Affairs (May). Luxembourg: Office for Official Publications of the European Communities.

European Anti-Poverty Network. 2002. *Making a Decisive Impact on Poverty and Social Exclusion: A Progress Report on the European Strategy on Social Inclusion.* (June). Brussels: EAPN. For more information see www.eapn.org.

Fitzpatrick, Tony. 1999. *Freedom and Security: An Introduction to the Basic Income Debate.* London: Macmillan.

Focus on the Global South. 2003. *Anti Poverty or Anti Poor: The Millennium Development Goals and the Eradication of Extreme Poverty and Hunger.* (December). Bangkok, Thailand: Focus on the Global South. Note: Focus on the Global South, a regional program of policy research and action, was founded in 1995 and is attached to the Chulalongkorn University Social Research Institute (CUSRI) in Bangkok, Thailand.

Foner, Philip S., editor. 1999. *The Life and Major Writings of Thomas Paine.* (February) Bridgewater, New Jersey: Replica Books.

Food and Agricultural Organization. 2000. *The State of Food Insecurity in the World.* Rome: FAO.

Food and Agricultural Organization. 2000(a). *The State of Food and Agriculture 2000.* Rome: FAO.

Foster, James; Joel Greer; and Eric Thorbecke. 1984. "A Class of Decomposable Poverty Measures," *Econometrica* 52:761-765.

Fourier, Charles. 1967. *La Fausse Industrie.* First published in 1836. Paris: Anthropos.

Frankman, Myron J. 2004. *World Democratic Federalism. Peace and Justice Indivisible* (March) London: Palgrave.

Frankman, Myron J. 1997. *Planet-Wide Citizen's Income: Antidote to Global Apartheid.* Paper published at the author's website. (October) See www.arts.mcgill.ca/programs/econ/frankman.html.

Freeman, Samuel, editor. 2002. *The Cambridge Companion to Rawls.* London: Cambridge University Press.

Friedman, Milton. 1968. "The Case for a Negative Income Tax," pages 202-219 in Melvin R. Laird, editor. *Republican Papers.* New York: Anchor Books.

Friedman, Milton. 1962. *Capitalism and Freedom.* Chicago: University of Chicago Press.

Gale, Fred; Bryan Lohmar; and Francis Tuan. 2004. *China's New Farm Subsidies.* Electronic Outlook Report from the Economic Research Service, U.S. Department of Agriculture. WRS-05-01 (February). Available at www.ers.usda.gov.

Garfinkel, Irwin; Chien-Chung Huang; and Wendy Naidich. 2002. *The Effects of a Basic Income Guarantee on Poverty and Income Distribution.* (February 22) Paper prepared for Conference on Rethinking Redistribution, sponsored by the Real Utopias Project, University of Wisconsin, May 3-5, 2002. See www.ssc.wisc.edu/havenscenter.

Gemmell, Norman and Oliver Morrissey. 2003. *Tax Structure and the Incidence on the Poor in Developing Countries.* CREDIT Research Paper No. 03/18. Nottingham: Department of Economics, University of Nottingham. Note: CREDIT is the University's Centre for Research in Economic Development and International Trade.

Gemmell, Norman with Oliver Morrissey. 2002. *The Poverty Impacts of Revenue Systems in Developing Countries: A Report to the Department for International Development.* (March 11). Nottingham: Department of Economics, University of Nottingham.

Geremek, Bronislaw. 1997. *Poverty—A History.* English translation from the Polish by Agniewska Kolakowska. Cambridge, Massachusetts: Blackwell Publishers, Inc.

George, Robley E. 2002. *Socioeconomic Democracy: An Advanced Socioeconomic System.* Westport, Connecticut: Praeger Publishers.

Goldsmith, Scott. 2002. *The Alaska Permanent Fund: an Experiment in Wealth Distribution.* Paper (draft) prepared for the 9th International Congress of the Basic Income European Network (September). Geneva.

Gordon, David and Peter Townsend, editors. 2001. *Breadline Europe: The Measurement of Poverty.* Bristol, United Kingdom: The Policy Press.

Gorz, André. 1999. *Reclaiming Work: Beyond the Wage-Based Society.* Cambridge: Polity Press.

Gray, John and Emma Chapman. 2001. *Evaluation of Revenue Projects: Synthesis Report (Volume I)*. Evaluation Report EV636 (February). London: Department for International Development.

Greenstein, Robert. 2003. *What is the Magnitude of EITC Overpayments?* (July 23, revised version). Washington, DC: Center on Budget and Policy Priorities. www.cbpp.org.

Groot, Loek F. M. 2004. *Basic Income, Unemployment and Compensatory Justice*. Dordrecht, The Netherlands: Springer.

Grosh, Margaret E. 1994. *Administering Targeted Social Programs in Latin America: From Platitudes to Practice*. Washington, DC: World Bank.

Grosh, Margaret E. and Paul Glewwe. 1995. *A Guide to Living Standards Measurement Surveys and Their Data Sets*. Washington, DC: World Bank.

Guttman, Amy and Dennis Thompson. 1996. *Democracy and Disagreement*. Cambridge, Massachusetts: Harvard University Press.

Handoussa, Heba and Zafiris Tzannatos, editors. 2002. *Employment Creation and Social Protection in the Middle East and North Africa*. Cairo: The American University in Cairo Press.

Hannan, Michael T. and Nancy Brandon Tuma. 1990. "A Reassessment of the Effect of Income Maintenance on Marital Dissolution in the Seattle-Denver Experiment," *American Journal of Sociology* 95 (5) 1270-1298

Hannan, Michael T., Nancy Brandon Tuma, and Lyle P. Groeneveld. 1977. "Income and Independence Effects on Marital Dissolution: Results from the Seattle and Denver Income Maintenance Experiments," *American Journal of Sociology* 84 (3) 611-633.

Hansen, Henrik and Finn Tarp. 2000. "Aid Effectiveness Disputed." *Journal of International Development* 12 (3) 375-398.

Harrington, Michael. 1962. *The Other America: Poverty in the United States*. New York: Macmillan.

Harrod, Roy F. 1939. "An Essay in Dynamic Theory," *Economic Journal* 49 (March):14-33.

Haveman, Robert H., editor. 1974. *A Decade of Federal Antipoverty Programs: Achievements, Failures and Lessons*. New York: Academic Press.

Hazlitt, Henry. 1973. *The Conquest of Poverty*. New Rochelle, New York: Arlington House. Reprinted 1986. Lanham, Maryland: University Press of America and Irvington, New York: The Foundation for Economic Education.

Healy, Sean and Brigid Reynolds, editors. 1994. *Towards an Adequate Income for All*. Report prepared for the Justice Commission of the Conference of Religious of Ireland. Dublin: CORI.

Heikkilä, Matti and Elsa Keskitalo, editors. 2001. *A Comparative Study on Minimum Income in Seven European Countries: Synthesis Report on the Role of Social Assistance as a Means of Social Inclusion and Activation - Synthesis Report*. Note: This comparative research project was financed by the European Commission and coordinated by Finland's National Research and Development Center for Welfare and Health (STAKES). The seven countries were Austria, Denmark, Finland, Germany, Italy, Spain and Sweden. Helsinki: STAKES.

Heston, Alan, Robert Summers and Bettina Aten. 2002. *Penn World Table Version 6.1*. (October) Center for International Comparisons at the University of Pennsylvania (CICUP).

Holtzblatt, Janet and Janet McCubbin. 2003. "Complicated Lives: Tax Administrative Issues Affecting Low-Income Filers." (January). Paper by U.S. Treasury Department analysts to be published in a volume forthcoming from the Brookings Institution on tax administration.

Hooke, A.W. 1980. *The International Monetary Fund: Its Evolution, Organization and Activities.* Washington, DC: IMF.

Hoover, Dennis R. 2001. "What Would Moses Do? Debt Relief in the Jubilee Year", *Religion in the News* (Spring) 4(1). Published by the Leonard E. Greenberg Center for the Study of Religion in Public Life, Trinity College, Hartford, Connecticut. Article is available at www.trincoll.edu/depts/csrpl/RINVol4No1/jubilee_2000.htm.

Horsefield, J. Keith. 1969. *The International Monetary Fund 1945—1965: Twenty Years of Monetary Cooperation.* Washington, DC: International Monetary Fund.

Hotz, V. Joseph and John Karl Scholz. 2000. "Not Perfect But Still Pretty Good: The EITC And Other Policies to Support the US Low-Wage Labour Market". *OECD Economic Studies.* 31/2000/II (May) 25-42. Paris: Organization for Economic Cooperation and Development.

Hum, Derek and Wayne Simpson. 2001. "A Guaranteed Annual Income: From Mincome to the Millennium", *Policy Options* (January/February) 78-82. Note: *Policy Options* is the journal of Canada's Institute for Research on Public Policy.

Huston, Aletha C., Cynthia Miller, Lashawn Richburg-Hayes, Greg C. Duncan, Carolyn A. Eldred, Thomas S. Weisner, Edward Lowe, Danielle A. Crosby, Marika N. Ripke, and Cindy Redcross. 2003. *New Hope for Families and Children: Five-Year Results of a Program to Reduce Poverty and Reform Welfare.* (June) New York: MDRC. Also, see www.mdrc.org/publications/345/full.pdf.

Inter-American Development Bank. 2000. *Social Protection for Equity and Growth.* Prepared by the IADB Poverty and Inequality Advisory Unit under the direction of Nora Lustig, editor. Washington, DC: IADB/Johns Hopkins University Press.

International Bank for Reconstruction and Development. July 1944. *Articles of Agreement of the International Bank for Reconstruction and Development.* Bretton Woods, New Hampshire.

International Development Association. 2002. *Additions to IDA Resources: Thirteenth Replenishment—Supporting Poverty Reduction Strategies.* Report from the executive directors of IDA to the board of governors (July 25). Washington, DC.

International Federation of Robotics. 2002. *IFR Newsletter.* No.47/48 (December). Stockholm: IFR Secretariat.

International Fund for Agricultural Development. 2001. *The Challenge of Ending Rural Poverty: Rural Poverty Report 2001.* New York. Oxford: Oxford University Press.

International Fund for Agricultural Development. 1993. *The State of World Rural Poverty: An Inquiry into Its Causes and Consequences.* New York: NYU Press.

International Labour Organization. 2004. *A Fair Globalization: Creating Opportunities for All.* Final report of the World Commission on the Social Dimension of Globalization. ISBN-92-2-115426-2. Geneva: International Labour Organization.

International Labour Organization. 2004a. *Global Employment Trends.* (January) Geneva: International Labour Organization.

International Labour Organization. 2004b. *Economic Security for a Better World.* Geneva: International Labour Organization.

International Labour Organization. 2003. *Working Out of Poverty.* Report by Juan Somavia, Director-General to the International Labour Conference, Geneva 91st Session. Geneva: International Labour Organization.

International Labour Organization. 2002. *A Global Social Trust Network.* Geneva: International Labour Organization.

International Labour Organization and United Nations Conference on Trade and Development. 2001. *The Minimum Income for School Attendance (MISA) Initiative: Achieving International Development Goals in African Least Developed Countries.* Report of the ILO/UNCTAD Advisory Group (May). Geneva: ILO.

International Monetary Fund. 2004. *Review of Technical Assistance*. Internal report prepared by the Office of Technical Assistance Management and approved by Claire Liuksila. (February). Washington, DC: IMF. See www.imf.org.

International Monetary Fund. 2000. *A Better World for All*. Washington, DC: International Monetary Fund.

International Monetary Fund. 1944. *Articles of Agreement of the International Monetary Fund*. (July) Bretton Woods, New Hampshire.

International Poverty Centre. 2004. *Dollar a Day: How Much Does It Say?* Theme of a series of articles by different authors in *In Focus*, the online publication of the UNDP's International Poverty Centre. (September) www.undp.org/povertycentre.

Ireland, Government of, Department of the Taoiseach. 2002. *Basic Income: A Green Paper*. Paper prepared by the Steering Group on Basic Income. September. www.taoiseach.gov.ie/department.

Japan, Ministry of Foreign Affairs. 2000. *Japan's Official Development Assistance Annual Report 1999*. (February) Report is available at www.mofa.go.jp.

Jazairy, Idriss; Mohiuddin Alamgir; and Theresa Panuccio. 1992. *The State of World Rural Poverty: An Inquiry into its Causes and Consequences*. New York: New York University Press.

Jenkins, Glenn and Rup Khadka. 2000. *Modernization of Tax Systems on Low-Income Countries: The Case of Nepal*. Discussion paper from the Consulting Assistance on Economic Reform II. Note. CAER II assists the policy process at the U.S. Agency for International Development and contributes to market-oriented growth in developing countries. The Harvard Institute for International Development (HIID) and its subcontractors provide services under U.S. AID Contracts PCE-C-00-95-00015-00 and PCE-Q-00-95-00016-00. This paper was funded by Contract PCE-C-00-95-00015-00, Task Order 39. Cambridge, Massachusetts: Harvard University.

Jones, Charles. 2002. *Introduction to Economic Growth*. New York, London: W.W. Norton and Company.

Jones, Gareth Stedman. 2004. *An End to Poverty? A Historical Debate*. London: Profile Books.

Jütte, Robert. 1994. *Poverty and Deviance in Early Modern Europe*. Cambridge: Cambridge University Press.

Kanbur, Ravi. 2001. "Economic Policy, Distribution and Poverty: The Nature of Disagreements," *World Development* 29 (6) 1083-1094.

Kapur, Devesh, John P. Lewis and Richard Webb, editors. 1998. *The World Bank: Its First Half Century*. Volume I: *History*, Volume II: *Perspectives*. Washington, DC: The Brookings Institution.

Karshenas, Massoud. 2003. *Global Poverty: National Accounts-based Versus Survey-based Estimates*. Employment Papers 2003/49. Geneva: International Labour Office.

Keynes, John Maynard. 1936. *The General Theory of Employment, Interest and Money*. London: Macmillan.

Knox, Virginia, Cynthia Miller and Lisa A. Gennetian. 2000. *Reforming Welfare and Rewarding Work: A Summary of the Final Report on the Minnesota Family Investment Program*. (September) . New York: MDRC. Note: This executive summary of the final report of the evaluation conducted by the Manpower Development Research Corporation is available at www.mdrc.org.

Kolko, Gabriel. 1962. *Wealth and Power in America*. New York: Frederick Praeger.

Kosters, Bart. 2004. "The United Nations Model Tax Convention and Its Recent Developments," (January/February). *Asia-Pacific Tax Bulletin*, publication of the International Bureau of Fiscal Documentation. www.ibfd.nl.

Kuznets, Simon. 1955. "Economic Growth and Income Inequality", *American Economic Review*, 45(1): 1-28.

Landman, J.P., coordinator. 2003. *Breaking the Grip of Poverty and Inequality in South Africa 2004-2014: Current Trends, Issues and Future Policy Options.* Executive summary of three longer research papers, prepared with the assistance of Haroon Bhorat, Servaas van der Berg, and Carl van Aardt. See www.sarpn.org.za.

Lavinas, Lena; Maria Lígia Barbosa; and Octávio Tourinho. 2001. *Assessing Local Minimum Income Programmes in Brazil.* Report prepared with the collaboration of Mariana Bitar, Eduardo Garcia, Daniele Manão and Marcello Nicoll (June). Geneva: International Labour Office.

Lee, Andrew and Robert Greenstein. 2003. *How the New Tax Law Alters the Child Tax Credit and How Low-Income Families Are Affected.* (May 29). Washington, DC: Center for Budget and Policy Priorities. www.cbpp.org.

Lenkowsky, Leslie. 1986. *Politics, Economics and Welfare Reform: The Failure of the Negative Income Tax in Britain and the United States.* Lanham, Maryland: University Press of America.

Lerner, Abba P. 1947. *The Economics of Control: Principles of Welfare Economics.* Third edition. New York: Macmillan.

Leube, Kurt R., editor. 1987. *The Essence of Friedman.* Selected writings of Nobel Laureate economist Milton Friedman. Stanford, California: Hoover Institution Press.

Lewis, W. Arthur. 1955. *The Theory of Economic Growth.* London: George Allen & Unwin Ltd.

Lieberson, Joseph and Jonathan Sleeper. 2000. *Poverty: A CDIE Experience Review.* (October 30). Paper prepared by U.S. Agency for International Development, Center for Development Information and Evaluation. Washington, DC: USAID.

Lipton, Michael with assistance from Shahin Yaqub and Eliane Darbellay. 1998. *Successes in Anti-poverty.* Geneva: International Labour Office.

Lipton, Michael and Martin Ravallion. 1995. "Poverty and Policy", Chapter 41 in Jere Behrman and T.N. Srinivasan, editors, *Handbook of Development Economics*, III-B:2551-2660. Amsterdam: Elsevier Science B.V.

Locke, John. 1690. *The Second Treatise of Civil Government.* London. Note: The book is in the public domain. One of several online versions can be found at www.constitution.org/jl/2ndtreat.htm.

Lustig, Nora and Ruthanne Deutsch. 1998. *The Inter-American Bank and Poverty Reduction: An Overview.* Washington, DC: IADB.

Maddison, Angus. 2001. *The World Economy: A Millennial Perspective.* Paris: Organization for Economic Cooperation and Development.

Majid, Norman. 2003. *Globalization and Poverty.* Employment Paper 2003/54. Geneva: International Labour Office.

Makino, Kumiko. 2004. *Social Security Policy Reform in Post-Apartheid South Africa: A Focus on the Basic Income Grant.* (January). Centre for Civil Society Research Report No. 11. Paper originally presented at 19th International Political Science Association (IPSA) World Congress in Durban, South Africa, June 29-July 4, 2003. Durban, South Africa: Centre for Civil Society.

Marris, Peter and Rein, Martin. 1982. *Dilemmas of Social Reform: Poverty and Community Action in the United States.* Chicago, Illinois: University of Chicago Press.

Marsh, Leonard. 1943. *Report on Social Security for Canada.* Ottawa: King's Printer. Republished in 1975, Toronto: University of Toronto.

McManners, John, editor. 1992. *The Oxford Illustrated History of Christianity.* Oxford, New York: Oxford University Press.

Mendez, Ruben P. 1992. *International Public Finance: A New Perspective on Global Relations.* New York and Oxford: Oxford University Press.

Michalopoulos, Charles, Doug Tattrie, Cynthia Miller, Philip K. Robins, Pamela Morris, David Gyarmati, Cindy Redcross, Kelly Foley, and Reuben Ford. 2002. *Making Work Pay: Final Report on the Self-Sufficiency Project for Long-Term Welfare Recipients.* (July) Ottawa: Social Research and Demonstration Corporation.

Mill, John Stuart. 1909. *Principles of Political Economy.* William James Ashley, editor. Note: This is based on the 7th edition. First edition published 1848. First publication of the 7th edition, 1870. London: Longmans, Green and Co. The complete text of the 7th edition is available at www.econlib.org/library/Mill/mlP14.html.

Milanovic, Branko. 2002. "The World Income Distribution, 1988 and 1993: First Calculation Based on Household Surveys Alone." *The Economic Journal* (January): 112:51-92.

Miller, Cynthia, Virginia Knox, Lisa A Gennetian, Martey Dodoo, Jo Anna Hunter and Cindy Redcross. 2000. *Reforming Welfare and Rewarding Work: Final Report on the Minnesota Family Investment Program. Volume 1: Effects on Adults.* (September) Minneapolis: State of Minnesota, Department of Human Services and New York: MDRC. Also see www.mdrc.org.

Milner, Dennis. 1920. *Higher Production by a Bonus on National Output: A Proposal for a Minimum Income for All Varying with National Productivity.* London: George Allen & Unwin.

Mitschke, Joachim. 2000. "Arguing for a Negative Income Tax in Germany," pp. 107-120 in van der Veen, Robert and Loek Groot, editors. *Basic Income on the Agenda: Policy Objectives and Political Choices.* Amsterdam: Amsterdam University Press.

Montesquieu [Charles Louis de Secondat, Baron de la Brède et de Montesquieu]. 1748. *L'Esprit des Lois.* As translated in Carrithers, David Wallace, editor. 1977. *The Spirit of Laws.* Berkeley, California: University of California Press.

More, Sir Thomas. 1516. *Utopia.* Penguin Books edition of 1965, translated with an introduction by Paul Turner. London: Penguin Group.

Mosley, Paul. and Ann Booth, editors. 2001. *New Poverty Strategies: What Have They Achieved, What Have We Learned?* London: Macmillan.

Moynihan, Daniel P. 1973. *The Politics of a Guaranteed Income.* New York: Random House.

Moynihan, Daniel P., editor. 1968. *On Understanding Poverty.* New York: Basic Books.

Muller, Pierre. 2003. "A History of National Accounting", *Courrier de Statistiques.* English Series No. 9, 35-50. This article, by a senior statistician at France's Institut National de la Statistique et des Études Économiques, provides an overview of the book: Vanoli, André, 2002, *Une Histoire de la Compatibilité Nationale,* Paris: La Découverte. (An English version of the book was published in 2005 by IOS Press, Amsterdam).

Munnell, Alicia, editor. 1987. *Lessons from the Income Maintenance Experiments.* Conference Series Number 34. Washington, DC: Federal Reserve Bank of Boston.

Murray, Michael L. 1997 " . . . *And Economic Justice for All": Welfare Reform for the 21st Century.* Armonk, NY: M. E. Sharpe.

Nasr, Seyyed Hossein. 2002. *The Heart of Islam: Enduring Values for Humanity.* New York: Harper San Francisco.

Nathan Associates, Inc. 2002. *The Effect of Economic Growth on Poverty and Income Distribution in Developing Countries: A Literature Review and Data Analysis.* Report prepared by Richard H. Adams, Jr. and submitted to U.S. Agency for International Development under contract no. 1-00-00-00013. Washington, DC: USAID.

Newberry, David and Nicholas Stern, editors. 1987. *The Theory of Taxation for Developing Countries.* New York: Oxford University Press.

Nissan, David and Julian Le Grand. 2000. *A Capital Idea: Start-up Grants for Young People.* London: Fabian Society.

Nozick, Robert. 1974. *Anarchy, State and Utopia.* New York: Basic Books.

Nussbaum, Martha. 2001. "The Enduring Significance of John Rawls," *The Chronicle of Higher Education: The Chronicle Review* (July 21). See chronicle.com/free/v47/i45/45b00701.htm

Nussbaum, Martha and Amaryta Sen. 1993. *The Quality of Life.* Oxford: Clarendon Press.

Organization for Economic Cooperation and Development. 2002. *Development Cooperation Review: Germany.* Paris: OECD.

Organization for Economic Cooperation and Development. 2001. *The DAC Guidelines: Poverty Reduction.* Paris: OECD.

Organization for Economic Cooperation and Development. 2001a. *The OECD's Project on Harmful Tax Practices: The 2001 Progress Report.* (November) Paris: OECD.

Organization for Economic Cooperation and DevelopmentDevelopment Assistance Committee. 1996. *Shaping the 21st Century: The Contribution of Development Cooperation.* DAC policy statement. (May) Paris: OECD.

Overseas Development Institute. 2004. *Measuring the Impact of Humanitarian Aid: A Review of Current Practice.* Humanitarian Policy Group Report 17 (June). Report prepared by Charles-Antoine Hofmann, Les Roberts, Jeremy Shoham, and Paul Harvey. London: Oveseas Development Institute.

Owens, Jeffrey. 2004. *Fundamental Tax Reform: The Experience of OECD Countries.* (November). Background Paper No. 47 (draft). A publication of OECD's Center for Tax Policy and Administration. Paris: OECD.

Oxfam International. 2005. *Paying the Price: Why Rich Countries Must Invest Now in a War on Poverty.* London: Oxfam International.

Patterson, James T. 1994. *America's Struggle Against Poverty: 1900-1980.* Cambridge, Massachusetts: Harvard University Press.

Pearson, Lester B. 1969. *Partners in Development: Report of the Commission on International Development.* New York: Praeger.

Pechman, Joseph A. and P. Michael Timpane, editors. 1975. *Work Incentives and Income Guarantees: The New Jersey Negative Income Tax Experiment.* Washington, DC: Brookings Institution.

Peters, F.E. 2003. *The Monotheists: Jews, Christians and Muslims in Conflict and Competition. Volume II—The Words and Will of God.* Princeton, New Jersey: Princeton University Press.

Pemberton, Malcolm and Nicholas Rau. 2001. *Mathematics for Economists: An Introductory Textbook.* Manchester and New York: Manchester University Press.

Planning Commission, Government of India. 2002. *National Human Development Report 2001.* (March) See http://planningcommission.nic.in/reports.

Planning Commission, Government of India. 2002a. *10th Five-Year Plan (2002-2007).* See http://planningcommission.nic.in.

Planning Commission, Government of India. 2001. *Approach Paper to the Tenth Five-Year Plan.* (September 1) The report is available at http://planningcommission.nic.in.

Premasiri, P.D. 1999. *Religious Values and the Measurement of Poverty: A Buddhist Perspective.* (January 12-14). Paper prepared for the "Consultation on WDR 2000/1 [World Development Report]: Poverty and Development," workshop in Johannesburg, South Africa, January 12-14, 1999. Note: This workshop was sponsored by the World Faiths Development Dialogue, Cornell University, Swiss Development Corporation, the MacArthur Foundation and the World Bank. www1.worldbank.org/prem/poverty/wdrpoverty/joburg/

President's Advisory Panel on Federal Tax Reform. 2005. *Simple, Fair and Pro-Growth: Proposals to Fix America's Tax System.* (November) Washington, DC. See www.taxreformpanel.gov.

President's Commission on the Management of AID Programs (Ferris Commission). 1992. *Report to the President: An Action Plan.* (April) Washington, DC.

Quilligan, James Bernard. 2002. *The Brandt Equation: 21ˢᵗ Century Blueprint for the New Global Economy.* Philadelphia: Brandt 21 Forum. Note: the Forum was established in 2001 to carry on the work of the original Brandt Commission, 1977-1984.

Radhakrishnan, S. 1989. *Eastern Religions and Western Thought.* First published in 1939. Delhi: Oxford University Press. Note: The Hindu scholar Sarvepalli Radhakrishnan (1888-1975), a former president of India who had been educated in Christian schools, sought to recast Hinduism as a universal religion, distinguishable in its essence from its socio-historical and sectarian roots in India.

Ravallion, Martin and Shaohua Chen. 2004. *China's (Uneven) Progress Against Poverty.* World Bank Policy Research Working Paper 3408b (September). Washington, DC: World Bank.

Ravallion, Martin. 2005. *Inequality is Bad for the Poor.* (June 23). Washington, DC: World Bank.

Ravallion, Martin. 2003. *The Debate on Globalization, Poverty and Inequality: Why Measurement Matters.* World Bank Policy Research Paper 3038 (April). Washington, DC: World Bank.

Ravallion. Martin. 2002. *How Not to Count the Poor? A Reply to Reddy and Pogge.* Paper available at www.socialanalysis.org.

Ravallion, Martin. 2001. "Comment on 'Counting the World's Poor' by Angus Deaton". *The World Bank Research Observer* 16(2) 149-156.

Ravallion, Martin. 1992. *Poverty Comparisons: A Guide to Concepts and Methods.* Working Paper No. 88. Washington, DC: World Bank.

Rawlings, Laura B. 2004. *A New Approach to Social Assistance: Latin America's Experience with Conditional Cash Transfer Programs.* Social Protection Discussion Paper Series - No. 0416 (August). Washington, DC: World Bank.

Rawls, John. 1999. *A Theory of Justice.* Cambridge, Massachusetts: Harvard University Press. Note: originally published in 1971.

Rawls, John. 1988. "The Priority of Right and Ideas of the Good", *Philosophy & Public Affairs* 17(4).

Reddy, Sanjay G. and Thomas W. Pogge. 2002. *How Not to Count the Poor!* Paper available at www.socialanalysis.org.

Reddy, Sanjay G. and Thomas W. Pogge. 2002a. *How Not to Count the Poor!—A Reply to Ravallion.* (August 15). Paper available at www.socialanalysis.org.

Reynolds, David. 2000. *One World Divisible: A Global History Since 1945.* New York, London: W.W. Norton & Company.

Rhys-Williams, Juliet (Lady). 1943. *Something to Look Forward To: A Suggestion for a New Social Contract.* London: Macdonald.

Rifkin, Jeremy. 1995. *The End of Work: the Decline of the Global Labor Force and the Dawn of the Post-Market Era.* New York: Tarcher/Putnam.

Romer, Paul M. 1986. "Increasing Returns and Long-Run Growth," *Journal of Political Economy* 94(5)1002-37.

Rostow, Walter W. 1960. *The Stages of Economic Growth: A Non-Communist Manifesto.* Cambridge, England: Cambridge University Press.

Rowntree, B. Seebohm. 1901. *A Study of London Town Life.* London: MacMillan.

Rural Research Agency. 1997. *Alaska's Permanent Fund: Legislative History, Intent and Operations.* Volume 5 of the Trustees' Papers of the Board of Trustees of the Alaska Permanent Fund Corporation. Note: The Rural Research Agency is an arm of Alaska State Legislature. This is an abridged but also updated version of an earlier history published in 1986. Volume 5 also contains a 1983 paper written for the Corporation by Joan Kasson titled *The Creation of the Alaska Permanent Fund: A Short History.* See www.apfc.org/library.

Sala-i-Martin, Xavier. 2004. *The World Distribution of Income: Falling Poverty and...Convergence, Period.* (March 31 draft version). See www.columbia.edu/~xs23/papers/WorldDistribution.htm.

Sala-i-Martin, Xavier. 2002. *The Disturbing 'Rise' of Income Inequality,* Working Paper 8904 (April) and *The World Distribution of Income,* Working Paper 8933 (May). Washington, DC: National Bureau of Economic Research.

Sala-i-Martin, Xavier and Arvind Subramanian. 2003. *Addressing the Natural Resource Curse: An Illustration from Nigeria.* (July). International Monetary Fund Working Paper WP/03/139. Washington, DC: IMF.

Sala-i-Martin, Xavier and Sanket Mohapatra. 2002. *Poverty, Inequality and the Distribution of Income in the G20.* Discussion paper 0203-10 (November). New York: Columbia University.

Salanié, Bernard. 2003. *The Economics of Taxation.* Cambridge, Massachusetts: MIT Press. English translation. Originally published in France in 2002 under the title *Théorie Économique de la Fiscalité,* Paris: Economica.

Salanié, Bernard. 2002. "Optimal Demogrants with Imperfect Tagging" *Economics Letters* 75:319-324.

Scholz, John Karl. 1994. "The Earned Income Tax Credit: Participation, Compliance and Anti-poverty Effectiveness", *National Tax Journal* (March) 59-8.

Sen, Amartya. 1999. *Development as Freedom.* New York: Knopf.

Sennett, Richard. 2003. *Respect in a World of Inequality.* New York & London: Norton.

Shane, Matthew and Fred Gale. 2004. *China: A Study of Dynamic Growth.* Electronic Outlook Report from the Economic Research Service, U.S. Department of Agriculture. WRS-04-08 (October). Available at www.ers.usda.gov.

Sheahen, Allan. 1983. *Guaranteed Income: The Right to Economic Security.* Los Angeles, California: GAIN Publications.

Simon, Herbert A. 1957. *Models of Man: Social and Rational.* New York: John Wiley and Sons, Inc.

Slack, Paul. 1995. *The English Poor Law, 1531-1782.* Cambridge: Cambridge University Press.

Slack, Paul. 1988. *Poverty and Policy in Tudor and Stuart England.* New York: Longman, Inc.

Smith, W. James and Kalanidhi Subbarao. 2003. *What Role for Safety Net Transfers in Very Low Income Countries?* Social Safety Net Primer Series. Washington, DC: World Bank Institute. Available at www.worldbank.org/poverty/safety.

Smolensky, Eugene. 2001. *On Fighting Income Poverty: Reflections on Six Country Evaluations.* September. The countries in question are Madagascar, Mexico, Mozambique, Nepal, the Philippines, and Vietnam. www.un.org/esa/coordination/SmolenskyPOV.pdf.

Solow, Robert M. 1956. "A Contribution to the Theory of Economic Growth," *Quarterly Journal of Economics* (February): 70:65-94.

Soubbotina, Tatyana P. with Katherine A. Sheram. 2000. *Beyond Economic Growth: Meeting the Challenges of Global Development.* (October) Excellent textbook published by the World Bank's Development Education Program. Washington, DC: World Bank.

South Africa, Government of. 2002. *Transforming the Present—Protecting the Future: Consolidated Report.* (March). Report of the Committee of Inquiry into a Comprehensive System of Social Security for South Africa. Pretoria: Department of Social Development. Note: This government-appointed committee is also known as the Taylor Committee after its chair, Professor Viviene Taylor. www.welfare.gov.za/Documents.

South African Council of Churches, Congress of South African Trade Unions, and South African Non-Governmental Coalition. 2003. *People's Budget: 2004-2005.* (February) Braamfontein, Johannesburg: National Labour and Economic Development Institute. www.sacc-ct.org.za/campaigns.html#big.

South African Council of Churches, Congress of South African Trade Unions, and South African Non-Governmental Coalition. 2002. *People's Budget: 2003-2004.* (February) Braamfontein, Johannesburg: National Labour and Economic Development Institute. www.sacc-ct.org.za/campaigns.html#big.

SRI International. 1983. *Final Report of the Seattle-Denver Income Maintenance Experiment: Vol. 1-Design and Result* (May) Washington, DC: SRI.

Srinivasan, T.N. 2000. *Growth and Poverty Alleviation: Lessons from Development Experience.* (December 8) Paper delivered at the High Level Symposium on Alternative Development Paradigms and Poverty Reduction, Asian Development Bank Institute, Tokyo. Also published in French under the title *Croissance et Allégement de la Pauvreté:Les Leçons Tirées de L'Expérience du Développement*, Revue d'Économic du Développement, 1-2, 2001:115-168.

Stanley-Clarke, Nicola. 1996. *The History of the Universal Basic Income.* www.geocities.com/ubinz/Nicola_UBI_history.html

Standing, Guy, editor. 2003. *Minimum Income Schemes in Europe.* A publication of the ILO's Socio-Economic Security Programme. Geneva: International Labour Office.

Standing, Guy. 2002. *Beyond the New Paternalism: Basic Income as Equality.* London: Verso.

Stigler, George J. 1946. "The Economics of Minimum Wage Legislation," *American Economic Review* (June) 36:358-65.

Stiglitz, Joseph E. 2002. *Globalization and Its Discontents.* New York and London: W.W Norton & Company, Ltd.

Strauss, John and Duncan Thomas. 1995. "Human Resources: Empirical Modeling of Household and Family Decisions." Chapter 34 in Jere Behrman and T.N. Srinivasan, editors, *Handbook of Development Economics*, III-A:1883-2023. Amsterdam: Elsevier Science B.V.

Subbarao, Kalanidhi. 1997. *Lessons of 30 Years of Fighting Poverty.* (September) Paper presented at the Conference on Economic Approaches Against Poverty, August 26-28, 1997 in Quebec City.

Sundquist, James. 1969. *On Fighting Poverty: Perspectives from Experience.* New York: Basic Books.

Swatos, Jr., William H., editor. 1998. *Encyclopedia of Religion and Society.* Walnut Creek, California: AltaMira Press. An entry titled "Preferential Option for the Poor" by Madeleine R. Cousineau is found in the authoritative printed version and on the web version of the encyclopedia, which is located at hirr.hartsem.edu/ency/web.htm

Tabor, Steven R. 2002. *Assisting the Poor with Cash: Design and Implementation of Social Transfer Programs.* Social Safety Net Primer Series No. 0223 (September). Washington, DC: World Bank Institute. www.worldbank.org/poverty/safety.

Tait, Alan A., Wilfrid L.M. Gratz, and Barry J. Eichengren. 1979. *International Comparisons of Taxation for Selected Developing Countries*. March. International Monetary Fund Staff Papers 26(1): 123-56. Washington, DC: IMF.
Tanzi, Vito. 1995. *Taxation in an Integrating World*. Washington, DC: The Brookings Institution.
Tanzi, Vito and Howell H. Zee. 2000. *Tax Policy for Emerging Markets: Developing Countries*. International Monetary Fund Working Paper WP/00/15. (March) Washington, DC: International Monetary Fund.
Tarp, Finn, editor. 2002. *Foreign Aid and Development: Lesson Learnt and Directions for the Future*. London and New York: Routledge.
Taylor Committee (Committee of Inquiry into a Comprehensive System of Social Security for South Africa). 2002. *Transforming the Present—Protecting the Future: Report of the Committee of Inquiry into a Comprehensive System of Social Security for South Africa*. Pretoria: Department of Social Development.
Theobald, Robert. 1965. *Free Men and Free Markets*. New York: Anchor Books. (Originally published in 1963 by Clarkson N. Potter.)
Titmuss, Richard M. 1962. *Income Distribution and Social Change*. London: George Allen and Urwin.
Tobin, James, Joseph A. Pechman and Peter M. Mieszkowski. 1967. "Is a Negative Income Tax Practical?" *The Yale Law Journal* 77(1):1-27.
Tomlinson, John. 2001. *Income Security: The Basic Income Alternative*. Queensland, Australia: Queensland University of Technology. Note: See especially Chapter 9, "History of Income Guarantees" and Chapter 10, "Basic Income". This interesting book can be found at www.geocities.com/ubinz/JT/IncomeInsecurity.
Townsend, Peter and David Gordon, editors. 2002. *World Poverty: New Policies to Defeat an Old Enemy*. Bristol, United Kingdom: The Policy Press.
Trattner, Walter I. 1999. *From Poor Law to Welfare State: A History of Social Welfare in America*. New York: The Free Press.
Ul Haq, Mahbub. 1976. *The Poverty Curtain: Choices for the Third World*. New York: Columbia University Press.
United Kingdom. 1997. *Eliminating World Poverty: A Challenge for the 21st Century*. White Paper on International Development. Command Paper 3789. (November). Presented to Parliament by command of Her Majesty. London.
United Nations. 2005. *Report on the World Social Situation, 2005*. UN General Assembly Report A/60/117 (July 13). New York: United Nations.
United Nations. 2003. *National Accounts: A Practical Introduction*. Series F, No. 85. ST/ESA/STAT/SER.F/85. Handbook prepared by Vu Quang Viet of the UN Statistics Division. New York: United Nations.
United Nations. 2002. *Implementation of the First United Nations Decade for the Eradication of Poverty*. Report of the Secretary General for 57th Session of the General Assembly. Advance unedited copy. (July) New York: UN.
United Nations. 2002a. *Report of the International Conference on Financing for Development*. Monterrey, Mexico. March 18-22, 2002. A/CONF198/11. New York: United Nations.
United Nations. 2000. *Basic Facts about the United Nations*. No. E.00.I.21 New York: UN.
United Nations. 2000a. *United Nations Millennium Declaration*. UN General Assembly Resolution A/res/55/2, 8th Plenary Session (September 8). New York: UN.
United Nations. 1997. *Report on the World Social Situation*. E/CN.5/1997/8 (Part 1). New York: United Nations. See www.un.org/esa/socdev/rwss.htm.

United Nations. 1995. *Report of the World Summit for Social Development.* (April 19) Copenhagen, March 6-12, 1995.

United Nations. 1992. *Report of the United Nations Conference on Environment and Development, Rio de Janeiro: Resolutions Adopted by the Conference, Resolution I, Annex II.* Sales No. E.93.I.8. (June 3-14) New York.

United Nations. 1970. *Towards Accelerated Development—Proposals for the Second United Nations Development Decade.* UN publication E.70.II.A.2. New York.

United Nations. 1962. *The United Nations Development Decade.* New York: UN.

United Nations. 1945. *Charter of the United Nations.* (June 26).

United Nations Children's Fund. 2002. *The State of the World's Children 2003.* New York: UNICEF.

United Nations Conference on Trade and Development. 2002. *The Least Developed Countries Report 2002: Escaping the Poverty Trap.* New York and Geneva: UN.

United Nations Conference on Trade and Development. 2000. *The Least Developed Countries: 2000 Report.* New York and Geneva: UN.

United Nations Department of Economic and Social Affairs, Development Policy and Planning Office. 2004. *Report on the Expert Group Meeting on Resource Mobilization for Poverty Eradication in the Least Developed Countries.* (March 8). Paper (draft) by Al Binger for the Sixth Session of the UN Committee for Development Policy, March 29-April 2, 2004. CDP/2004/PLEN/4. www.un.org/esa/analysis/publications/papers.htm.

United Nations Department of Economic and Social Affairs, Statistics Division. 2003. *Household Surveys in Developing Countries* (Draft). (April) See unstats.un.org/unsd/hhsurveys.

United Nations Department of Economic and Social Affairs, Statistics Division. 2002. *United Nations Millennium Development Goals: Data and Trends, 2002.* New York: United Nations. (May 31) Note: This report is not an official UN document but is based on a report of the Inter-agency Expert Group on MDG Indicators, April 2002.

United Nations Department of Economic and Social Development: Statistical Division. 1992. *Handbook of the International Comparison Programme.* Studies in Methods Series F, Number 62. ST/ESA/STAT/SER.F/62. New York: United Nations.

United Nations Development Program, Arab Fund for Social and Economic Development and Arab Gulf Program for United Nations Development Organizations. 2005. *The Arab Human Development Report 2004: Towards Freedom in the Arab World.* New York: United Nations.

United Nations Development Program. 2005a. *Human Development Report 2005: International Cooperation at a Crossroads—Aid, Trade and Security in an Unequal World.* New York: United Nations.

United Nations Development Program. 2003. *Human Development Report 2003 - Millennium Development Goals: A Compact Among Nations to End Human Poverty.* New York and Oxford: Oxford University Press.

United Nations Development Program. 1999. *The Way Forward: The Administrator's Business Plans, 2000-2003.* (December 15) Report to the Executive Board of the United Nations Development Programme and of the United Nations Population Fund, January 24-28 and January 31, 2000. DP/2000/8. New York: United Nations.

United Nations Development Program. 1998. *Human Development Report 1998—Consumption for Human Development.* New York and Oxford: Oxford University Press.

United Nations Development Program. 1997. *Human Development Report 1997—Human Development to Eradicate Poverty.* New York: Oxford University Press.

United Nations Economic and Social Council. 1995. *Poverty Eradication and Sustainable Development: Report of the Secretary-General.* (March 20) Commission on Sustainable Development, Third Session, April 11-28, 1995. E/CN.17/1995/14. New York: United Nations.

United Nations Economic Commission for Africa. 2003. *Economic Report on Africa 2003: Accelerating the Pace of Development.* Addis Adaba, Ethiopia: UNECA.

United Nations Economic Commission for Africa. 2002. *Economic Report on Africa 2002: Tracking Performance and Progress.* Addis Adaba, Ethiopia: UNECA.

United Nations Economic Commission for Europe. 2004. *World Robotics 2004.* Published in conjunction with the International Federation of Robotics. New York: United Nations.

United Nations Economic and Social Commission for Asia and the Pacific. 2002. *Economic and Social Survey of Asia and the Pacific, 2002/Economic Prospects: Preparing for Recovery.* (March) Sales No. E.02.II.F.25. New York: United Nations.

United Nations Millennium Project. 2005. *Investing in Development: A Practical Plan to Achieve the Millennium Development Goals.* New York: United Nations. Note: The UN Millennium Project, directed by Dr. Jeffrey D. Sachs, was commissioned by the UN Secretary-General and supported by the United Nations Development Group.

United Nations Millennium Project. 2004. *Interim Report of Task Force 1 on Poverty and Economic Development.* (February 10). The report's coordinators were Mari E. Pangestu and Jeffrey D. Sachs. Available at www.unmillenniumproject.org.

United Nations Population Fund. 2002. *The State of World Population 2002 - People, Poverty and Possibilities: Making Development Work for the Poor.* New York: United Nations Publications

United Nations Research Institute for Social Development. 1995. *States of Disarray: The Social Effects of Globalization.* Geneva: UNRISD.

United Nations Secretariat. 2003. *Institutional Framework for International Tax Cooperation.* (August 19). Paper prepared for the Eleventh Meeting of the Ad Hoc Groups of Experts on International Cooperation in Tax Matters, December 15-19, 2003, Geneva. New York: United Nations.

United Nations Secretariat - Department of Economic and Social Affairs. 2001. *Combating Poverty: Report of the Secretary-General.* (March 14) Report prepared by the Department of Economic and Social Affairs of the United Nations Secretariat for the UN Commission on Sustainable Development.

United Nations, Executive Board of the United Nations Development Program and of the United Nations Population Fund. 2002. *Annual Report of the Administrator on Evaluation 2001.* Second regular session of the Executive Board, September 23-27. (July 9) DP/2002/27. New York: UN.

United States Conference of Catholic Bishops. 2003. *Faithful Citizenship: A Catholic Call to Political Responsibility.* Washington, DC: USCCB. See www.usccb.org/faithfulcitizenship.

United States Conference of Catholic Bishops. 1986. *Economic Justice for All: Pastoral Letter on Catholic Social Teaching and The U.S. Economy.* Washington, DC: USCCB.

U.S. Agency for International Development. 2004. *Pro-Poor Growth: A Guide to Policies and Programs.* (January) Washington, DC: USAID. Note: This document was prepared by Development Alternatives, Inc. and the Boston Institute for Developing Economies for review by USAID. It does not necessarily reflect the views of USAID or the U.S. Government. The document is included on a 2005 CD produced by USAID's Poverty Analysis and Social Safety Net Team. For more information, go to www.PovertyFrontiers.org.

U.S. Agency for International Development. 2003. "Statement of the Administrator", *Congressional Budget Justification FY 2004.* (February 28) Washington, DC: USAID. See www.info.usaid.gov.

U.S. Agency for International Development. 2002. *Working for a Sustainable World: U.S. Government Initiatives to Promote Sustainable Development.* (July) Washington, DC: USAID.

U.S. Central Intelligence Agency. 2005. The *World Factbook 2005.* Available at www.cia.gov.

U.S. Central Intelligence Agency. 2002. The *World Factbook 2002.* Available at www.cia.gov.

U.S. Central Intelligence Agency. 2001. *Long-Term Global Demographic Trends: Reshaping the Geopolitical Landscape.* (July) Available at www.cia.gov/publications.

U.S. Congress, House of Representatives. 1989. *Report of the Task Force on Foreign Assistance.* (February) 101st Congress, 1st Session. House Report 101-32.

U.S. Department of Agriculture, Economic Research Service. 2005. *Food Security Assessment.* (April). Shahla Shapouri and Stacey Rosen, coordinators. Outlook report no. GFA-16. Washington, DC: USDA.

U.S. Department of Health and Human Services, Office of the Assistant Secretary for Planning and Evaluation. 1983. *Overview of the Final Report of the Seattle-Denver Income Maintenance Experiment.* (May) Washington, DC: USDHHS. Available at aspe.hhs.gov/hsp.

U.S. Department of the Treasury, Internal Revenue Service. 2002. *"Compliance Estimates for Earned Income Tax Credit Claimed on 1999 Returns"* (February 28). Paper written for 2002 IRS Research Conference. See www.irs.gov/pub/irs-soi/compeitc.pdf.

Note: The U.S. General Accounting Office is the former name of the U.S. Government Accountability Office. The following references use the name of the organization as it stood when the reports were issued.

U.S. General Accounting Office. 2002a. *Foreign Assistance: USAID Relies Heavily on Nongovernmental Organizations But Better Data Needed to Evaluate Approaches.* (April) GAO-02-471. Washington, DC.

U.S. General Accounting Office. 2001. *Foreign Assistance: Lessons Learned from Donors' Experiences in the Pacific Region.* (August) GAO-01-808. Washington, DC.

U.S. General Accounting Office. 2001a. *U.S. Agency for International Development: Status of Achieving Key Outcomes and Addressing Major Management Challenges.* (August) GAO-01-721.Washington, DC.

U.S. General Accounting Office. 1994. *Multilateral Development: Status of World Bank Reforms.* (June) GAO/NSIAD-94-190BR. Washington, DC.

U.S. General Accounting Office. 1993. *Foreign Assistance: AID Strategic Direction and Continued Management Improvements Needed.* (June) GAO/NSIAD-93-106. Washington, DC.

U.S. General Accounting Office. 1991. *Foreign Assistance: Progress in Implementing the Development Fund for Africa.* (April) GAO/NSIAD-91-127. Washington, DC.

U.S. General Accounting Office. 1988. *Foreign Aid: Problems and Issues Affecting Economic Assistance.* (December) GAO/NSIAD-89-61BR. Washington, DC.

U.S. General Accounting Office. 1986. *Foreign Assistance: U.S. Use of Conditions to Achieve Economic Reforms.* (August) GAO/NSIAD-86-157.

U.S. General Accounting Office. 1983. *Donor Approaches to Development Assistance: Implications for the United States.* (May 14) GAO/ID-83-23. Washington, DC.

U.S. Department of the Treasury, Internal Revenue Service. 2003. *Child and Dependent Care Expenses*. IRS Publication 503 for use in preparing 2003 returns. Washington, DC: IRS.

Van der Veen, Robert and Loek Groot, editors. 2000. *Basic Income on the Agenda. Policy Options and Political Feasibility*. Amsterdam: Amsterdam University Press.

Van Parijs, Philippe with Cohen, Joshua and Joel Rogers, editors. 2001. *What's Wrong with a Free Lunch?* Boston: Beacon Press.

Van Parijs, Philippe. 2001a. *A Short History of Basic Income*. Available at http://www.bien.be/BI/HistoryBI.htm.

Van Parijs, Philippe. 2000. *Basic Income: A Simple and Powerful idea for the 21ˢᵗ Century*. Paper prepared for Basic Income European Network, VIIIth International Congress, Berlin, October 2000.

Van Parijs, Philippe. 1995. *Real Freedom for All: What (If Anything) Can Justify Capitalism?* Oxford: Clarendon Press.

Van Reisen, Mirjam. 2002. *Directing EU Policy Towards Poverty Eradication: From Commitments to Targets to Results* (ECDPM Discussion Paper 35). Maastricht: European Centre for Development Policy Management.

Velásquez Pinto, Mario D. 2003. *The Bono Solidario in Ecuador: An Exercise in Targeting*. Extension of Social Security (ESS) Series Paper No. 17. Social Security Policy and Development Branch, International Labour Organization. Geneva: International Labour Office. See www.ilo.org/public/english/protection/socsec.

Ventry, Dennis J., Jr. 2001. *The Collision of Tax and Welfare Politics: The Political History of the Earned Income Tax Credit, 1969-1999*. (March). Joint Center for Poverty Research Working Paper 149. Evanston, Illinois (Northwestern University) and Chicago, Illinois (University of Chicago): JCPR. www.jcpr.org/eitcinfopage.htm.

Vives, Juan Luis. 1526. *On the Assistance to the Poor*. English translation by Alice Tobriner (1999, with introduction and commentary) of Vives' *De Subventione Pauperum*. Toronto and London: University of Toronto Press (Renaissance Society of America Reprint).

Waddington, Hugh and Rachel Sabates-Wheeler. 2003. *How Does Poverty Affect Migration Choice? A Review of Literature*. Development Research Centre on Migration, Globalisation and Poverty - Working Paper No. 13 (December). Brighton, United Kingdom: University of Sussex. www.migrationdrc.org.

Wade, Robert Hunter. 2002. *Globalization, Poverty and Income Distribution: Does the Liberal Argument Hold?* (July). Development Studies Institute Working Paper Series 1, No. 02-33. Draft of paper prepared for Conference on "Towards a New Political Economy of Development", University of Sheffield, July 4-6, 2002. London: London School of Economics and Political Science. Also see www.lse.ac.uk/depts/destin.

Walter, Tony. 1989. *Basic Income: Freedom from Poverty, Freedom to Work*. London: Marion Boyars Publishers Inc.

Watts, Martin. 2001. *Basic Income versus the Job Guarantee: a Review of the Issues*. Centre of Full Employment and Equity Working Paper No. 01/09. (July) Callaghan NSW 2308, Australia: University of Newcastle.

Weiss, Edith Brown. 1989. *In Fairness to Future Generations: International Law, Common Patrimony, and Intergenerational Equity*. Dobbs Ferry, N.Y: Transnational Publishers, Inc.

Widerquist, Karl; Michael Anthony Lewis and Steven Pressman editors. 2005. *The Ethics and Economics of the Basic Income Guarantee*. Aldershot, United Kingdom: Ashgate.

Widerquist, Karl. 2002. *A Failure to Communicate: The Labour Market Findings of the Negative Income Tax Experiments and Their Impact on Policy and Public Opinion*.

(September) Draft of paper prepared for 9th International Congress, Basic Income European Network, Geneva, September 12-14, 2002.

Wilson, Harold. 1953. *The War on World Poverty*. London: Victor Gollancz.

Wogaman, J. Philip. 1968. *Guaranteed Annual Income: The Moral Issues*. Nashville, Tennessee: Abingdon Press.

World Bank. 2005. *Global Monitoring Report 2005—Millennium Development Goals: From Consensus to Momentum*. Advance Edition. Note: Second in a series of reports assessing progress toward the Millennium Development Goals. Washington, DC: World Bank.

World Bank. 2005a. *Global Economic Prospects: Trade, Regionalism and Development - 2005*. Washington, DC: World Bank.

World Bank. 2005b. *World Development Report—2006: Equity and Development*. Washington, DC: World Bank and New York: Oxford University Press.

World Bank. 2004. *Global Finance Development: Harnessing Cyclical Gains for Development. Volume 1 — Analysis and Summary Tables*. Washington, DC: World Bank.

World Bank. 2004a. *Inequality in Latin America: Breaking with History?* (February) The authors are David D. Ferranti, Guillermo E. Perry, Francisco Ferreira and Michael Walton. Washington, DC: World Bank.

World Bank. 2004b. *World Development Report —2005: A Better Investment Climate for Everyone*. Washington, DC: World Bank and New York: Oxford University Press.

World Bank. 2003. *Global Economic Prospects and the Developing Countries*. Washington, DC: World Bank.

World Bank. 2003a. *2003 World Development Indicators*. Washington, DC: World Bank.

World Bank. 2003b. *Global Economic Prospects 2004 —Realizing the Promise of the Doha Agenda*. Washington, DC: World Bank.

World Bank. 2002. *Global Development Finance 2002:Financing the Poorest Countries*. Washington, DC: World Bank.

World Bank. 2002a. *Poverty Reduction and the World Bank: Progress in Operationalizing the WDR 2000/2001*. Washington, DC: World Bank.

World Bank. 2001. *Global Economic Prospects and the Developing Countries 2002*. Washington, DC: World Bank.

World Bank. 2001a. *Global Economic Prospects and the Developing Countries 2001*. Washington, DC: World Bank.

World Bank. 2001b. *World Development Report 2000/2001: Attacking Poverty*. Washington, DC: World Bank.

World Bank. 2001c. *Global Development Finance 2001: Building Coalitions for Effective Development Finance*. Washington, DC: World Bank.

World Bank. 2001d. *African Poverty at the Millennium: Causes, Complexities and Challenges*. Washington, DC: World Bank.

World Bank. 2001e. *Social Protection Sector Strategy: From Safety Net to Springboard*. Washington, DC: World Bank.

World Bank. *Voices of the Poor* Series—

- Rademacher, Anne; Kai Schafft; Raj Patel; Sara Koch-Schulte; Deepa Narayan. 2000. *Can Anyone Hear Us?* (March) Volume I. London and New York: Oxford University Press.

- Shah, Meera; Patti Petesch; Robert Chambers; Deepa Narayan. 2000(a). *Crying Out for Change*. (September) Volume II. London and New York: Oxford University Press.

- Narayan, Deepa and Patti Petesch, editors. 2002. *From Many Lands*. Volume III. London and New York: Oxford University Press. (January) See www.worldbank.org/poverty/voices/index.htm. Note: This three-volume series draws from discussions with 60,000 poor women and women from sixty countries.

World Bank. 1993. *East Asian Miracle: Economic Growth and Public Policy.* Washington, DC: World Bank.

World Bank. 1992. *World Development Report 1992: Poverty.* New York: Oxford University Press

World Bank. 1990. *World Development Report 1990: Poverty.* New York: Oxford University Press.

World Bank. 1981. *Accelerated Growth in Sub-Saharan Africa: An Agenda for Action.* Report 3358. (Also known as the Berg report, since it was prepared by the World Bank African Strategy Review Group under the direction of University of Michigan economics professor Eliot Berg). Washington, DC: World Bank.

World Bank, Africa Region. 2002. *Africa Human Development Action Plan.* Report 26372 (June). Washington, DC: World Bank.

World Bank, Operations Development Department. 2005. *2004 Annual Review of Development Effectiveness: The World Bank's Contributions to Poverty Reduction.* Washington, DC: World Bank.

World Bank, Operations Evaluation Department. 2002. *IDA's Partnership for Poverty Reduction: An Independent Evaluation of Fiscal Years 1994-2000.* Washington, DC: The World Bank.

World Bank, Operations Evaluation Department. 2002a. *Social Funds: Assessing Effectiveness.* Washington, DC: The World Bank.

World Bank, Operations Evaluation Department. 2000. "Development Effectiveness at the World Bank: What Is the Score?" *OED Reach.* (Spring) Number 24.

World Bank, Operations Policy and Country Services. 2001. *Adjustment Lending Retrospective: Final Report.* (June 15) Washington, DC: World Bank.

World Bank, Operations Policy Department, Learning and Leadership Center. 1997. *Handbook on Economic Analysis of Investment Operations.* Washington, DC: World Bank.

World Bank, Social Protection Group. 2002. *Reducing Vulnerability and Increasing Opportunity: A Strategy for Social Protection in Middle East and North Africa.* Washington, DC: World Bank.

World Trade Organization. 1994. *Agreement Establishing the World Trade Organization.* (April 1) See www.wto.org.

Wresinski, Joseph. 1994. *Chronic Poverty and Lack of Basic Security: The Wresinski Report of the Economic and Social Council of France.* Landover, Maryland: Fourth World Publications. Note: Originally published in February 1987 as *Grande Pauvreté et Précarité Economique et Sociale* in the *Journal Officiel de la République Française.*

Yunus, Muhammed (with Alan Jolis). 1999. *Banker to the Poor: Micro-lending and the Battle Against World Poverty.* New York: Public Affairs.

Zee, Howell H. 1999. *Inequality and Optimal Redistributive Tax and Transfer Policies.* Working Paper of the International Monetary Fund WP/99/60. (April) Washington, DC: International Monetary Fund.

Index

Robert F. Clark is a writer and consultant living in Fairfax County, Virginia. He has a doctorate in public administration and has written on program evaluation, disability, aging, long-term care and poverty. His previous books on poverty include *Maximum Feasible Success: A History of the Community Action Program* (Washington, DC: National Association of Community Action Agencies, 2000); *The War on Poverty: History, Selected Programs and Ongoing Impact* (Lanham, MD: University Press of America, 2002); and *Victory Deferred: the War on Global Poverty (1945-2003)* (Lanham, MD: University Press of America, 2004). He has also published two novels.

www.ingramcontent.com/pod-product-compliance
Lightning Source LLC
Chambersburg PA
CBHW070417270326
41926CB00014B/2833